Counting on Hope

Counting on Hope

Five Adoptions, Four Lasagnas,
Three Miscarriages, Two Trips to Russia,
and One Group of Friends

Laura Schmitt, Jen York, Amy Bowman,
Ginger Marten, and Grace Moretti

Introductions by Jenny Kalmon

To order additional copies of this book, contact:
Xlibris Corporation
1-888-795-4274
www.Xlibris.com
Orders@Xlibris.com
71214

Contents

We dedicate this book to our children and all those who love them.

INTRODUCTION

by Jenny Kalmon

I was *that friend*, the fertile one whose uterus others secretly envied. While I have not personally experienced the frustration of infertility, my friends, one by one, endured the unimaginable pain of miscarrying, the trials of fertility treatments, and the humiliation of invasive medical exams. Through it all, there I was, *that friend*, the one who got pregnant without even trying. The one who didn't know the right words when misfortune and loss weakened their hopes.

As we met to put together this book, I was warmly welcomed into this group of mothers, some of whom I'd known for over ten years, others who were co-workers. In a ridiculously short time, we became *those friends*, the ones who cried and mourned together while recalling lost pregnancies. The ones who supported each other while exposing our rawest emotions. The ones who laughed out loud as humor emerged despite talk of sperm counts and failed adoptions.

Once a month, we would gather together, and my friends would take turns sharing their newly written chapters. Since I had no writing to share, I took on an editor's role. I'd interrupt the reader with suggestions like, "add an analogy about magic beans here," "change the word *tried* to *struggled*," and "remind the audience who that person is again." Mostly I just listened, amazed and bewildered at the years of heartbreak, hope, anxiety, and joy that each of my friends would go through to bring their babies home.

Through the creation of this book, we found the common ground we'd been waiting to find. We all remembered the joy of seeing our child for the first time. We all celebrated the homecoming of our children. We all experienced the thrill of milestone moments. We all kept our fingers crossed and leapt heart-first into the dawn of motherhood.

PART I

Laura

"Patience is the art of hoping."

~Marquis De Vauvenargues

I was that friend, the one carefully and thoroughly completing the adoption recommendation form in hopes that my responses would help my dear pal along in her pursuit of becoming a parent.

When Laura called and asked me to complete a recommendation for her and her husband to be adoptive parents, I felt honored to be included in their journey. Though conflicted about the paperwork itself, my rational mind did grasp the necessity of documentation and following through with the process. I would gladly describe my friend as organized, responsible, and physically healthy. I would attest to the fact that she kept a safe, secure, not to mention, creatively decorated home. I would brag about the fun parties she hosted, complete with homemade games and unique themes.

Yes, I would write the recommendation, yet my heart triggered a defensive response. I struggled to understand the excessive paperwork required for potential adoptive parents. A furnace inspection? Written recommendations from friends with requests such as "describe the health and wellness habits of the prospective parents?" At my first prenatal visit, I don't recall one question related to the status of my home heating system, and while my doctors asked a few personal questions about my health habits, I certainly wasn't expected to bring a friend along to vouch for me. I was sure these adoption agencies had no idea what my friends had already been through on the long road to becoming parents.

~Jenny Kalmon

CHAPTER 1

Easy Prey

It smothered me—latched on tight like tentacles that wrap and squeeze and bind their prey. Though most women controlled this fierce, maternal urge, mine controlled me—devoured me actually, for six long years. Over time it enticed me, convinced me I not only wanted motherhood, I craved it, needed it, required it to live contently.

My daunting quest to tame this unrelenting urge begins with a mind-made timeline. With sufficient might, I can close my eyes and literally see a penciled line, significant dates, and obvious captions. My timeline, though thirty-five years in length, appears relatively brief, but it only highlights life's two extremes—days of bliss and days of grief. Fortunately, I'll begin with the bliss. My eyes shut tight, I spot the first noteworthy date and its appropriate title.

February 2, 2005—No Way

My lengthy adoption story, oddly enough, began in a bathroom, for to chronicle my path to adoption, I must first divulge my fertility woes. I must first reveal the unexpected truth.

By February 2, 2005, my husband John and I had been trying to get pregnant for approximately five years. Every single month, whether we attempted sex thirty times, one time, or not at all, I'd convince myself that I was pregnant—I'd even experienced intense cravings for salt, painful swelling in my nearly B breasts, and extreme delays in my menstrual cycle. I bought pregnancy tests as often as I bought a new tube of toothpaste, and if my period stalled by just one day, we most certainly, in my irrational mind, had produced life. But in reality, we hadn't. Whether I bought a $14.99 test or a ninety-nine cent one (yes, a local dollar store sold pregnancy tests for one dollar), I never saw a second line—until the second day of February.

My period, like it had for so many months, refused to show up on its expected day, so that Friday afternoon, I stuck to my one-day-late testing policy. After veering left rather than right out of my school's parking lot, I stopped by the nearest discount chain and purchased yet another dollar store test. Soon after pulling into my garage, I threw my coat on a kitchen chair and downright scampered to the master bath.

Keep in mind that even though my tests never posted positive results, I always felt a surge of giddiness with the prospect of seeing two lines. Like the previous month, I held a target the size of a stick of Trident gum between my legs, covered the stick with warm pee, and rested the test on the flat bathroom counter. In a very short amount of time, much faster than the suggested two minutes, two dark lines transpired.

"No way," I said aloud. My husband, not yet home and not expected for two more hours, could not validate the shocking results. I had to tell someone; I suddenly needed witnesses. "No way," I said aloud again, maybe to my neatly hanging towels. But before I could refute the evidence to another inanimate object, I suddenly realized there *was* a way.

Thanks, Mom. My eyes instinctively tilted upward. Though my mom had been dead since September 24, 2002, the positive test only solidified my belief that she had somehow intercepted my nightly prayers—my pleas to God that begged for a beloved child. This had to be her doing—it was all there in her letter.

My mom, who died of cancer at the young age of 60, had written each of her six children a final letter before leaving this world. About a week before she passed away, my sister Donna informed me of this, and in all honesty, I remember feeling shockingly thrilled. I envisioned savoring pages of favorite memories and undisclosed aspirations.

On the day of her funeral, I received my mother's letter, a surprisingly brief correspondence. Rather than writing it on eight by ten stationary, she had scrawled it on a five by seven piece of memo paper (her message only filling half the page). When I first read the note, I actually felt cheated. I had selfishly expected more from my dying mother and didn't even treasure her words enough to keep them in a safe place. I immediately lost her note and could not for the life of me find it for more than two years after her funeral.

It reappeared in late December 2004, like a beloved missing earring that camouflages itself within carpeting but then suddenly gleams in just the right light. While ducking under my bed to find an unused picture frame, I spotted the envelope and immediately recognized the unsteady handwriting. Curious to revisit her letter, I unfolded the note and read the now profound message:

Laura,

You have grown to become a very caring and loving person. God Bless you and John. Your life is full of meaning. Your generosity is overwhelming. I hope you have children you can raise as I did. I pray for you and John. May God Bless you and I'll see you in heaven.

Love,
Mom

I couldn't believe I had once dismissed these prophetic seven sentences. I remember thinking, after reading the note, that she had somehow known I would need to hear those exact words, not on the day of her funeral, but years later. On that day, I felt such a strong sense that, perhaps as a reward for good behavior, she had been permitted to visit earth. She had come with predictions that I drank in with refreshing ease.

Standing in my bathroom, a month after rereading the letter, I felt certain my mom deserved the bulk of the credit. I believed, with baffling confidence, that she had personally petitioned God on my behalf, brown-nosed Him even, to produce this longed for grandchild. Still pondering her insights, I felt a strengthened bond between us, as if my mom now possessed omniscient powers, able to come to my aid whether summoned or not.

The moment, though sentimental, proved wholly short-lived. Struck by a fit of skepticism, I cursed the cheap, get-all-my-hopes-up dollar store test, doubting its accuracy. Again I insisted, "There is no way," this time to the mirror, to my reflection actually. And my reflection couldn't believe it either. She blushed and grinned, and we both decided our next step—call the hospital. Take a blood test.

After a twenty second phone call, I drove eight miles to the local clinic, trying to fully grasp my emotional state. One part of me, my pessimistic self, wanted me to remain neutral until otherwise notified. "You took a dollar store test, Laura. You are *not* pregnant." The other part of me, my optimistic self, denied such advice. "If I'm pregnant now . . . February, March, April, May, June, July, August, September, October? Would the baby be born in October? Wait, if I got pregnant in January . . ." By the time I pulled into the parking lot, I couldn't calm that second self. I had wanted to enter motherhood for five years now, and maybe, just maybe, I had finally arrived.

After slight complications with supplying a urine sample, my pee likely wasted on my dollar store find, a nurse in Mickey Mouse scrubs filled a paper cup with water, guided me to the waiting room, and told me to come back whenever I was ready. When the urge finally hit, I trickled out just enough drops.

"How soon do you think you will have the results?" I asked, not realizing that on Friday afternoons even doctors leave when their shifts end.

"I'm not sure we'll get to it today, but we might be able to call you tonight. Will you be home?"

I sighed heavily. Would I have to wait an entire weekend for this news? My face collapsed. "I actually won't be home tonight. I'm leaving town at six o'clock."

"If it's okay with you, we can call and leave a message on your phone."

"That'd be great." As I left the hospital, renewed optimism again surfaced. Fueled by women's intuition and Pandora's escaped hope, I drove home certain I was driving for two.

When I pulled into the garage and did not see John's truck, I convinced myself I could hold my tongue. We would spend the night playing cards with his family, a cluster of strong personalities who would create a raucous enough environment to distract my curious mind. More than any in-law, I dreaded passing the night in the strong company of two uninvited guests, Wonder and Doubt.

*

On that chilly February night, just after twelve, John placed the car in park, and I scooted out the door and towards the phone. A glowing red dot indicated the arrival of a message, and I snatched the phone from its handle to enter a series of numbers.

"You have one new message," an automated voice announced.

Though a typical answering machine proclaimed information to anyone three rooms away, we owned a voicemail system, which gave only the person on the phone the ability to hear the recorded message. By now John had nestled into his side of the bed, exhausted from driving 50 miles on wintry Wisconsin roads. I, on the other hand, stood in our spare bedroom on the other side of the house, establishing complete privacy, and following the final automated instruction.

"Press one-one to hear your messages."

One. One. And there it was.

"This is Wendy from the clinic. Your lab results from today are in. The test is positive. You are pregnant." The woman's voice clicked out, and the automated one stated, "If you'd like to delete this message, press seven. If you'd like to replay this message, press four."

Elation, exhilaration, disbelief. I literally polkaed to the bedroom door intending to hand the phone to my husband, so he could hear the news firsthand. To my utter disappointment, however, John didn't even have his table lamp on, lighting the pages of the latest John Grisham novel. Instead he lay with his back to me, blankets up to his chin, the faint smell of sleep settling in the air. No way was I waiting until sunrise to share my news. Again my mind shouted silently, *No way*, as I flicked on my own bedside lamp.

"John," I whispered loudly. "You need to hear this weird message on our answering machine."

This plea did nothing to stir my annoyed husband, who shooed me away like a bothersome insect that buzzed in the opening of his uncovered ear.

"Seriously, John," I buzzed, "Please listen to this message."

John turned in my direction engulfed in irritation. This was not going well.

"Give me the phone," he said begrudgingly.

"Press four," I urged.

I watched him listen to the doctor's life-altering test results, waited to exchange a life-altering embrace, and studied how his face digested the life-altering news. Oddly enough, he remained unmoved.

"It's a wrong number, Laura. Just delete it and go to bed."

In all of the times I'd fantasized about this momentous event, I never once prepared for this reaction. "No way!" my inner self screamed.

"John, it's not a wrong number. I have to tell you something. I need you to sit up and listen to me. Something big happened today."

John leaned on one elbow, still squinting at the light that I had turned on when I first entered the room.

"That message was from our clinic. I took a pregnancy test today. It was positive. I'm pregnant!"

I should have known, after eight years of marriage, what he would say. I guess all couples after a while share certain phrases, borrow similar words, and ultimately form their own private language. I reached my arms around him, but he pushed me back to face him. Still in shock and somewhat sleepy, he looked in my eyes and stated simply, "No way."

*

By March 27, 2005, I had known about the precious cargo inside my belly for approximately ten weeks and had yet to utter a word to my unsuspecting co-workers. Since John and I felt it taboo to announce my pregnancy too early, we only told our immediate families and closest friends. By sheer coincidence, I planned to meet with my book club the day after the doctor's confirmation call, so we both knew I'd be sharing our news the moment they arrived. My entire club consisted of merely three dear friends, the three women I'd graduated with from college, stood beside in weddings, and called upon weekly for cooking tips, movie reviews, or marital advice. Among Jen, Amy, and Jenny, I sensed that Jenny would most appreciate my status. A mother of two already, she likely longed to discuss parenting dilemmas with actual parents. Although a select few knew my delightful secret, John and I both agreed the time had come to confess our condition to colleagues. The day before spring break, we revealed our thrilling news at work.

As expected, by the end of that Friday, the entire high school where we both taught, including a student body of over 1300, had directly or indirectly learned the news. We couldn't leave the building without faculty, custodians, or students exchanging a hug, slapping a high five, or offering a spirited congratulations. Our lives teetered on the brink of tremendous change, people warned. Little did we know the truth of this prophecy.

When glancing at my retrievable timeline, I see the next significant date: March 29, 2005. Rather than finding the expected heading, "Easter Sunday," I see the title, "Make it Stop." I remember the day well. I remember the day beginning with such undeniable possibility and ending with such unexplained loss.

March 29, 2005~Make it Stop

On the eve of that particular Easter, John and I shared a renewed zest for the upcoming holiday. Sure it would be nice to visit with our families the following day, but to partake in an organized egg hunt through a child's perspective again—that's what we craved. Though we were still months away from holding a child, and years away from helping him locate eggs of a designated color, we both enjoyed our heightened sense of children. Each day that passed, we instinctively began paying more attention when a nephew requested a piggyback ride or a niece needed her shoe tied. Like two eager rookies reporting for practice, we wanted authentic training—special drills that tested our stamina. Bring on the jelly-bean highs and chocolate stained T-shirts. All of a sudden, after years of being responsible and relatively boring adults, we longed to rediscover the charms of childhood. Ten years had passed since John or I had dipped hardboiled eggs into vinegar-based dye and decorated a single Easter egg. We were ready for this conversion. At least I knew that I was.

With most holidays, John and I had to divvy up our time between our large immediate families, sometimes celebrating on the exact day with his family and often celebrating two or three days before the holiday with mine. On this Easter, we planned to visit my family, who lived only thirty miles away. Our contribution to the traditional menu of ham, cheesy potatoes, and hot buns included a green bean casserole that I intended to prepare before leaving at noon. But as soon as I woke up that morning, I couldn't will myself to think of food. I felt abnormal pangs of pressure cramping my lower stomach, as if someone was using a plastic fork and poking me for a good laugh. I wanted to laugh and simply shrug the ominous feeling away like a kinked neck after sleeping on a crooked pillow, but I knew this was no sprained ankle I could wrap in an Ace bandage and keep elevated so the throbbing blood could drain away. That's when the thought occurred, *blood*. I instantly recognized the feeling—I was about to have my monthly period. And once I identified this reality, the heaviness on my belly intensified. "Make it stop," my inner voice scolded, an earnest appeal aimed at my malfunctioning body.

Around nine that morning, I talked to John about my concerns. "I don't feel right," I tried inadequately to explain. "It's like I feel pressure on my stomach, cramping even."

My problem-solving husband suggested we call our doctor. For some reason, I disagreed. Was I being paranoid? Were we overreacting? I hated the idea of wasting my doctor's time with some insignificant plastic fork symptoms.

After a brief discussion, John called the clinic. He didn't mind; he wanted to help. And I knew deep down why I couldn't call myself. As soon as he started dialing, my throat tightened. My eyes ached. Tears outlined the edges of my contacts. With my eyelids blinking madly, I willed the tears back in. This time my will held its own, my poor, unsuspecting, unprepared will.

With his right hand holding our portable phone and his other holding the phone book, John called the hospital. At this point I remained lying on our bed, not about to give gravity any advantage in the situation. Once connected, John delivered up his best professional-teacher/soon-to-be-father voice. "Yes, my wife is ten weeks pregnant, and she's experiencing some cramping. Do you think we need to be concerned about this?"

John waited for a reply and then turned to me and asked, "Have you had any bleeding?"

I shook my head no, convinced that a verbal response would stimulate those burning tears still bullying my will. John listened attentively to the nurse on the phone, adding polite okays and offering thanks before ending the call.

He set the phone down on the nightstand, patted my hand with a soft tap, and relayed the information he'd just absorbed.

"As long as there's no bleeding, they aren't very concerned."

"Am I supposed to lie down or something? Take any medicine? Should we even be going to my dad's house today?"

John shrugged his shoulders with genuine uncertainty. "They said you could lie down if you wanted to, but you didn't have to. I think we need to decide if we should cancel for today. What do you want to do?"

What did I want to do? I wanted to stop worrying, stop allowing my pessimistic self to badger my easily bruised optimism. I wanted to stop this cramping. "Make it stop," I demanded silently addressing, not my will, but Jesus personally. I knew about His special day and all, but this was getting serious. My pesky woman's intuition had teamed up with my mother's instinct, and both surged like two mutts pleading for someone to open the back door and let them in already. I sensed hackles rising, claws scratching, voices whining.

An unknown presence beckoned me to stay on guard. What did I want to do? I had triggered an alarm that only I could hear. Some time within the last ten hours, I had tripped a switch in my body, a dreadful switch. I needed to find the off button. I needed to make it stop.

"I don't think we should go today. I just want to lie down all day and relax and not really move until I feel normal again. Is that okay with you?"

John completely understood and even offered to deliver the casserole while I continued resting.

"I'll call and explain what's up. If they need the dish to complete the meal, you can run it over, right? I doubt they'll want you to do that though."

I dialed my dad's number and thankfully Leisa, one of my older sisters, answered. I didn't really think my dad would truly understand the nature of my excuse to ditch Easter (even though he had raised five daughters and knew far more than he would admit about tampons, Midol, and "female plumbing," as he liked to call it). But I knew Leisa would identify with my situation as she had endured a miscarriage just a few years ago.

"No worries!" Leisa chimed (always the optimist, a lifelong member of the glass half full club.) "You just rest all day if you need to. I'm sure there's nothing to worry about. Tell John to go rent some movies. We can get by without the green beans."

I hung up the phone with my fears in check. A part of me even contemplated Leisa's suggestion. A day of renting movies, sharing buttered popcorn, and brainstorming baby names sounded wonderfully worry-less. I found the day's new motto: *No worries.*

Just as I turned to share this carefree philosophy with my husband, I felt it. It crawled down my body like a thin drop of water slowly leaking from a tired faucet. I sprinted to the bathroom to confirm my suspicion.

There it was.

A
d
r
o
p
of
red
blood.

That damn switch.

I was leaking.

I needed to flip a valve.

"Make it stop," I prayed, "please."

Now that I had produced one drop, I wanted John to call the doctor again. I wanted these professionals to look in some kind of maternity manual, diagnose the severity of the situation, and offer detailed instructions involving a switch or a plug. This could not turn into the alternative. It was Easter. Too much holiness hung in the air. Today of all days, even the most frequently absent church members outfitted themselves in new, pastel apparel, slid into hard, wooden pews, and worshiped their chosen Savior. I could hear the organ led hymns, smell the Cheerios smuggled in through white purses, taste the incense itching my nose, and touch the invisible prayers hovering towards heaven. Maybe this was all just an elaborate test of faith. Fine then. I had always been a good test taker, with the exception of pop quizzes. And wasn't this more of a pop quiz? Then what was the first question? How badly do you want this baby? My Maker already knew the answer to that.

John picked up the phone and again dialed the hospital. This time he spoke directly to a doctor, already a bad omen that we had graduated beyond a nurse's expertise. Two questions into the conversation, John handed me the phone.

"Hello?" I said, choking down the burning clump of tears now strangling my vocal chords.

"Laura, how would you describe your bleeding? Would you say there are drops of blood or is there heavy bleeding?"

"Only a couple drops of blood," I replied, "but I'm feeling like I'm getting my period. Would you suggest I lie down or something? Should I come in?" I wanted immediate answers and instant reassurance. I couldn't believe the steady, cool voice on the other line. He didn't seem the least bit concerned. Maybe this was a normal, no worries kind of pregnancy hiccup. I half expected him to tell me to drink a glass of water upside down and enjoy the holiday.

"Here's what I would suggest. If you want to lie down, you can, but you don't have to. Just make sure you refrain from having sex, and, if the bleeding increases, call us back."

I couldn't get over the sex comment. From a medical standpoint, I'd heard that sex could induce labor, but I, along with my bloated body, wanted nothing to do with sex. (I would refrain from sex for the next seven months if that's all it took.) The advice seemed as obvious as if he just casually suggested, "Refrain from running a marathon today." I appreciated his candor though. His concise, levelheaded response relaxed me.

"Okay, I can do that. Thanks," I stated, my internal alarm quieting a bit.

I hung up the phone and broke the news to John. "No sex today, doctor's orders."

"Like we were having sex today anyway."

"I know, right?" We both shared a laugh for the first time since waking that morning.

"I'm gonna lie down for about an hour and try to de-stress. Will you stay by me?"

Without hesitation, John grabbed his book off the nightstand and lay on his back. I followed suit. We had spent countless Sunday afternoons like this—reading for a while, allowing printed words to seduce us into sleep. After dozing off twenty minutes at a time, we'd awaken with a slight jolt only to repeat the process again. If this wouldn't disarm my system, nothing would.

I had not known it at the time, but nothing would.

*

Though my once hostile body stayed dormant for the rest of the afternoon, it eventually confronted the basic physics of life: an object in motion stays in motion. I, to this day, don't know what I did to initiate the sequence. At seven that evening, despite my persistent will, I ran to the bathroom, trying to prevent a gush of blood from staining my beige sheets.

When I reached the toilet and looked down, I discovered streaks of burgundy, cherry, and crimson swirling together, darkening the once clear water.

"John!" I screamed in a piercing, helpless screech. "John, I need help!"

Shards of pain stabbed my lower stomach causing me to slouch on the stool, bury my head, and wrap my arms around my legs. Each surge of pain released a thick, warm fluid, a blood red discharge that flowed involuntarily.

"It's happening!" I screamed. "Please come in here!"

My husband sprinted through the bathroom door and stopped at the sink.

"John, I think we lost it," I cried. He took in the scene—my red face, my red eyes—I was an overexposed photo of too much red. "I need you to look. I can't look."

Urgency. Hysteria. Despair. All of these emotions crowded together in my small and increasingly polluted bathroom, but Fear consumed the most space. I needed John to intervene. I needed his tall, muscular frame to barge in and chase off these unwelcomed demons. I needed John's strength, courage, and hope.

With endearing gentleness, he tilted me forward and looked down into the water. "I've never seen that much blood before," he admitted, his face nearly colorless.

"I know!" I wailed, bawling uncontrollably. "Call the hospital."

As John rushed off to the make the call, I sat in that cramped bathroom, my legs trembling, my faith faltering.

Please, Lord. I prayed. *Please don't take this baby from me.*

Salty tears, salty snot. All I could taste was salt and sadness. Nothing seemed fair, yet nothing seemed final. "Make it stop," my inner voice begged. And that's when I sank my lowest yet. "Please, Mom," I prayed, "if you're up there in heaven, *please* make it stop." In my desperate state, I resorted to the one person who I thought could offer help. The longer I stayed in that crouched position in my desolate bathroom, however, the closer I came to accepting that she had not been summoned. My deceased mother may have returned to earth and helplessly witnessed my current crisis, but this time she did not petition God, or if she did, He ignored her pleas. He had His plans. Moments after I sent the desperate prayer, another surge of blood passed. The harsh truth became clear; no one on heaven or earth could make it stop.

After another hour of bleeding, I showered quickly and threw on one of John's oversized sweatshirts and a pair of dingy running pants. John and I headed to the hospital, and after hearing the results of a fruitless ultrasound, returned home at two a.m.

A few days later, when the intense grief decided to sleep and even jabs of anger couldn't wake it, John sat me down and shared a brutally honest confession. He, in the aftermath of all of this, realized that he didn't truly want the baby until we had lost it. I found it difficult to relate to this revelation, but still weak and exhausted, decided not to judge.

"But more importantly," he continued to explain, "I am now one hundred percent certain that I want to be a dad. I want a baby."

I still can't accept that a miscarriage had to happen for John to appreciate the fragile gift of fatherhood, but it gave me some sense of purpose, some sense of why it happened. Today I know exactly why we were never meant to keep that child, but I didn't know it three years ago. And I didn't know it until one more bathroom incident, possibly the most powerful incident yet. This story, not saturated with sadness, is coated with a more shameful ingredient, envy.

*

As I peek at my timeline, I now notice the expected initials B.C., yet they don't signify Before Children nor do they symbolize more dreaded Birthday Candles. At this point in my life, B.C. referred to my biological clock, that internal mechanism that I chose to ignore in my twenties, a time when I kept busy by completing and checking off my "Goals to Achieve" list.

As a typical woman with modest life ambitions, I had progressed through my twenties reaching the expected milestones. Milestone #1, age 23, graduate from college; Milestone #2, age 23, find a teaching job; Milestone #3, age 24, get engaged; Milestone #4, age 25, get married; Milestone #5, age 26, purchase a starter home; Milestone #6, age 27, own a dog; Milestone #7, age 28, produce the first of 2.5 children. The only glitch along the way occurred at Milestone #7. But to use the term glitch somewhat weakens the severity of the problem. I was fast approaching the dreaded 3-0, the notable age when my inability to produce viable, healthy eggs began concerning everyone. Once polite compliments such as, "You and John will make great parents someday," suddenly changed into blunt inquiries such as, "Have you two checked to see if John's *boys* are swimming upstream?"

People meant well. At least I think they did. But concerned sisters, an eager mother-in-law, and curious co-workers didn't press and pressure as often as my very own B.C. did. And from age 28 to age 31, my craving for a baby intensified to an unbalanced point. Getting pregnant and staying pregnant became an all consuming priority.

For roughly the first five months following my miscarriage, from April through August, my body took its precious time in healing, probably because I never underwent a Dilation & Curettage, more commonly known as a D & C. (I passed on the optional medical procedure where a doctor will force a woman's cervix to dilate and then scrape the uterus of any remaining tissue.) Once I finally stopped bleeding, my body then refused to produce regular menstrual cycles, which made knowing when to have sex a complete and utter chore. By the start of September, I began working with a more aggressive gynecologist, and that's when I really noticed a change, in myself and in my surroundings. I couldn't pump gas, check out groceries, or walk through a parking lot without sighting every single pregnant woman within a half-mile radius. Why was this so easy for others and so hard for me? Gradually, I viewed the task as downright pointless. Was I forcing something that was never meant to be?

From September through March, my once determined mind became skeptical of what I chose to do to my body. For example, I sensed my mind raising its brow when I underwent an invasive procedure involving the flushing of my fallopian tubes. Worse yet, I noticed my mind scrunch its face when I entered my gynecologist's office within twenty-four hours after a very scheduled, very passionless session of sex. My disapproving mind opted to turn away when the doctor extracted the still moving sperm inside of me, a medical method that helped evaluate the number and mobility of my husband's *swimmers*. Somewhere between Point A and Point B (and when I say point, I'm literally talking about the pointy metal instruments that poked and prodded my lower region all in the name of science), I became a cynic. Though I could have very easily blamed my mood-shifting alter ego on my newly prescribed drugs, I knew it was me. A raw, bitter, unpleasant version of me had emerged from the darkness.

This pious, spiteful self began questioning God's existence and judging those around me, especially inept mothers. Though I kept my comments to myself, I worried that people could hear my unspoken criticism. My distain lingered like bad breath. It sat on my tongue like the residue that builds from eating spiced, black jellybeans. I'd study mothers and think: *why not me?*

During this time, I could spend hours pondering the random way God dispersed birth certificates, and I *did* spend hours, mostly at night, right before bed. I felt so conflicted about the whole pregnancy process, a process I thought only worked with the help of God, with His blessing. I used to hold my own nieces or nephews, or stare at the tiny toenails of a friend's newborn, and believe wholeheartedly in the miracle of life, in God's will. For the first eighteen years of my life, I attended a Catholic church, bowed my head every Sunday, and recited with sincerity, "Thy kingdom come, Thy will be done on earth as it is in Heaven." But getting pregnant boiled down to pinpointing my once-a-month ovulation schedule, having sex one to two days prior to ovulating, hoping my husband's swimming sperm remained alive and kicking, releasing a hardy egg from my ovaries, and praying at least one sperm penetrated my egg and produced a fetus. Once sex became a scientific experiment, obligation replaced romance, need replaced want, and unnatural replaced natural. By Friday, March 24, 2006, irrational had replaced rational, no thanks to my B.C.

March 24, 2006—So Unfair

The fast approaching month of April, much like January, brought out deep introspection. That may seem odd, but April now contained two depressing dates: Easter, the one-year anniversary of my miscarriage, and my birthday, another year closer to less viable egg production. Though sometimes Easter fell in March, this year it landed on April 16, one day before my thirty-third birthday. Towards the end of March, my cynicism reached record heights. While the deliberate tick of my annoying B.C. refused to back off, a baby boom had struck in all departments but mine. On Friday, March 24, I entered school with expected dread. It was the last day before a much needed spring break, a day when most students brought too much energy and most teachers too little patience. (I was no exception.) I didn't know exactly what would happen, but frustrating mornings usually begin with a starving stomach finding no cereal in the cupboard, no egg in the fridge, or no bread in the drawer. It was that kind of day.

If I consult my timeline, I can make out the heading, "So Unfair." It happened on that Friday. It happened after the bell rang to end fourth hour and another bell rang to begin fifth. It happened in another stinky bathroom, the one on second floor, right across from the volunteer center, the one near the library. That's when I saw the former student. That's what triggered, as Oprah would say, my "aha moment."

I stood waiting for an open stall, and she casually walked through the door, all belly, all smiles.

"Oh, hi, Mrs. Schmitt," she said. Then we both stood there a moment as I took in her condition. She looked quite far along, though I was no expert at guessing due dates. Her T-shirt, made of a stretchy green fabric, clung to her basketball figure making it more pronounced than if she'd buried it under a sweater. I guess she's not hiding the child was my first thought. Was she keeping it? I knew I couldn't ask that question, of course, but I knew I needed to inquire about the obvious.

"Hey there. Look at you. How far along are you?" I figured this was a safe question, not too nosy, not ignoring the elephant in the room, or the elephant-like tummy to be more accurate.

"The baby's due in June," she replied, again with the smile, the beaming, proud smile.

"Wow," I responded lamely, "This should be a busy summer for you." I heard the loud flush of a toilet, saw the orange door open, pointed to it as if to signal an end to our chat, and ducked inside, a bit irked, moderately peeved.

As I sat in my stall, shaking my head, I couldn't help having a word with the Big Guy. "Okay, God." I prayed, "What's the deal here? I'm turning 33 in three weeks, I'm married, college educated, earning a steady income . . ." I kept rambling off my parenting qualifications like some interviewee applying for a job. Had he misplaced my résumé or something? How in the world did this seventeen-year-old get blessed with a child instead of me? Was it that whole egg meets sperm, sperm creates fetus thing? Was it really just that? "So unfair," I told myself, my eyes rolling. *It was all so unfair.*

I stepped to the half-oval sink that spat out water to three pairs of hands at one time. My left palm triggered the spray as my right palm punched the walled soap dispenser. While I lathered and rinsed, she exited her stall, scooted up to the sink, and scrubbed her small hands. I snuck another glance at her bulging belly. It struck me as beautiful, a cashmere sweater I wanted to try on and leave with.

"See ya, Mrs. Schmitt," she said, wiping her damp hands on her pants, smiling wide. Enough with the smile.

"Bye now," I offered, still at the sink, still catching the falling water, still struggling to silence my pious, judgmental self. But once she left the bathroom, and I rubbed my hands beneath an automatic dryer, I had to look my horrid self in the mirror, all skin and bones, all jealousy. That was one disadvantage to being thin. When my slim body filled up with emotion, it filled up fast. The envy didn't linger in my hips or cling to any cellulite. It heard some sort of starting gun, raced through each vein and capillary, and within seconds, consumed my every cell.

I left that high school bathroom filthier than it had ever been. I didn't add to the misspelled graffiti carved into the stalls; I didn't literally vandalize a cubicle, but I felt so utterly drenched in envy that I suspected I had dripped some on the tiles or smudged some on the door. The last thing teenage girls needed was to touch this infectious toxin. They all knew its unyielding power.

Convinced that gooey resentment was trickling out my pores, I stayed quiet at lunch, (a relatively easy task when surrounded by eight articulate women, all English teachers, all verbally gifted). I finished half my turkey sandwich, smiled politely at the shared anecdotes, but for fifteen minutes straight, I kept eyeing up the day's treat that sat in the center of the table. There they were—spiced, black jellybeans. Without anyone commenting (or maybe even noticing), I ate one black jellybean after another, transforming my tongue into a thick layer of blackish green. I didn't even like the bitter licorice taste. Was I punishing myself for merely thinking the horrid, critical thoughts I'd been spewing out into the universe? Even though no one could hear them, I still created them, and who knows the chain of negativity my mind set in motion. It was a far cry from pulling a Hester Prynne, but how else can I explain my irrational behavior? Just before the lunch hour ended, when I returned to the same bathroom and looked in the exact same mirror, sure enough, my tongue bore my sin. My black-green tongue now matched my black-green attitude, and that's when I decided I loathed my pathetic self.

Something had to change—I had to change. That Friday, after surviving the last day before my much needed break, I drove home serenaded by a soft buzz, an unusually inspiring hum. It wasn't until I pulled into my gravel driveway that I could name the sound. Sure enough, it was right there almost tangible to the touch—a small, yet brilliant light bulb. That very afternoon I sat my husband down to discuss some realistic options, including adoption—option number two.

CHAPTER 2

Built on a foundation of eight years of marriage, eight years of observations, and eight years of daily choices, I affectionately dub John a "cheese and sausage" kind of husband. What I mean, quite literally, involves John craving Canadian bacon, pepperoni and cheese, or spicy, garlic chicken, and politely, yet adamantly, voicing his preference. After a brief debate, however, John consents to ordering my personal favorite, cheese and sausage, on any given evening from any given business. To simplify the theory into a concise thesis: if I beg, John caves. Eight years of negotiating confirmed my assumption. How odd that a theory, eight years in the making, could crumble to pieces, eight seconds into our "options" discussion. But crumble it did, as soon as I mentioned my views on option number one: in vitro fertilization.

There we sat, feet on our ottoman, lips cooling pizza, trading the highlights of our last day before break. I relived the semi-meltdown in the school bathroom—the pregnant teen, my horrid spite. John described visiting college students—former graduates, bursting with facial hair.

By the second slice of pizza, I eased into my thoughts about in vitro fertilization, yet in all honesty, we had visited this topic before. By now we rarely pronounced the enormous term—we left it at "in vitro"—as if referring to some college friend we knew so well we assigned a nickname. Up until now in vitro had always been debated under purely hypothetical circumstances. If we needed to kill time in a long car ride, for instance, our buddy in vitro could always add spice to a stale conversation. Now that it resurfaced as a realistic option, however, I felt passionate about expressing my concerns.

"In vitro is probably out of our price range," I began, as if we intended to buy a home rather than produce human life. I think that's what bothered me the most. I felt like those people who spelled Christmas as X-mas, who later overheard complaints about how they took "Christ" out of the word. This whole concept, even my first point, led to a discussion fraught with logistics rather than ethics. Back to becoming specimens in some elaborate and pricey experiment, we needed to ponder some disturbing questions. Couldn't we equate this procedure to someone opting for plastic surgery? From a moral standpoint, should we even partake in such an artificial operation? Didn't such medical miracles somewhat distort God's natural plan for us? I had no desire, at this point, to think seriously about the religious compromises attached to this decision, but before I could state my next concern, John caught me off guard by pointing out our financial status.

"If we wanted to do it, we could afford it," he affirmed, and for the next ten minutes, we mulled over how we could pool together our hard-earned savings to purchase butt shots and sperm injections. There were enough statements beginning with, "We could . . ." and "If we would . . ." coming from John's end that I sensed he had pondered this topic on more than just a few car rides.

Besides the financial burden, I brooded over another concern—needles. I knew deep down I couldn't poke myself with a shot on a daily basis, nor could John. When I admitted this to my husband, he gave me a look, but I gave it right back. Sure John provided a sperm sample a few months ago, but not even in a doctor's office. I guarantee, besides a slight stab to his ego, he experienced no pain whatsoever. The true lab rat lately was my vagina. A trooper since last March, even she'd had enough—enough exposure, enough prodding.

"Laura, if there was any way medically that I could help, I would. If I were you, I'd do anything and everything I could to have a child."

Would he *really*? I wanted to dare him to twist his penis in thirds and then hold it there in a pinched position for an undisclosed amount of time, for that's what my vagina felt like when they inserted the instrument that flushed out my fallopian tubes. Instead I offered my final line of reasoning.

"Here's my biggest worry," I confessed, "that we could do it all—suffer through every shot, endure the side effects of every drug, finally get pregnant, and then, twelve weeks later, end up with another miscarriage."

"That would suck," John admitted.

"I know," I said. And we both just sat there, remembering the damn bathroom, the devastating ultrasound, the dead silent drive home. We never once played the game, "our child would be so-and-so years old by now." Maybe individually we did, at least I did. Only a year ago our lives glowed with potential, yet now life centered around recapturing that lost gem. I couldn't help but envy characters in fiction who simply followed a treasure map, deciphered an ancient riddle, or stumbled upon an obscure key. No matter how perilous their journey, they always unearthed their answer. I guess I didn't need a squat, cloaked elf to guide me away from in vitro. I just couldn't decide how best to discover John's views on option number two.

"Would you ever consider adoption?" There. I said it—finally throwing it on the table like a last minute hors d'oeuvre squeezed in before the main course. It had been consuming my thoughts ever since lunch, teasing my optimistic self who had taken quite a beating lately and was not used to getting any attention at all. That whole concept, that a teenager or grown woman may be yearning to rid herself of a baby as much as I yearned to hold one—it struck me as powerful, faith-full even, one or two steps closer to God's will. Phrases like, "meant to be," and "everything happens for a reason," started nudging themselves from the cubbyholes of my mind as if they'd been playing a yearlong game of hide-and-seek but once again wanted to be found and contemplated. I caught my optimistic self trying to holler, "Come out, come out, wherever you are" in an attempt to summon other faith-based mantras and uncover more buried beliefs.

Adoption. In all fairness it, too, wasn't a new topic of discussion for John and me, but it was never quite this relevant, never this serious. Unfortunately, after about five minutes of conversation, both John and I found ourselves posing plenty of unanswerable questions. Rather than searching the web for unreliable advice, John proposed we phone Jim, his road biking buddy who adopted a little girl from Korea.

"Maybe he could come over for supper tomorrow night, and you could meet Kendra for yourself." I loved the idea.

My greatest question mark surrounding international adoption involved the health and the age of the adopted child. As teachers, John and I had taken classes on brain-based learning, so we understood how fast an infant's brain develops. My friend Jenny researched the topic for her master's project, and I sat through the entire presentation. She noted that experiencing neglect or stress at a young age can produce too much cortisol, a stress hormone that may lead to impaired memory or delays in cognitive abilities. In our minds, couples who pursued an international infant, at best, took home a twelve-month-old. This, to me, was a toddler, already acquiring language, eating solid foods, walking on unsteady limbs. To go this route meant surrendering the first 12, 18, maybe 24 months of my child's life to a perfect stranger, or strangers. I heard some unwanted infants lived in overcrowded orphanages. According to my own sister-in-law, her niece came to the United States from China with a flat head, supposedly from so much time spent lying in an unattended crib. A part of me longed to adopt such a child, scoop her in my arms and rescue her from these harsh conditions, but another part just couldn't imagine plucking a child from her surroundings, no matter how desolate, and plopping her in my arms.

I could close my eyes and envision our first encounter. As I'd anxiously reach for a tender embrace, she'd shrink from my grasp. There'd be bending and kicking and bucking of sorts—tears of dread and bewilderment fleeing her eyes. "No! No! No!" She would shriek (in her own language, of course) yet with a cry so universal it would surpass the need for translation. Was this an accurate prediction, or would Jim negate my misconceptions? I prayed he would.

That following day, that dinner, and that four-year-old diva made such an impact on me that Saturday, March 25, 2006, remains etched in my timeline along with the title, "Inconceivable."

March 25, 2006—Inconceivable

I must begin with the diva's grand entrance, as she wouldn't fit the title had she cowered behind her father's leg or clung with might to his tall, long neck. The three foot princess strutted boldly through the front door, discarded her purple Dora coat, and immediately welcomed herself in. Within seconds she had surveyed the living room, found our oversized leather chair, and perched upon the seat like a queen on her throne. "I'm going to kindergarten next year," she pronounced proudly, but I cannot emphasize enough the perfect articulation of each word. "What are we having for dinner?" she inquired with eloquence, and right then and there I just wanted to eat her up, nibble on all of her sweetness and poise or serve it on a platter with a bright, pink bow. Even her giggle sounded delicious, as I watched my husband tap her shoulder, then duck behind her enormous chair. She smiled a scrumptious smile, reminding me of a delicately iced gingerbread cookie, the kind that people long to eat but leave untouched for others to admire.

"I hope you like spaghetti," I answered, resonating with enthusiasm as one usually does when addressing children.

With the meal ready and the table set, I ushered everyone into the dining room with garlic and basil guiding the way. It didn't take long to tower our plates with food and for bright orange sauce to stain the corners of my husband's mouth. Without our prompting, Jim began stuffing us with personal views and researched knowledge, some of it quite factual, though much of it a bit slanted.

To avoid an open adoption, he explained, he decided to adopt internationally. Neither John nor I truly understood the two terms, *open* and *closed* adoptions, so Jim backed up and defined both words. According to Jim, a birth mother nowadays looks through portfolios that prospective adoptive couples create, and the birth mother decides who will parent her child.

"You can get picked simply because you drive a red sports car." This was the subjective commentary that weaved its way into an otherwise enlightening conversation. Jim couldn't disguise his obvious bias. Though he didn't always use the colors I'd have chosen, he painted a picture we asked him to paint.

"It's called an open adoption," he continued, "because you keep in close contact with the birth mother. You send her pictures or even visit with her, and the adopted child knows exactly where he or she came from." I could tell Jim didn't approve of this arrangement, and I didn't know if I liked it either. If our intellectual, common sense friend opted for a closed adoption, I didn't know enough about the alternative to disagree. Consumed by curiosity and ignorance, I hung on Jim's every one-sided word.

"Do you know anything about whether the birth mother can change her mind?" I interrupted.

Jim didn't know the exact amount of time that must pass, but he thought the birth mother could change her mind and decide to keep the baby even after placement in a couple's home. For this reason, he and his now ex-wife preferred to adopt internationally. Once they left the country, no birth mother could change her mind or even contact them. Plus, agencies simply put couples on a waiting list, and when they reached the top, they qualified for the next available baby. There was no portfolio, no red sports car.

The passionate way Jim discussed international adoption brightened that brilliant bulb I had recently found glowing within me. Maybe it wasn't a bulb at all. Maybe *renewed hope* spread through my veins like the tingling pricks of an unused limb that falls asleep and then wakes up numb, surrounded in needles. Sure enough, I sensed Hope jolting from her lengthy slumber, slightly disoriented, but, nonetheless, wide-eyed and present.

At this point in the conversation, Jim emphasized the reason he adopted from Korea. Apparently through his chosen agency, the children destined for potential adoption lived in foster care rather than in an orphanage. That might explain Kendra's impressive demeanor—intelligent, curious, content. That's what I saw when I looked at this girl, a resilient and determined soul.

As forks scraped along our near empty plates, we stayed at the table, debating on dessert. That's when it happened.

I remember her sitting on the chair to my left. I remember her prattling on about the upcoming holiday. I remember her inquiring about the Easter bunny, the hiding of baskets, and the coloring of eggs. In the midst of our sharing, she declared the word.

"Inconceivable!" she yelled. And then she giggled.

I turned to her Dad, too stunned to speak. But finally I asked, "Did she just use the word *inconceivable*?" The whole exchange was just that. This night, too, was just that. This four-year-old child just correctly used a word that some of the sophomores I teach could not even define. *Inconceivable*. It truly was.

Jim chuckled aloud but then shrugged off the feat. "She did say the word, but I doubt she knows what it means. It's a line in one of the movies she watches every day." He asked the miniature genius in a raised, childlike tone, "Is that from *The Princess Bride*?"

She nodded yes and giggled some more, and I soaked in the moment, as if knowing its significance. Right then and there I knew with certainty that John and I would pursue adoption. The night had begun with unlimited questions but ended, inconceivably, with one clear answer.

*

On the third day of our vacation, we drove along Hwy 54, traveling ninety miles to a recommended adoption agency. After an entire Sunday of negotiating, John agreed to accompany me to a free consultation on Monday, March 27, with a woman named Sally. I vowed not to sign any papers or commit to any services.

"We are merely gathering data," my husband warned. "Please don't get your hopes up."

I understood the terms of our finalized verbal contract, but deep down I held fast to my pizza inspired theory. Did John not recall the time I begged him to visit the humane society, *insisting* we would only *look*? Did he not remember the day I convinced him to tour the newly constructed house just down the road, *promising* we would *not* make an offer? Did he not recollect the afternoon I persuaded him to browse through a furniture warehouse sale, *swearing* we would leave with *nothing*? How could he forget our first dog, our second home, and our three reclining theater seats? Whether John realized it or not, I was stepping into that office oozing with hope. Verbal contract or not, I oozed.

*

After nervous introductions and a brief interview about our intentions, we all took turns asking the delicate questions. While Sally inquired about our infertility, John focused more on the health of adopted babies, and I shared my concerns about an adopted child's age. Within the first ten minutes, Sally transformed into a talking adoption handbook slash travel agent, complete with colorful brochures and various pricing charts. The majority of the meeting centered around international adoption. (Jim had done all the leg work. We only needed a second opinion.)

In an extremely matter-of-fact way, Sally confirmed many of the stereotypes that Jim and others had mentioned. Yes, she had seen flat-headed children come from China. Yes, many international adoptions began in an orphanage. Yes, some babies from Russia suffered from fetal alcohol syndrome. Time and time again, she assured us, these adopted children, when placed in a nurturing environment, thrived within a short time. Thanks to Sally's candid comments and Kendra's precocious vocabulary, I couldn't silence my optimistic self who kept whispering, "Adopt from Korea. Adopt from Korea." But just as my mind started purchasing a plane ticket, hiring a translator, and envisioning a delicate Korean daughter sporting an Americana sundress, Sally asked the life-altering question.

"Have you two considered domestic adoption?"

No lights flickered. No alarms rang. No celestial signs of any kind rained down from heaven. But perhaps they should have, for that one question set into motion events that would forever change our lives.

Once we expressed a willingness to learn more about adopting domestically, Sally, again in a blunt fashion, broke down the process. Expectant birth mothers indeed searched through a couple's portfolio, possibly identifying most with a wife squeezing a Golden Retriever or a husband clad in army threads. No one could guess what might prompt a match. Deal breakers, however, could come down to careers.

"Teachers?" I asked, "Do birth mothers hate teachers?"

"No, not especially," Sally began. "Most of them like teachers—it's sometimes policemen they tend to shy away from." I couldn't explain the relief I felt. Something within me straightened tall—curiosity, perhaps—possibility, maybe.

As if to soften her frank responses, Sally accompanied most of them with specific examples gleaned from years of experience. When emphasizing that the agency only dealt with open adoptions, she described the two extremes. While some adoptive parents simply exchanged pictures via mail, others arranged visits on a monthly basis. One child ended up as a ring bearer in his birth mother's second wedding.

The more insights Sally shared, the more intrigued my B.C. grew. It decided to chime in midway through the meeting, which surprised me since I hadn't noticed it for three full days. It approved of this proactive approach to parenthood. "Time's a tickin'," it reminded, as if to suggest that domestic adoption might produce faster results.

Even though a part of me agreed with my B.C., another part of me stayed cautious. My pessimistic self kept waiting for the unavoidable—the reality of how often birth mothers changed their minds after giving birth. We'd watched enough made for TV movies together to know it happened—just how often? We both wanted to know.

Like all her answers, Sally didn't dip the message into any type of sweetener so we could swallow it with ease. She used clear and direct language as she had throughout the session. A birth mother had every right to change her mind and keep her baby. Even if a couple initially took the baby home and bonded with it for a month, the birth mother could decide not to legally give up her rights. In the state we lived in, couples needed to wait at least thirty days before the birth mother terminated her parental rights in an open court proceeding known as a TPR.

Thirty days. 720 hours. It seemed like a lifetime. In more precise terms, a birth mother could exhaust 43,200 minutes reflecting on her decision. If in just one of those minutes she longed for her baby back, all would end. A miscarriage seemed mild compared to pain that raw.

Just as my pessimistic self began pleading to veer the discussion back to adopting from Korea, Sally pulled out some sample portfolios. Pointing and stopping after every page, she offered some insights into the mind of a birth mom.

"One time a girl came in," Sally explained, "and only wanted to see women with blond hair." My attention peaked. "She wanted her child to fit in."

Comments like these cued the most bizarre thoughts. *I have blond hair; maybe I would have been picked.*

As if Sally read my mind, she added another unexpected shocker. "You two would be good candidates for domestic adoption. You're young, attractive, and active. That's what a lot of birth mothers are looking for."

At the same time, John and I turned towards each other as if to confirm whether the other had heard this revelation. I could tell from his eyes that he had, though he refused to register any added reaction. Over the years I had observed John perfect the acquired art of feigning interest out of sheer courtesy. Taking a cue from John's polite guise and my inquiry for specifics, Sally shared the portrait of a typical birth mother.

Much to my surprise, this agency usually worked with birth mothers in their early twenties, many of whom had children of their own, had little family support, and who didn't think they could financially and emotionally raise another baby. Most women chose the adoptive couple during their last trimester, so couples might get invited to a final ultrasound and then, within a month or so, get a call to come to the hospital and meet the newborn baby.

"Do birth mothers know the sex of the baby? Is it harder for them to know they might be giving up a boy or girl?" I asked random questions such as these with sincerity, yet all the while I ran the risk of sounding senile as well as stupid.

Sally reassured us that the agency counseled all birth mothers throughout their pregnancy. Consequently, though some did change their minds, most birth mothers stayed committed to adoption.

By the end of our meeting, my pessimistic self sat brooding on one side of my mind while my optimistic self stood pacing on the other. The internal dialogue volleyed back and forth, serving up cons then spiking back pros.

"The birth mother could change her mind."

"That's why she doesn't pick until late in the pregnancy."

"What about the birth father?"

"Sally said that many of the girls don't identify the dad, or if they do, he often signs away his rights."

"What about the health of the child—would a woman who didn't even want the baby take care of herself and her unborn infant?"

"According to Sally, *you* could have an unhealthy baby yourself."

From the moment we left the agency. I heard one voice pleading no, one voice insisting yes, both silently debating, a dress rehearsal for that night's dialogue at dinner. John and I had decided the previous day to make a night of this entire trip. After visiting the agency, we planned to eat out at a nearby restaurant, then relax and reflect at an area hotel. By six p.m. that evening, we had settled into a booth at a quaint café, ordered black coffee, and saturated our tongues with the sobering drink. "Cheese and sausage," my optimistic self whispered. May John please revert back to his cheese and sausage tendencies.

Anxious. Overwhelmed. Hesitant. Little did I know until our fourth sip of caffeine that John sat basking in all of these emotions, as well as excitement. Drunk from the smells of French fries and apple pie, we held hands and chattered incessantly, relishing the peak of a natural high. And in a very real way, we were quite high. High on the possibility of holding a newborn. High on the knowledge that we possessed certain qualities that might appeal to potential birth mothers. That instant rush that tickles the gut—that's what we felt. I couldn't contain this thrilling gust of electricity that threaded itself through every vein. My head had consulted my heart, and all of my body now radiated one truth: we should try domestic adoption. For one year, we should give it our all.

The following day, after checking out of our hotel and breakfasting on omelets, we returned to the agency, drunk once again on intentions and hope.

"We'd like to pursue domestic adoption," we confessed to our tour guide Sally, who escorted us into a different room, the room that would heighten my rising high. Right there on the wall to my left hung a bulletin board splattered with smiles, a collage of faces grinning with pride, chosen couples embracing their children, chosen children emitting joy. Would we some day make this wall of fame, this collection of success, this hodgepodge of happiness? My optimistic self, now fixated on each family, stood captivated by the display. We headed home completely changed, yet one constant remained—I oozed with hope. Again, I oozed.

*

The adrenaline high that coursed through my blood the entire way home gradually evaporated the way a balloon leaks helium. Though I crept into bed practically touching the ceiling, I woke the following morning, essentially deflated. It didn't take long to find the pin that punctured my zeal—the bulging, manila envelope lay near our bags in the entryway.

"Are you ready for this?" I asked John, breaking the seal of the heavy package. But before he could answer, I skimmed the material, astonished at its meticulous demands, stunned at the hoops we'd committed to jump. When I glance at my timeline, I spot the next date.

March 28, 2006—Hoop Jumping Begins

From the end of March to the middle of July, my husband and I resembled obedient circus poodles, jumping through a row of hoops only to encounter another row. But unlike a puppy, we savored no meat flavored biscuit after each successful leap. Motivated by a more abstract reward, the abundant love of a newborn babe, we performed as instructed. Would all of this hurdling eventually pay off? We questioned the process on a weekly basis, but what could we do? We simply jumped.

Hoop #1: Create a Profile. While an outsider may view a portfolio as a glorified and slightly boastful scrapbook, I cannot emphasize enough the importance of this personal binder. Snapshots of past events, roasting marshmallows while camping with a nephew, resting near a palm tree while vacationing in Florida, cradling a Godchild while sitting on Santa's lap, actually meant glimpses into future escapades. The wording of each caption, the description of each photo could very well turn one potential birth mother on and one completely off. What could we possibly do to make our portfolio, essentially our ticket to parenthood, surpass the competition? Because in all reality, it could come down to a red sports car, and if it did, we would not make the cut.

The most difficult aspect about this time-consuming hoop involved the undeniable marketing factor. Parts of our portfolio even read like local ads—and weren't they just that—advertisements? As if reviewing a real estate brochure, a birth mother might comment, "Here's a three bedroom, two bath couple with a finished basement and large backyard." Or another girl, as if skimming the personals, might think, "Here's an ambitious couple who share a passion for teaching, a love of family, and an interest in long walks around a nearby lake." To make matters worse, I decided our portfolio, in an attempt to emerge unique, needed a running theme. Unfortunately, my finished product likely appeared more corny than creative. I actually presented our A,B,C's and 1,2,3's of adoption. ("A" stood for Anticipation, Active, Anything is Possible and so on.) I guess if that appealed to someone, then that someone would appeal to us. Deep down, however, I despised the task. It catalogued every possible qualification we possessed as potential parents, but wasn't it just another reminder that we might not be good enough? Would we ever be worthy? For four months we stumbled upon doubts and tumbled through hoops.

The mother of all hoops, technically known as The Home Study, actually contained so many elaborate exercises that it's best to discuss it as a set of hoops. This overwhelming series of tasks, our detailed obstacle course, could only be managed one jump at a time, so heads held high, like well-trained pups, we scaled each hoop, regardless of height.

Hoop #2: Submit Requested Paper Work. As part of the application process, we had 30 days to provide the following forms: Financial Statement, Pregnancy Policy, Foster Care License, Medical Reports, Health Questionnaires, Health Insurance Verification, Background Disclosure, Water Inspection, Furnace Inspection, Pet Vaccination Verification, and Autobiographies.

By far the autobiographies proved to be one of the most daunting tasks. Our agency asked us to write descriptive narratives on ten questions, yet each question required a very layered response. For example, the first question initially asked us to describe our immediate family, but then a parenthetical addition invited us to describe, in detail, our parents, their upbringing, their influence on us, each sibling (I have five and John has eight), the specific roles they play in the family, and the amount of time spent with each one. Four hours and two single-spaced pages later, I had completed my first question. Was I supplying irrelevant information? The more time I spent summarizing my courtship with John or formulating my parenting philosophies, the more resentment rose within me. Did other adoptive couples see any irony here? In the time it took us to type out our discipline procedures, someone in the world conceived an unplanned, and worse yet, unwanted child. Who was doing a background check on that potentially jobless, insuranceless, penniless pair? Contemplating such circumstances, however, merely distracted me, and I couldn't afford distractions. I had hoops to jump, and jump I did.

Hoop #3: Sign the Pregnancy Policy. A simple signature on yet another form, for one primary reason, initiated a temporary crisis. The pregnancy policy confirmed our nonpregnant status, our commitment to no longer pursue fertility options, and our official medical diagnosis—*unexplained infertility*. Of course we had admitted these truths verbally a number of times, but my irrational mind kept insinuating that signing this form meant surrendering all hopes of having a biological child. I would never share crayons with a blue-eyed, blond haired daughter genetically destined to inherit my chicken legs and John's beak of a nose. I would never sing the alphabet to a blue-eyed, blond haired son genetically destined to inherit my long face and John's broad shoulders. Sure, there were outlandish tales of women who got pregnant soon after adopting a child, but I didn't put much stock into these claims. My rational self knew that I, as well as John, needed to come to peace with our fate. (I also resolved to stop begrudging every pregnant person who crossed my path.) Enough with the envy.

Hoop #4: Pass the Home Inspection. I thoroughly understood the agency's policy to visit the home of an adoptive couple. Hygiene horrors, space concerns, and pungent smells could all reveal themselves the minute someone walked through a front door. Thanks to Oprah and the producers of the Home and Garden network, I believed wholeheartedly that a home reflected the true essence of its owner. No thanks to these people, I felt a compelling urge to spruce up our landscaping, reorganize our cluttered closets, and scour with zeal all exposed surfaces. In my paranoid mind, I pictured our social worker honing in on every crevice, swinging wide each closet door, and rejecting our application because, while scrutinizing the contents of our refrigerator, she spotted an outdated container of cottage cheese. (Of course she had no intentions of even opening the fridge, but, to be on the safe side, it too would not escape my sanitizing frenzy.) We would spend five weeks preparing for an appointment that would last one hour. Who could blame us? In hoop jumping terms, the home visit represented the circus finale. Once we completed this remaining leap, we'd at last be admitted into the adoption pool where prospective birth mothers could select our portfolio.

*

On July 18, 2006, we officially entered the coveted pool with guarded optimism, all thanks to Tina, our assigned social worker.

"Don't create a nursery. Don't buy any baby clothes. You can call us once a month to see how many times your portfolio has been shown." We appreciated Tina's wise words, her trusted insights, her complete sincerity. "Hopefully you'll hear from us soon," she added. "Just sit tight."

So there we sat like obedient poodles, patiently waiting for a morsel, a nugget, a table scrap of any kind.

Ring, phone, ring.

For two and a half months, time crawled with great effort while we growled over our position—the phrase, "throw us a bone," now relevant and used.

Ring, phone, ring. And then it did.

CHAPTER 3

On Wednesday, October 4, 2006, at six p.m., John spotted the name on the caller I.D. and yelled from the kitchen, "It's Tina calling. You might want to get in here." Of course, this could have been another false alarm, as had happened on two previous occasions, but I bolted into the dining room.

"Hello?" John stated, as more of a question than a greeting.

"Yes, I am," he replied. Then he whispered, "She asked if I was sitting down." By now we both sat rigid at our oval oak table, hands held, faces flushed.

"Yes, she is," he replied. "She wants to know if you're right here." Then John tipped the phone, so I could lean in with my right ear while he leaned close with his left.

"I hope you can both hear me because I'm calling to tell you that there was a baby boy delivered yesterday, and his birth mother picked you two to adopt him. We'd like you to meet us at the hospital tomorrow to take him home."

John and I both heard the words but, paralyzed by shock, labored to process the bizarre situation. Thirty seconds ago, we were childless. Was this really happening?

"No way," I thought. "Inconceivable."

An untraceable amount of time ticked away before I found myself half-jumping, half-pacing, and half-dancing as if my bewildered limbs matched my confused mind. My two hands cradled my hot cheeks then dropped down to cover my open mouth. My head shook back and forth, still doubting the news. Then, instantly, I needed answers. Was the baby healthy? What was the birth mother like? What about a nursery? We had taken Tina's words to heart. We had no crib, no sleeper, not a single diaper! *Inconceivable*!

"Ask her about the baby! Ask her about the birth mom!"

While I jumped-paced-danced, John stayed on the line gathering specifics. He waved his hand to silence me, trying to focus his attention on Tina. As he learned essential details, he tossed them back to me. Each tidbit of information entered the room like a fragile bubble floating on air. I listened with awe, so worried the fantastic moment might burst prematurely.

"He's seven pounds, four ounces. Caucasian. Healthy. Beautiful. His birth mother is sixteen years old, a junior in high school. She has a very supportive family, her dad and grandparents. The birth mother's name is Amanda, and she has not yet seen the baby. We really want her to hold him and maybe feed him before you two come, but she denied her entire pregnancy. No one knew she was pregnant until yesterday."

The implausible facts again disrupted our processing. We paused on our end, exchanging raised brows, wide eyes, dropped jaws.

"Her dad didn't even notice she was pregnant?" I asked in disbelief.

"Apparently not."

Another awkward silence emerged.

This time Tina broke it. "The plan is to meet at the hospital at 4:00 p.m. tomorrow."

"Should we call our principal so we can arrange maternity leave?"

"Actually, I don't want you to tell anyone because once she sees the baby, she might change her mind. I'll call you at ten in the morning, and if all goes well, you can talk to your principal then. In the meantime, you will need to get a few items before tomorrow. Borrow the items though. Don't buy anything."

John grabbed a pencil and pad to scribble down a list. I again snuggled up to the portable phone, planning to interject about this "no tell" policy. As I glanced at the list materializing before my eyes, I couldn't grasp the concept of borrowing these supplies while at the same time not admitting their immediate use. I negotiated with Tina.

"My sister Donna just had a baby boy within the last year. I know I could borrow all of this from her, but can I tell her what it's for? She'll keep it secret."

"Okay," Tina agreed. And once John confirmed the directions to the hospital, Tina added one last thrilling detail that heightened our blissful mood.

"Amanda hasn't named the baby, so it's up to you to choose a name."

Brainstorming baby names—the already abundant pheromones in my body multiplied at this new development. Was I leaking bliss?

When John hung up the phone, we fell into each other's arms. My head tucked naturally in the familiar crook above his left shoulder, allowing his cotton shirt to catch the tears that pushed out when I blinked. "Can you believe this?" I asked John, still digesting the astonishing phone call.

"In all of the scenarios that Tina described, I never imagined this one," he confessed. We both laughed the kind of nervous-elated laugh that accompanies a state of giddiness.

"John, I have to call Donna. She may not even be home. If she is, we need to drive to her house, pick up what she has, and then go to Wal-Mart—we're gonna buy *some* things, right? Like bottles? Can I buy a new outfit for the baby to wear home?"

"Sure, we'll buy a few things," John replied. I grabbed the phone.

With anxious fingers, I dialed my levelheaded, take-charge sister, who insisted she would have all we needed ready to pick up by the time we arrived. John and I lived thirty miles away, but that long drive could do wonders for our over-stimulated minds. We could create a shopping list for Wal-Mart all the way to Donna's house or even contemplate baby names. In reality, however, we would likely pass the time debating if the birth mother would change her mind. I couldn't fathom that someone could psychologically dismiss all signs of pregnancy. Did she not get her monthly period? Did she never once vomit? If she truly *did* deny the pregnancy and was only *now* admitting the existence of a child, when would she have had time to accept her decision to place the baby for adoption? Did she make this life-altering choice in nine hours when most women pondered it for nine months? Tina's tentativeness troubled me. One look at that baby, and wouldn't the birth mother yearn to keep it?

When John slowed for a patch of construction, I read an orange sign, "PROCEED WITH CAUTION." How absurdly fitting, my pessimistic self scoffed, but I ignored the thought. Now a hostage to adrenaline, my body and mind surrendered the questioning and began accepting the exhilarating reality. We were chosen. By this time tomorrow, we could be driving along a different highway with our son in the back seat. Inconceivable.

As promised and expected, Donna greeted us with much more than a congratulatory hug. Neatly labeled boxes blocked our entrance, but we eventually finagled through her front door, inventoried the supplies, and anxiously loaded up our borrowed goods. With one item checked on our overwhelming "To Do" list, we thanked my sister and traveled down the road to the closest Wal-Mart.

Once the automatic glass doors pried themselves apart, I sped to the baby section, leaving John behind to grab a cart.

"Slow down already," John pleaded. But I paid no mind to his request. For the past year I dreaded merely glancing in the direction of baby clothes, and if I dared browse through the department, it was for the sole purpose of purchasing a shower gift for an expectant friend or relative. Finally, I could adore giraffe print bibs and polka dotted blankets for a reason.

A few sleepers, a couple of bottles, a stack of diapers, a container of wipes—we intended to stick to a shopping list of necessities, but maternal instincts kicked in hard—paternal ones too. "Can we get him this stuffed dog? Can we buy this rattle? What about these booties? I think he needs this hat—or this one with the footballs on it." I assumed John, stoic when willed, would remove each luxury the second it hit the cart, but he fueled my fervor instead of smothering it.

Aside from one pink bottle of baby lotion, the cart filled fast with various hues of blue. At the check-out, we smirked with guilt. How in the world would we fit all of this into our already packed vehicle? That didn't concern us. We relished the moment—a pair of frazzled parents on the eve of giving birth—that's what it felt like. Halloween Eve, Christmas Eve, Easter Eve—the eves that make young bodies squirm with anticipated glee could no longer compare to our euphoric eve. We were drunk again—on a refreshing cocktail spiked with possibility.

*

After three separate trips of unloading the car, I stared at my kitchen, my pheromones waning. This chaotic collection of new and used items now struck me at once as despicable clutter. How could I welcome our newborn son into a home so void of order? I couldn't, I decided, simple as that.

For the sake of efficiency, not to mention sanity, I rummaged through my entire house, searching for woven baskets presently displaying decorative towels, already read novels, and half burned candles. On a quest to organize, I used my newly acquired containers to transform my living room into a pathetic changing station. After filling one basket with essentials including diapers, baby powder, and Velcro bibs, I set aside two more baskets to pile high with receiving blankets and footed sleepers. Both items, however, currently sloshed about in my washer, soaking in the unscented detergent my sister Donna insisted I use. While waiting for my baby blue laundry, I carried empty boxes to the basement, vacuumed the carpets, and gave in to the intense urge to scour the toilets.

Approximately two hours later, I sighed at the progress, then retired to my bedroom where I slipped into my walk-in closet, studying my insufficient wardrobe. What sweater-pants combo emitted a trendy, yet maternal first impression? I held up various shirts, keeping the ones with a motherly vibe. Finally I committed to a blue turtleneck sweater with khaki pants—it didn't scream Mom, but it complimented my eyes.

Refusing to peek at the clock on my nightstand, I crawled gingerly into my side of the bed, envying my stress free husband who slept soundly to my left. Rather than indulge in some much needed rest, I instead began the absurd task of skimming the 806 page reference guide entitled, *What to Expect the First Year*. I desperately needed a crash course on bottle feeding, sleep patterns, and bathing an infant. Though I knew never to shake a baby and to always secure the neck, I had no recent practice with changing a diaper and no idea how to care for a newly cut umbilical cord, much less a freshly circumcised penis. The more I read, the more panic pulsated within me. How could I possibly appear confident when deep down I felt like an incompetent fraud?

Somewhere between page 162 and 208, while reading the section called, "What You May Be Concerned About," my eyes fell victim to my exhausted mind, and soon my body surrendered as well. A few hours later, my alarm rang, signifying the arrival of October 5, the next date highlighted along my personal timeline. The caption beside the date reads, "Meeting Wyatt." But from 5:50 a.m. to 9:33 a.m., we still didn't know if we had a meeting, nor had we agreed upon a winning first name.

October 5, 2006—Meeting Wyatt

We started the day with feigned normalcy, afraid that outright optimism might jinx our newfound luck. As I taught my first two classes, my secret simmered inside me, like agitated, boiling water continually nudging a flimsy lid. I shared my room with another English teacher, so not to inform her of my astounding news required immense restraint—luckily she had a habit of spreading gossip, so this fact alone helped me hold my eager tongue.

After the third hour bell rang, at approximately 9:30 a.m., I headed out of my classroom, intending to correct essays in the English office during my fifty minute prep. As soon as I stepped out the door, however, I heard John call my name, and we both leaned against the nearest lockers, whispering both for privacy and not to disrupt the classes now started.

"Laura," John began, "I just got a call from Tina on my cell. They don't want us to come at four o'clock this afternoon; they want us to come *now*. I guess Amanda's grandparents are there, and they really want to meet us. Plus, she's held the baby and is still on board with the adoption."

I couldn't believe my husband's update. Thank God I didn't have a class to teach that hour; we needed to go see our principal. Were we going to be allowed simply to leave the building and pick up a baby? Who would teach our classes? Time moved faster than usual—"Hurry up!" my pessimistic self ordered, "Get to that baby before she changes her mind." I couldn't help but agree.

Lucky for us, we found our principal in the building, in his office, and in an exceptionally compassionate mood. Though he had encountered plenty of shocking situations throughout his administrative career, he appeared startled by our predicament and then incapable of holding in genuine tears.

With decisive authority, he proposed a plan. "We will take care of everything here. Eventually we'll arrange a more permanent sub for Laura, but for now I'm sure there are plenty of co-workers who will help your subs out."

We all walked out of that office wiping our eyes and our starting-to-drip noses. Would everyone embrace our glorious news with such acceptance? We could only hope.

*

On the way to the hospital on that early October day, sheer joy overwhelmed us. The autumn hues staining every leaf left us gasping at times as we pointed out hills or picturesque farms. We rode with the sun warming our arms through the car's closed windows. Plus we produced our own inner heat—nervous energy—the kind that if harnessed could power small, rural towns. I could tell we both felt it—that ticklish, hooky feeling that follows those who cut class on such gloriously sun-drenched days. Stirring underneath slight pangs of rebellion, adding to our helpless giddiness, sat all the thrills associated with keeping a marvelous secret. *Wait until we tell our friends and family. Wait until they hear our news.*

About thirty miles into our ninety-mile drive, we at last got down to the business of naming our son, a trying task since we'd not seen his boyish face, smelled his newborn skin, or cradled his delicate limbs. In Tina's initial phone call, she described a dark-haired, blue-eyed beauty, but what social worker in her right mind would offer any less to potential parents? Although we didn't know if we could trust our only source, what choice did we have? The closer we got to the hospital, the more urgently I wanted a name. Forty miles in, we had a narrowed list of five options handwritten on a yellow post-it. Now the time came to study the origins.

"How do you like Jonah?" I asked John, then turned the volume down on the radio until the twang of country music evaporated to nothing.

"I love it," John replied.

"It means," I held up the paper to decipher my notes in the margin, "someone who brings bad luck."

"Where did you hear that?"

"I searched my top picks on the Internet this morning, and I always loved the name, but seriously, that's a horrible meaning."

After a brief digression on the validity of Internet sources, John agreed to veto Jonah, and I shared the other names on the list along with their assigned meanings. Eventually, we found a name that passed our two-pronged criteria. (One, neither of us had ever taught a deviant student by our selected name, and two, we approved of its origin.)

"So our baby's name will be Wyatt then?" I asked John for official confirmation.

"Yep!" he agreed. "I love it."

"Me, too." And we drove the rest of the way, constantly mentioning the new name and speculating whether it would miraculously match the baby's facial features and still unidentified personality.

*

Once we pulled into the hospital parking lot, unwelcomed company gathered inside me, harassing my central nervous system, like a gang of punks out to ruin prom. The usual crowd gathered within—Fear, Doubt, Paranoia even. I thought the tentacle-like grip of my maternal urge might come to my aid, but she lay low, probably conserving energy for the moment she met Wyatt.

In new-parent fashion, I awkwardly swung a bulging diaper bag over one shoulder and my purse and digital camera over the other. John led the way, carrying the hand-me-down car seat that my sister assured us would safely transport a newborn. Despite my unease, I couldn't quit smiling. Were we really about to meet our son? Was I really two floors away from motherhood?

Once we meandered through the first floor and found our way to the maternity ward, our social worker Tina waved us over and greeted us with a hug.

"Do you want to see him before you meet Amanda?"

"Can we do that?"

"Sure, he's right here." I followed Tina's finger until it pointed to a double door, each with its own glass window. About four feet away, a flawless baby lay in a hospital bassinet, wrapped snuggly in a white blanket with a blue knitted cap on his tiny head. I tiptoed close to that narrow window and could not believe the bundled lump of perfection sleeping so soundly, entirely unaware of the significance of the day.

"Hi, Wyatt," I whispered to my son, but no one else heard the exchange, for I don't even know if I spoke the words aloud. I know *now*, since I carry the knowledge of how our future unfolds, that I will never forget that brief, potent moment—the same instant that poets for centuries have attempted to describe in lines of prose. It's a question I often get asked from curious relatives or even close friends, "So when did you think of Wyatt as your own son? Did you just love him the minute you saw him?"

"I can't explain it," I confess, "but I loved him immediately—I think it was the knitted hat that got me."

Before I could savor my son any longer, Tina touched my elbow and led me in the opposite direction.

"We should go in and meet Amanda and her dad," she suggested.

As excited as we were to finally meet Wyatt's birth mother, we were slightly more apprehensive. Throughout this whole process we continually sought the approval of others, but no person's opinion carried more weight than the sixteen-year-old girl just two doors down on the right side of the hall. Would she meet our expectations? More importantly, would *we* meet *hers*?

Awkward cannot begin to accurately describe the aura that hung in the air of that typically sterile hospital room. Like two weather patterns trying to cross the same plane, we trotted in the room all smiles and sunshine only to intersect a sad, unsettled front. As soon as I emptied my arms, however, they filled up again—this time with an unexpected embrace from a watery-eyed, bald man who I would much later refer to as Grandpa Joe.

"We're Amanda's grandparents," the man's wife announced. Then she too offered the kind of honey-smelling hug that emits grandma, banana bread, and powder based make up. I knew immediately this was not a typical birth mother. This girl had connections—family ties—a support system.

"This is hard for us, you know," Grandma said. "We sure love babies."

The entire scene, now so unlike the choreographed interview I'd recently envisioned, left me somewhat speechless. In the middle of the room, in a chair rather than on her bed, Amanda sat with a solemn look upon her tired face. To her left stood her equally exhausted father, another weary face complete with bloodshot eyes resting upon two heavy bags. In the same corner sat Amanda's close friend, a spindly, timid teenager, yet another ally to offer support.

"It's so nice to meet you," I finally responded to sweet-smelling Grandma.

"And this is Amanda," Tina said, stepping near the dark-haired girl who attempted to smile a polite grin.

"Hi, Amanda," I said, leaning down and hugging the complete stranger who had endured hours of labor to produce the perfect child all in the room wanted to hold and keep for themselves.

"Hi," she replied.

I scooted over so John could offer a hug, but thankfully he offered much more.

"Hi, Amanda," John began, but to my surprise, he slid an empty chair smack dab in front of Amanda and spoke the words all sixteen ears in the room needed to hear. "Do you have any idea what this means to us?" He paused for effect, or maybe just to articulate exactly what he truly felt. "This means the world to us. You are giving us the world. We cannot thank you enough."

After an intense moment of absolute silence, we all blinked back tears and allowed John's words of gratitude to unite the room of strangers with the power of an inside joke. The shared laughter at our sobbing broke the initial spell of awkwardness, and it didn't take long for conversation to fill the room, most of it centered around the seemingly ideal birth mother.

"Amanda here's a B student," her dad boasted.

"Any favorite classes?" John asked.

"What do you two teach again?" Grandpa interrupted.

"I teach history. Laura teaches English."

"Say history and English," Grandpa suggested with a wink. Then we laughed again in unison, appreciating the effort at lessening the tension. After a few more comments and more semi-forced laughter, John and I must have passed an unspoken compatibility test, for Ryan, Amanda's protective dad, signaled for a nurse to bring in the baby.

"Are you ready to meet your son?" Ryan asked, and just the wording of the question helped relieve my skeptic side.

"He's referring to the baby as *your* son!" my optimistic self affirmed. Delirious happiness filtered through me.

"Oh, he's just a doll," Grandma added proudly. "You're going to love . . ."

But before she could even finish her thought, the nurse had carted the blue-knitted-capped boy to the front of the room, lifted him from the bassinet, and positioned him into my long, thin arms. John snuggled close behind me, and as we stared with awe at our potential son, I heard the click of a camera and saw the immediate glow of a bright white light.

"I hope you don't mind," Ryan stated, holding up an expensive looking camera and shooting another photo of our stunned, yet beaming faces.

"We don't mind at all. Can you take a few shots with *my* digital camera?"

Standing there, my arms gentling cradling seven pounds of unconditional love, I still couldn't fathom the type of birth family surrounding this baby. Ever since we began the process of adoption, I selfishly viewed the situation from my angle only. Adoption, an act of pure altruism, would surely rescue a child from an environment fraught with either alcoholism, drugs, abuse, neglect, poverty, or maybe all of the above. Until now, I had mistakenly allowed my ego to catapult me to near sainthood status for saving a birth mother from an unwanted burden and saving a baby from a disadvantaged life. I couldn't have been more wrong. We weren't saving Amanda or Wyatt. Truth be told, Amanda was saving us. One look at her family and the realization hit me in the gut like sudden insights usually do. Amanda could have kept this baby and never exposed it to the evils of the world. God knows Great Grandma and Grandpa would have stepped up to the plate, dousing the child with so much love he would have reeked of indulgence.

The more I learned about the birth mom, the more foolish I felt. B-student Amanda not only planned to attend college after high school, she admittedly hoped to be the first person in her family to graduate with a university degree. Hearing this only solidified the fact that we had found the Holy Grail of adoption. Motivated, bright, generous—we never imagined meeting a birth mother with these lofty attributes. The only flaw in this seemingly perfect situation involved the birth father, or more accurately, a lack thereof.

From the beginning, Amanda has never identified Wyatt's biological father, a decision that has proved a blessing and curse. Curse-wise, by not knowing the birth father, we would never obtain medical background or genetic dispositions that Wyatt might have inherited. Blessing-wise, a nonexistent birth father meant fewer biological family members to ogle over him and pipe up with motions to keep the baby and veto the adoption. Every second I spent in that hospital room, every minute I held my stunning son, a part of me wanted to bolt for the door before Amanda and her allies came to their senses.

"It was nice meeting all of you," I would say on my way out. "Let's keep in touch."

But even though I longed to strap Wyatt in our car seat and smuggle him out the door, I literally couldn't go through with it—nurse's orders. In our complacent attempt to follow Tina's advice, we dutifully borrowed an outdated, completely unusable car seat. That may sound unrealistic since my sister had a baby so recently, but little did I know, she had borrowed a car seat as well, one purchased within the last decade. Mine, on the other hand, was not used by my sister Donna, but by my oldest sister Monica, whose daughter turned 21 in 2006. After one look at our ill equipped hand-me-down, the nurse in charge insisted we head to a local shopping center and purchase a brand new car seat, preferably one with a five-point harness. *A five point what?* Of course, I didn't reveal my incompetence—the fact that I brought a car seat older than the birth mother herself took care of that. I nodded politely to the nurse's instructions but inwardly prayed that John understood her unsolicited advice sprinkled with jargon.

"Do you mind staying here with the baby while we pick up a safer car seat?" I asked the birth family. All amiably agreed we should take our time.

As we got into our compact car and began maneuvering through the parking lot, my paranoia peaked.

"Doesn't Amanda have an awesome family?" John stated.

"Yeah—and that's exactly why we need to hurry up and get back there before they change their minds!"

"I know! I feel the same way!"

"You *do*? You're supposed to say I'm being freakishly paranoid."

"Laura, did you see that baby? He's perfect. Let's just get to the store, pick out a car seat, and get the hell back."

Semi-startled by our combined insecurities, I realized that holding our son, maybe even feeding him, had likely kick-started John's paternal urges at the same time they rebooted my maternal ones. Naturally, our incentive to rush back to the hospital caused the kind of excessive stress that backfires in the end. As soon as we reached our parked car, easily manageable problems escalated into one immediate crisis after another.

Here we were, two educators with master's degrees, and neither one of us could figure out a way to get the newly boxed purchase to fit in the trunk or backseat of the car. Then, once we finally decided to simply remove the seat and discard the box, we again felt like imbeciles when we attempted to install the multi-strapped contraption. At last, after watching the sun fade fast into the horizon, I heard John announce, "It's in! Let's go!"

"Is that thing supposed to be reclining like that?" I questioned.

"Just get in already. Let's pray to God I installed it right."

After moderately speeding back, John found an adequate parking space, slid out of the car, and released the top portion of the zoo printed car seat. We both scurried to Amanda's room, half expecting to find an abandoned bed and a simple, "Decided to keep the baby" note. Fortunately, our fears proved unfounded. Though the room had cleared of some of the company, one less social worker, one less friend, and one less nurse, it still contained Amanda, her dad, and her two endearing grandparents.

Just as before, no sooner had we emptied our arms did they fill up again with this affectionate pair. I got Grandpa's hug first and then Grandma's—such a sincere, warm embrace that some of her down home, made from scratch scent rubbed off on my sweater and reappeared unexpectedly on the long drive home.

The unsettled front we initially felt reentered the room, causing an unspoken cloud of gloom to linger in our midst. Where was the rulebook on this sort of arrangement? On what page could I find the words to remind these red-eyed strangers that we'd all see each other again sometime soon? Someone, somewhere, needed to assure me that my spoken intentions were not empty promises laced with a hint of pity. But in all honesty, as I watched these newfound relatives exit the melancholy room, I had no idea how much our futures would collide. Would we visit Amanda twice a year, and during those times, meet with her grandparents as well? Would it be completely inappropriate to add them to our Christmas card list and send a photo of their biological great grandson, no doubt donning a Santa hat or peeking out of an oversized stocking? Would such correspondence bring sorrow rather than joy? I didn't know for certain the answers to any of these weighty questions, but I knew after our brief encounter that these people radiated goodness, so why *wouldn't* I expose Wyatt to them? Why deny him such unconditional love?

The moment the grandparents left, a solemn type of energy emerged in the room. All joking subsided. Even smiling seemed wrong.

"Amanda's about ready to check out of her room. Do you guys just want to all walk out together?" These suggestions came from Amanda's dad, which explained the sudden bend in both of their moods.

I turned to John, and we nodded in agreement. "Yeah, that'd be great. We're all set, too."

Amanda emptied a corner closet, and I scooped up Wyatt to try out his new car seat. We all left with our hands full, but not quite as full as our nervous, aching hearts. Silence settled on us now, following us down the long, straight corridors and hovering close throughout the elevator ride. Finally we reached two large glass doors, the exit we needed, though Amanda and Ryan parked elsewhere. We stopped in unison, and again I craved a trusted adoption handbook, this time with a section on leaving the birth mother.

Until this point, stoic Amanda showed little emotional attachment. She hugged us without a single tear, smiled politely if we looked her way, and stood patiently while we made more small talk. Maybe she sensed we were prolonging the good-bye, the kind of farewell that needed attention, required respect, and signaled finality. Just when I thought we would turn to leave, Ryan bent down to kiss tiny Wyatt, asking Amanda, "Well, aren't you gonna say good-bye?"

Slowly, Amanda, too, crouched down and kissed her biological son on the forehead. Without a glance in our direction, without the least bit of warning, she stood up and unexpectedly collapsed in her father's arms, releasing a deeply instinctual cry, the muffled yelps of a wounded animal. As she clung to Ryan and gasped for breath, we stood there stunned, sick with pain and sick with joy. We gathered our son and left the scene, like guilt-ridden bandits fleeing a crime, glancing behind in a paranoid fashion, glancing down at our priceless loot. This wasn't the way it was supposed to be. I felt so selfish, so sinful, so sad.

"That was the saddest thing I have ever witnessed," I told John in the car, still visualizing the scene. And that's when I realized the magnitude of the day, not from my standpoint, but from Amanda's instead. She'll relive that moment again, I thought to myself, just as I will. Yet I hoped that eventually the image would not invoke regret, but a sense of pride, a flood of generosity.

"Do you think she'll change her mind?" I asked my husband.

"We have thirty days to find out."

CHAPTER 4

Five miles into the drive home, I still couldn't shake feeling like a dirty thief. A part of me, of course, felt insanely elated—*that* part sat in the backseat beside my newly obtained treasure. But another part felt that intuitive, gut-twisting nudge that usually comes when I've forgotten to unplug my curling iron or realized I'd left a swimming suit drying on a hook behind a hotel's bathroom door. What had I forgotten? What had I misplaced? Or rather than forgetting something, maybe I simply felt guilty, like when I lied to my husband about how much I spent at a craft fair or how little I cared that he rarely rinsed his breakfast bowl. An unsettling knot had burrowed its way into my intestines, so there I sat, my insides tangled in a heap of remorse, a pile of shame.

Ten miles into the drive home, John made the obvious suggestion, the one that would weaken my guilty conscience.

"I think it's time we called our friends and family." Then he dug into the shallow pocket of his light khaki pants and handed me the cell phone.

My sister Donna would get the first call. When we visited her the day before, I mentioned the possibility of stopping on our way home from the hospital. I had mistakenly assumed we'd be on the road by suppertime at the latest. Instead, we'd be dropping in closer to eight p.m., the precise hour she begins her son's bedtime ritual. I dialed her number, fully expecting to arrange a rain check in a day or two.

"Hello?" Donna answered.

"Hey, Aunt Donna, are you still game for meeting your newest nephew?"

"Why, absolutely!" she replied, and that's when I heard a few voices in the background. "I actually took the liberty of calling Dad and Leisa, so there's somewhat of a welcoming committee sitting in my living room anxiously waiting to see you." I should have known a secret of this magnitude wouldn't stay captive for long, but rather than feeling she had stolen my surprise, I felt delighted that Wyatt would receive a last minute homecoming.

Since we had many more calls to make, I ended the conversation as quickly and politely as possible, and a new surge of exhilaration ran through me. I couldn't wait to tell our dearest friends the bizarre, joyful news that we were not only chosen to adopt a child, we were driving him home this very minute. John's family knew nothing of our miracle either. I smiled as I imagined the overzealous howls and catcalls that would vibrate through the ear of the phone after we revealed the truth to his boisterous siblings. As the two of us pondered who to phone next, John proposed a clever plan.

"Why don't we hold off telling my family about Wyatt tonight, and then tomorrow, I can call them all up and tell them to gather together because we have a big announcement? They'll think we're announcing that we got picked to adopt, but then we can bring in Wyatt and surprise everyone in person!"

"Are you sure you want to wait that long to tell your family?"

"Yeah, what's another day?"

With nine fewer family members to personally call, I held up the glowing phone and asked with enthusiasm, "Okay, who's next?"

John would suggest a name, and I'd dial away, bursting with bliss. The majority of every phone call contained the same exchange. I would explain our call from the agency, our trip to the hospital, and then close with the shocking kicker, "I'm sitting in the backseat right now looking at our son, Wyatt."

The recipient of this call, whether friend or family member, refused to believe the news. Most people responded with "What? Are you kidding me?"

Once each friend or sibling eventually conceded that John and I were not pulling some elaborate, tasteless hoax, they immediately shared our joy, many of them requesting visual confirmation in the near future. And we, too, couldn't wait for the world to meet our son because, as odd as this may sound, he was *all ours*. From the instant I met him, I felt the bond. If Amanda changed her mind at this point, I was in deep, irreversibly so. I wanted every person who met him to embrace him with the same unconditional love. During those initial nights home with my newborn, I added a footnote of gratitude to my ritualistic bedtime prayer. Just after giving thanks for my open-minded friends and family, I extended genuine appreciation for Wyatt and a brief plea for all to accept him. Despite these sincere efforts, one significant family member remained sheepishly reluctant, the one I'd always struggled to please.

*

I didn't notice the hesitancy at first. When John and I arrived at my sister's house, we stepped inside a room full of smiling teeth and wide open arms. I never once tired of comments such as, "He's just adorable" or "Look at all that hair." Luckily, our son took the attention in stride. Jostled from one aunt to the other, passed from one uncle to the next, squeezed in between a cousin and his dad—nothing much unsettled him, except for the persistent strobe light effect from my camera's flash. And in the midst of all this photography, all this fuss over the unexpected blessing, I never really noticed my own dad's reaction. When it was time for him to hold his grandson and smile for my scrapbook, I didn't think twice when he immediately surrendered Wyatt to the next awaiting relative. I thought the gesture generous.

It wasn't until that following week, during my dad's next visit, that I started to see a pattern forming. Within minutes of handing my father his grandchild, he'd offer him up for someone else to hold. Once he did this on a third occasion, I decided to investigate, to call my one sister who was always the closest to our somewhat private dad.

I dialed Donna's number during one of Wyatt's naps. She answered on the third ring.

"Hey, Donna, I have a question for you."

"Is this going to take more than five minutes because I was just about to change Luke's diaper?"

"Probably not. I was wondering if you've talked to Dad at all about Wyatt. He seems really disinterested in him, like he doesn't even want to hold him."

There was a definite pause in the conversation.

"Well . . ." she began, another pause passing between us. "I guess you could say he's a bit worried that this might all fall through, so I think he's basically guarded about the situation."

"He thinks the birth mother is going to change her mind?"

"Yes, and he's worried about you too, about how attached you're getting."

The whining in the background helped us keep the conversation short. After a hurried good-bye, I clicked the off button on my cordless phone and dropped it on the couch nearby. *My dad thinks it's going to fall through.* A stab of resentment poked me in the side. Why couldn't he just be happy for me like everyone else? Why couldn't he just support me? I hated to admit it, but we'd had some definite issues when it came to support. As a typical large family, we knew who migrated to Mom and who adhered to Dad. Although I respected my dad's opinion, appreciated his traditional values, and admired his work ethic, I never felt the urge to *adhere* to him. We just didn't have a lot in common, not even during my childhood.

Rather than sulk over my dad's worries, I decided to review some lesson plans for my designated sub. While skimming over the materials for an upcoming mythology unit, I smirked at the tale of Daedalus and Icarus, one that reminded me of my own situation, of a father and a child with little in common.

Throughout my youth, I had always struggled to connect with my dad, a man whose passions I either feared or despised. In the spring, while he savored an afternoon casting for spawning fish, I felt petrified each time he used a worm as bait. Rather than watch my bobber, I cringed at the night crawlers escaping the cottage cheese container that he always forgot to close. In the summer, while he recruited help with weeding the garden, I volunteered to stay indoors folding laundry, eager to avoid the daddy longlegs lurking under each lettuce leaf. In the fall, while he played "P-I-G" using our shoddy basketball hoop outside, I spelled the shameful alternative, "H-O-R-S-E" since most of my shots either hit the rim or missed the net completely. In the winter, while he sped down marked snowmobile trails, I clung for my life in our pull-behind sleigh, my hands and feet stinging with frostbite.

That poor, poor Icarus—the more I thought of him, the more I realized our similarities. According to the myth, the father and son ended up imprisoned in a maze. To escape their fate, Daedalus gathered feathers, created wings, then advised his son Icarus to stay away from the sun which would melt the wax that held his wings together. Although Icarus initially agreed, he found himself drawn to the glorious sun, ignored his father's warnings, and fell to his death.

"Don't fly too close to the sun," the father in the myth warned, and that's when it hit me that my protective father was offering the same advice. "Don't get too close." That was his exact message too.

For a few minutes, I allowed my revelation to sink in and somewhat sting—like peroxide does as it cleans a wound with its bubbling fizz and putrid smell. If Amanda changed her mind within the next twenty-some days, as she had every right to do, I would most likely die emotionally. I would grieve the child as I had mourned my dead mother. I would wake in the middle of the night, aching with loss. Maybe my dad was right after all. I hated to admit it, but maybe, unlike Icarus, I should just back off and withhold my love.

Fat chance of that happening. Withholding love had never been my strong suit. (Just ask my teenage self who fell hard and fast for Rick Springfield, Michael J. Fox, and a diary full of unsuspecting classmates.)

My sole hope now rested in the hands of Wyatt's selfless biological mother. A couple of weeks had passed, yet we only received a few modest updates from our social worker Tina. We knew Amanda attended her school's Homecoming, a possible sign that she wanted to be a teen and not a mom, but only those who witnessed that final good-bye could truly comprehend that this girl loved

Wyatt. She may have denied the pregnancy, but at some point between giving birth and placing him for adoption, she let her guard down. Amanda couldn't withhold her love either, and that became my main worry.

For me, the hardest part about domestic adoption was waiting for the termination hearing; the stress that ensued feasted on my paranoia. Even though I had no grounds to think it, I began picturing Amanda pulling up in my driveway, unannounced, ringing my front door bell, sauntering up to Wyatt's bassinet, and removing him with instinctual grace. After exchanging pleasantries, she'd scamper out the door, clutching my son in her left arm and waving good-bye with her right. I didn't know her well enough to trust that she'd keep her word. I assumed she missed Wyatt. I had no indications to think otherwise. I'll never forget the call that confirmed my worst fears. It came from Amanda's father, and it set into motion even more unsettling stress, even more unmanageable paranoia.

The call came about mid October, a frantic time of bottle feedings every two hours and nonstop visitors offering gifts. I must admit that our adoption, our abrupt leap into parenthood, had triggered a flood of goodwill from close friends to mere acquaintances. That first week, Jen delivered a diaper bag full of supplies, Grace dropped off a chicken and broccoli casserole, Amy made cheeseburger soup, and Jenny brought over her new son Ben, born only three weeks prior to Wyatt. Once John returned to school and shared our surprising circumstance, that we were instant parents functioning with the bare essentials, our supportive colleagues amazed me as well. Every day, John came home with pastel colored gift bags containing needed sleepers, handmade blankets, and bestselling children's books. Before long, we had a baby thermometer, a working monitor, and an infant bathtub. Since Tina still warned us not to create a nursery until after the termination hearing, our living room continued to look like the baby section in a cluttered corner of some secondhand consignment shop. Whenever another guest came for a quick peek at Wyatt, I cringed at the mess around me and couldn't help wonder if my company left commenting on the shambled condition of my usually tidy home. Just when order seemed furthest from my reach, the inevitable phone call came. Amanda and her father Ryan wanted to visit Wyatt. Two days notice—that's what they gave us.

I heard John say midway through the call, "That sounds great." And when he finally looked in my direction, I widened my eyes and gave him my best, "Are you kidding me?" face. I held up two fingers and mouthed silently, "Two days?" My husband nodded yes.

Once John hung up the phone, I immediately came to a decision. "Okay, here's the deal. When Amanda walks in that door, I want her to feel absolutely convinced that she made the right decision. I want this place looking better than it ever has, and I want a nursery."

With only forty-eight hours to convert a home office into an infant's hideaway, I spared little time arguing my plea. The following morning, I headed to a local strip mall to purchase a bed-in-the-bag crib set, and later that evening I sped to Wal-Mart for another hefty shopping spree of necessities. One artificial wooden crib and one almost all particleboard dresser later, I drove home with my right foot steady on the gas pedal. Hopefully I could convince my cheese and sausage husband to assemble my bargain finds.

After minimal begging, John pulled out the directions to the crib and began organizing the pieces. All at once, I felt a wave of relief. Wyatt was going to get a nursery—hopefully in time for Amanda's visit. Sure enough, by ten that night, John had built the furniture, leaving a wake of cardboard and Styrofoam littering the carpet.

With the speed of a small jet, I recycled the waste and began altering the space into a sports lover's paradise. After dressing the crib, hanging a quilt, and displaying framed photos, I felt wired rather than exhausted. Fueled by anxiety, I decided rather than lying in bed with an over-stimulated brain, I might as well stay up and sanitize until the sun poked through the blinds.

A part of me wanted so much to impress Amanda, not one-up her in any way, not convey the attitude that we had so much *more* to offer. (We certainly didn't lead a wealthy lifestyle.) But I'd expected to give her a tour of our modest home, to point out the framed pictures in the basement, to nod at our support system hanging right there on the wall. Maybe the longer I stayed up working, the quicker tomorrow would come, and then the next day, and then the next day, and finally it would be November 6, Amanda's court date. Would tomorrow's visit change all that? I didn't know if she'd been having doubts, but why risk it? Why give her any reason not to think Wyatt belonged right here, in my home?

By two in the afternoon the following day, John and I sat awaiting our company with damp palms and alert nerves. I, a frazzled mess, had already put in a day's work vacuuming the upstairs rooms, maneuvering through the crowded grocery store, bathing and dressing Wyatt in his most flattering sleeper, and baking a batch of chocolate chip cookies. (Sure, they were the refrigerated kind that required no mixing, but technically I baked them in my oven, so I fully planned to claim *homemade* status if anyone pressed.)

"We should have kept Wyatt up all night so he'd have been really cranky during the whole visit," John suggested jokingly.

"*Now* you tell me."

Before we could devise other ways of bringing out the worst in Wyatt, we heard the slamming of car doors and the familiar ring of the door bell. This was it. The mother of all visits, literally and figuratively.

Though I can remember few details from that initial visit, some specifics do stand out. As soon as Amanda took off her jacket, I noticed she chose to wear the necklace we gave her at the hospital, and this I interpreted as a sign of genuine respect. (It didn't quite match the rest of her trendy attire, which showed, in my mind, even more character on her part.) I also remembered immediately surrendering Wyatt to her, so she could savor him during her limited stay. When he fussed for his bottle, I asked if she wanted to feed him, and with natural ease, she offered him his formula. To this day, I don't remember many specific conversations, any prolonged, awkward pauses, or the guided, grand tour, but I'm certain we encountered all of the above.

I do remember, however, the fragile nature of our relationship. Not that I could compare it to glass—for glass breaks and produces shards, which not only cut and poke but cause dreadful images of scars and blood. That's not the fragile I'm referring to. I'm talking about the delicate way John and I communicated during the visit—exchanging deliberately kind comments, laughing lightly at each other's lines. We understood the potent power of spoken words and the even more impressionable mark that body language left behind. When John told a story, did I roll my eyes or possibly leave the room? Did I laugh at the tales I'd heard him tell and then again retell, the original version always greatly skewed with exaggeration and wit. Did I interrupt, as I'd been known to do, and did this cause *him* to roll *his* eyes or fumble the ending of one of his winning anecdotes?

It's not like we meant to trick Amanda into liking us—our behavior wasn't as artificial as it was sugary sweet, like adding sprinkles to a vanilla donut or candy corn on a Halloween cupcake. We meant to delight rather than deceive. Common courtesy doesn't always come as naturally in the eighth year of marriage—it's almost like fancy china that's pulled out on special occasions. We could use it every day, but it's so much easier to revert to paper plates.

Besides worrying about Amanda assessing the strength of our marriage, I worried even more about her assessment of our parenting skills. Did our treatment of Wyatt bother her in any way? Did we appear overbearing, overprotective, not protective enough?

Amanda, so quiet at our initial visit, reminded me of an analyst compiling data to later dissect and examine. During one story in particular, I wondered if she listened passively, yet at the same time, gathered red flags about our ability to parent. The story itself involved John and I revealing the glorious news about Wyatt to John's large family.

We had called all eight siblings and asked them to meet at his mom's house for a special announcement. I entered into the main hallway with a video camera I borrowed from my friend Grace already recording the special event. As John quieted the crew, I spanned the family room with an unsteady hand, trying to capture the three sisters, two brothers, two sister-in-laws, countless cousins, and one anxious mother-in-law who waited with tentative smiles. Finally, John addressed the crowd, "Well, glad all of you could make it."

He paused for a moment, then added with pride, "This week Laura and I were placed. There's a girl who picked us to be Mom and Dad."

A chorus of screams and clapping rose up, then deflected off the ceiling.

"She's really awesome," John continued. "We got a chance to meet her."

"Hey, we have her picture," I interrupted as planned, "go get her picture from the car."

As John went searching for a nonexistent picture, his family bombarded me with questions that neither of us expected. Our plan involved John revealing, rather than a photo of Amanda, our adorable, sleeping son, snug and content in his car seat, but with no dress rehearsal for the gig, we forgot to prepare my end of the charade.

"How old is she?" one sister asked.

"She's sixteen-years-old."

"How far along?"

"*Very* far along," I fumbled, "it could be a nice birthday present for John."

"So she's due in a few days then?"

"Yeah."

"You guys don't get to know the sex of the baby, do you?"

"Yep, it's a boy. We think it is anyway . . ."

But before I could fib my way through another half-truth, John had arrived with our waking son Wyatt, and shrieks and gasps soon filled the room.

"Oh, my God!" most people exclaimed, and then they offered their congratulations, followed by a fierce hug. The entire scene, now transferred to a DVD, complete with appropriate background music, still incites tears for whoever dares view it, but after we shared the story with the receptive birth family, I couldn't help but wonder which part Amanda might dwell on later. Would she reflect on the accepting nature of Wyatt's extended family, or, more importantly, would she ponder over this seemingly unreliable couple who abandoned a newborn in a parked car?

No matter how carefully John and I tried to speak or act, we couldn't quite read our polite, equally apprehensive guests. After about an hour into the visit, the thought hit me that maybe I couldn't blame Amanda for scrutinizing my every move. All along, I couldn't help but monitor her demeanor just as carefully.

Probably my sharpest memory of the birth mother involved a stint when Wyatt experienced an episode of crabbiness. When he decided to vocalize his frustrations, Amanda had him in her arms, yet when I attempted to rescue her from his shrill screams, she turned me down. In no time at all, she had soothed our distressed baby, and though this should have instilled extreme relief, it instead ignited intense fear. This girl could parent this child, I thought. She had *it*—the natural, nurturing finesse of a potential daycare owner or future maternity nurse. This girl secreted goodness, reminding me so much of her honey-smelling grandma that I backed away from her and my content son in order to serve my pseudo-homemade cookies. I think for the first time I felt a little like a pseudo-mom. I began wondering whether Wyatt would someday prefer his biological mom over me. Or maybe we could somehow meld into the ultimate duo. I'd provide the daily doses of reading and affection, and she'd keep him young and hip while at the same time inspiring him to pursue college and not shirk responsibilities. I suddenly wanted all her good qualities to rub off on him each time I saw her rubbing his arm, leg, or back.

As I sat in our oversized, leather chair, enjoying the last cookie left on the plate, an insight slithered through me—Amanda and I had a lot in common. We both liked each other, we both loved Wyatt, and we both wanted this adoption to succeed. When I closed the door after saying good-bye, I felt overwhelmingly lucky, yet it wasn't luck after all, coursing through my body and generating a wide smile. Maybe this was simply hope. Within minutes, however, my pessimistic self reminded me of the unsettling truth. She still had 16 days before the hearing, 384 hours to ponder her options, 23,040 minutes to change her mind.

November 6, 2006-Amanda's Call

This was it. The day had come. At 3:45 p.m. on that mild autumn day, Amanda would appear in front of a judge and decide whether or not to terminate all parental rights. And during the entire day, and during the court proceedings, I would sit at home and do what I had learned to do since the adoption process began—wait.

I would sit, and I would wait.

I would feed Wyatt his bottle, and I would wait.

I would play with a rattle, and I would wait.

I would watch T.V., and I would wait.

When John came home on that incessantly long day, I finally had an adult to talk with, to worry with, but most importantly, to wait with. And with crossed fingers, we did just that. We waited for the final results. We held Wyatt, we cooked dinner, we ate dinner, and there we sat, waiting.

Just after I cleared our plates into our garbage, the phone rang.

CHAPTER 5

The long awaited arrival of November 6, 2006, reminded me of the cruel paradox of Christmas Eve *day*. As a child, I'd awaken on Christmas Eve morning with such excessive anticipation for Santa to leave his stash of gifts that each minute of the interminable day seemed to double in passing. While I had heard of other families exchanging some, or better yet, all of their presents on Christmas Eve *night*, my family saved the whole shebang for Christmas morning. Sure, the sight of several wrapped boxes for all six children never disappointed, but what torture it was to get so close and still be told, not only to wait, but also to wait with patience (for Santa saw every indiscretion on that dreadful day). Waiting for the phone to ring, for the news about Amanda's fateful decision, brought me back to my impatient youth, to a girl who not only peeked at her present, but who had also been holding the gift for over a month.

If this were a piece of fiction, the weather outside would have indeed matched my solemn mood. Sheets of sleet would have entered the forecast to serve as a symbol of indecision, a foreboding sign from above that even nature couldn't decide whether to rain or whether to snow. But since this is a memoir, I must admit, the weather held no grim premonitions. Unseasonably warm, calm temperatures passed through the region. I encountered no freak ice storms, early blizzards, or torrential rains, except those brewing, for much of the day, in my overanxious body.

Just after six p.m. on that excruciatingly long day, John and I both stood up when the telephone rang for a second time.

"You get it!" I told John, so he removed the phone from the wall, pushed the on button, and greeted the caller. It was Amanda. She wanted to inform us personally that the hearing had ended—she had signed away her parental rights.

John, of course, thanked Amanda in his loud, expressive voice, but I couldn't help but wonder why the important expression "thank you" contains merely two syllables when it undoubtedly deserves more substance. Even after

John hung up the phone, I felt a need to return Amanda's generosity. She gave us Wyatt. She gave us a family. Were we simply supposed to say thank you in a brief phone call? How could we express our endless gratitude?

When our social worker Tina called within minutes of hanging up with Amanda, I asked her about sending the birth mother a package. (Despite the misconception that birth mothers get compensated monetarily for their loss, I knew that the agency, and even state laws, set limits on how much adoptive couples can give to a birth mother.)

"A thank you card?" I pleaded with Tina, "Am I only allowed to send her a thank you card?"

After discussing some ideas, Tina approved of me sending Amanda a CD of a singer we both liked. I didn't know why I thought this the ideal gift, probably because I remembered discovering that Amanda and I not only watched the reality-based singing competition where this person found stardom, but we also attended his concert. How odd to think that in 2003 we were in the exact same place at the exact same time—perhaps even brushing up against each other's shirt sleeves as we meandered down a crowded aisle. When the artist released a second CD in September of 2006, I instantly wanted to share it with Wyatt's birth mother. In retrospect, I can't believe I felt proud of my exchange. Amanda gave me a child, and in return, I gave her a Clay Aiken CD. What was I thinking? I honestly didn't know the protocol to follow. I didn't know if Amanda held certain expectations on my end, and I certainly didn't want to disappoint her.

From the very beginning, we had no clear idea of how *open* our own open adoption would be. Would we trade pictures, letters, phone numbers, addresses, e-mails, or even trendy text messages? Would we visit on holidays, birthdays, special occasions, or any random weekend? When I thought of the word *open*, I never associated it with the word *adoption*. I simply pictured a sign that typically leans on the inside of a store window and often contains in large print, *OPEN* and in smaller print, *Come on in*. Ironically, our relationship has developed into a very similar concept. And though I think we may be more open than most adoptive couples and birth families, we have fallen into a familiarity that merges friendship with kinship. We didn't just adopt Wyatt; we adopted Amanda, along with her entourage of supportive allies who we first met at the hospital. On all of Wyatt's special occasions, from birthdays to holidays, we invited our newfound birth family; Wyatt's baptism was no exception.

March 4, 2007—Wyatt's Baptism

Not long after Wyatt's abrupt arrival, John and I started reevaluating our need to attend church. Did belonging to a congregation for the first eighteen years of our lives shape us into the decent, law abiding people we had become?

Didn't our wholesome values stem from Sunday trips to a long, wooden pew where our families spread out like neat rows of planted peas, ready to seep in nutrients and blossom to our full potential? We both agreed they had.

Since the beginning of December, John and I had abandoned our slothful habit of sleeping in on Sundays and had begun visiting a local Lutheran church. After joining the congregation in February, we scheduled a baptism for the beginning of March. As the celebration drew near, we saw the event as an intimate opportunity to unite our immediate families with Wyatt's birth family. The guest list, however, totaled an alarming 55 people. Whether a party of that size would impress or alienate the birth family, we would soon discover, but as certain siblings on both sides began apologizing for having other commitments, I feigned disappointment. Secretly, I hoped twenty of the guests would cancel, providing a less chaotic setting for the three families to mingle.

When March fourth finally arrived, I spent so much time offering food, refilling drinks, and introducing relatives, that the afternoon slipped by much faster than expected. The service itself left John and me beaming, and I could tell my traditional Catholic guests appreciated the lively church band (of which my friend Ginger played her violin and winked as I walked passed for communion). After the festive ceremony, our families gathered at our humble home. I remember the smell of hot beef and the constant hum of six separate conversations, but I don't recall relaxing and taking the time to enjoy my assembled company. Though I longed to stay near our friends Amy and Richard, Wyatt's godparents, I would hear my name called, followed by a request for paper towels, more ice, or directions to the bathroom.

Midway through the gathering, I made a point to sit in the chair next to Grandma Betty, Amanda's jovial grandmother. Although we met with Amanda at least once a month, we hadn't seen Grandma Betty since Christmas. Most of the time, if we met at Amanda's house, I could sense that Grandpa Joe and Grandma Betty worried that they were interrupting our time with Amanda and Ryan, for they rarely stayed for more than an hour and always thanked us profusely for sharing our precious Wyatt. But in all honesty, I couldn't get enough of this merry, affectionate couple who immediately greeted us with bear hugs and gentle pecks on our cheeks. No adults in my family, mother or father, grandmother or grandfather, even aunt or uncle dispensed love so freely. During every visit, I found myself drawn to Joe and Betty—every easy embrace worked like wood filler covering a crack—I hadn't realized my childhood, so void of physical affection, had left so many empty holes. With Grandpa Joe and Grandma Betty, I knew that Wyatt would never experience such voids—so many people loved our son—a basement full to be exact.

When the last guests had located their coats and waved good-bye, I sat down with John to assess the afternoon. Did it look like everyone got along? Did our families get a chance to meet Amanda's family? Wasn't the cake delicious? Yes, yes, and yes. From our viewpoint, everyone enjoyed the gathering, yet, in reality, everyone had not. The splendidly mirthful Grandma Betty could not stop weeping throughout the visit. I hadn't even noticed. (And I wouldn't know it until a year and a half later.) Why did I not detect her discomfort? Was I far too engrossed in my hosting responsibilities? When I thought back on the day, I could conjure up only one alibi, my newly acquired parental tunnel vision.

A mere month after we brought Wyatt home, I became excruciatingly aware of the parenting styles of siblings and strangers. Who disciplined fairly? Who belittled intentionally? Who should I emulate? Who would I ignore? Preoccupied by my new focus on parents, I missed Betty's tears entirely and noticed other tears instead, a whining nephew's or a tired niece's. I suddenly possessed some hidden Mom gene that now heightened my awareness of how the world treated its children. Often before I drifted to sleep, my newfound vision led me to recall the ways in which I was parented, especially throughout childhood. Although I had always felt closest to my mother, I remembered with more clarity the times I spent with my dad who didn't hesitate to get down on all fours and simulate horseback rides.

Instead of a verbal "I love you," my dad displayed his love in deliberate acts of kindness. On certain Saturday mornings, Dad would line our oblong griddle with six bubbling pancakes. After flipping the bacon frying in one pan, he stirred the maple syrup heating in another. I couldn't say what I enjoyed more, the actual feast or the smell that lingered in the house for a good two hours after the breakfast. In the winter, Dad, not Mom, squeezed into our narrow, five-seater toboggan, and in the summer, Dad, not Mom, built a tree swing, the kind with the coarse, thick rope that left slivers in our palms. Though each sibling gradually outgrew the swing, I never tired of it, not even of the occasional sliver.

March 23, 2007—Adoption Day

I guess it was natural to appreciate my parents more once I had become one. And on March 23, 2007, the day that I *officially* became one, who stood right by my side, in a pressed buttoned shirt and belted pair of trousers? My very own father. After Amanda formally waived her parental rights, my dad responded to Wyatt just as I had wanted. In true Grandpa style, Dad held him, tickled him, tossed him about until formula-based drool trickled down one side of his mouth, and asked him repeatedly, "So how ya doin', big guy?"

Neither John nor I knew what to expect when we walked into the courthouse to adopt our son, but we surely wanted to share the momentous occasion with our parents, who by now had both found significant others to accompany them (the very people they would eventually marry). So surrounded by grandparents and grandparents-to-be, Wyatt entered the judge's office on John's arm, and the rest of us followed. John and I scooted two leather chairs up to the judge's desk while my dad, John's mom, and her fiancé squeezed into a row of chairs behind us. Jan, my dad's fiancé, stood to the side, a camera raised and aimed at our squirrelly, nearly six-month-old son who pawed at the documents, picture frames, and stray pens set atop the mahogany desk. After raising our right hands and answering a few questions, we signed official documents and snapped enough photos to fill a small album. Later that day, brimming with excitement, I developed the photographs and swore I could see, standing dead center in each picture, Pride himself, his smile as wide as his long arms that stretched to include every torso in every frame. So many characters had left the scene—Paranoia, Fear, Doubt, and my true nemesis, Stress. Pride had pushed them all aside, Pride and his cohort Joy.

At the end of that meaningful day, as Wyatt rocked in my arms savoring his bedtime bottle, I couldn't imagine my life with any other child. Adoption, a porthole to a world of tummy time and lullabies, altered me, transformed me basically, from resentful to grateful. My heart burst with as much love for Wyatt as gratitude for Amanda so much so that I found myself sobbing for no better reason than I felt overwhelmingly happy.

None of my contentment could have surfaced without Amanda's generosity, so another feeling assaulted me, a feeling of eternal debt. How would I ever repay this girl? How would I ever convey my appreciation? Deep down inside I knew the answer—I knew what she wanted, and I knew I would give it to her. On the night of Wyatt's baptism, I whispered a promise to my sleeping son. I would wholeheartedly commit to a *very* open adoption. Whenever and wherever Amanda wanted to see her biological son, I would be there. Moments after my declaration, consumed by tenderness, I thought of my dad, a man who raised his children to get down on all fours, go sledding, and swing high. Though I legally couldn't pay for Amanda's college tuition or purchase for her a used yet reliable car, I could do as my dad had taught me—I could spend time with her and her family and allow her to spend time with Wyatt and mine. Affection through action. That's how she'd feel the depth of my gratitude.

Four months later, with Amanda's seventeenth birthday fast approaching, we received a call from Ryan with a memorable request. He wanted to throw Amanda a surprise birthday party, which also presented the opportunity for us to meet his immediate family.

"We'll be there," I responded, knowing exactly what the day would mean to Amanda—how much she would wish for acceptance from her uncles, her aunts, and her adorable cousins. I see the date etched in my mental timeline beside the title, "Amanda's Birthday." More allies, we were about to meet even more.

July 16, 2007—Amanda's Birthday

Waking to blinding sun on that mid-July day in no way replenished my exhausted body, which remained gripped in anxiety throughout the sleepless night. I could not belittle the magnitude of the day, for my worrisome self became acutely aware that Amanda's family may not have any interest in meeting the two greedy vultures who feasted on her vulnerability and flew away with their missing kin. How accepting were Amanda's relatives who, in one fell swoop, found out she was pregnant, gave birth, and placed the baby for adoption? Though no one at this point could undo what had already been done, they could certainly still voice disapproval or silently scowl at us throughout the afternoon. Thank God I had John to accompany me, an extrovert who shined in these situations and glowed with enough self assurance to make up for my deficiency.

When describing my husband, friendly does not sufficiently capture John's social personality. The man has a presence about him, an invisible aura of positive energy that settles on anyone who shakes his hand. More often than not, his optimism works like a contagious germ that transfers quickly and infects instantly, and in most situations, he's the tallest and the loudest, and the one entertaining the small crowd of people who have already fallen victim to his incurable, cheerful disposition.

The more I sit back and watch my animated husband, the more I see the source of his popularity. Either John will find all of the commonalities between a speaker and himself, or he will discover the speaker's greatest passion and ask a slew of questions pertaining to that topic. When a break in the conversation signals the need for a funny story, John adds one with ease, yet he deliberately returns to the speaker's favorite subject, no matter how boring. On Amanda's special day, I appreciated my husband's gift for gab and banked on the prospect that it would charm the most reluctant members of Wyatt's birth family.

When John and I pulled along the curb to park outside Amanda's home, a rush of familiar faces walked over to welcome Wyatt. Grandpa Joe, Grandma Betty, Ryan, and both of Ryan's Springer Spaniels edged their way to the right, rear window where Wyatt slouched in his car seat, groggy from an interrupted nap. As we exited our car, I spotted Amanda out of the corner of my eye, a huge smile of surprise planted on her face.

"I didn't know you were coming!" she said as I gave her a hug before opening the back door to rescue our fidgeting son. Though everyone reached to intercept Wyatt, the overwhelmed child turned away from their attempts, then immediately pointed to the two jumping dogs and slithered loose to pet the canines.

"Oh, look at how he loves Chocolate and Butters," Grandma Betty cooed, and everyone oohed and awed at Wyatt, who continued to point his finger and squeal with delight when Chocolate left it drenched in slobber.

We must have spent ten minutes in the front yard, stalling possibly, while transitioning Wyatt from a quiet car ride to the commotion of company. Unfortunately, large gatherings provoked our son to act clingy and needy, unattractive traits in the cutest of children. At family events, rather than play ball with an uncle or build blocks with a cousin, Wyatt typically clamped his legs and arms around Mom or Dad, leaving relatives of all ages with the sting of rejection.

In my ignorant days, I foolishly worried that during visits Wyatt might prefer his birth mother over me, yet now I prayed that Wyatt would accept Amanda, fall willingly into her arms when she requested a hug or kiss. The older Wyatt grew, the quicker he warmed up to his birth family. (By his second birthday, he even uttered genuinely, "I miss Amanda," if too much time had passed between visits.) On this particular occasion, however, Wyatt was only nine months old, so it took him longer to recognize Amanda, her dad, and her always doting grandparents.

I couldn't help but notice that our hosts didn't seem overly interested in escorting us to the hub of the party, the small backyard. Too enthralled by Wyatt's obsession with his new furry pals, they simply watched our son, marveling at his gleeful expressions and captivated by how tall he'd grown. Amid our enormous families, Wyatt blended in, another tiny ant in a large, bustling colony. Here Wyatt received everyone's attention, an appreciated change of pace (though I felt a bit guilty at how the party focused on Wyatt rather than the birthday girl).

When we finally decided to venture to the back of the house, the oldest of Ryan's brothers, Mike, greeted us with a firm handshake and mighty voice. His tall, athletic stature, predominately bald head, and boisterous, natural charisma mirrored John's in every way, so not surprisingly, the two connected instantly, jawing on about fatherhood and football.

"Did I toss and turn the previous night for this?" I asked my pessimistic self. She just shrugged her shoulders as if disappointed in our unexpected success.

As John and Mike continued to form a quick camaraderie, another brother approached our conversation, Eric. Had I met Eric in a poorly lit parking lot, I almost certainly would have labeled him creepy if not deranged and dangerous. The man, much slimmer and slightly shorter than Mike, had adorned his arms, legs, and chest with tattoos, including a sizable octopus with colorful, sprawling tentacles. Not to stare offensively at these markings was as difficult as resisting a glimpse at a protruding zit on someone's nose or an escaped crumb on someone's chin. Lucky for me, Eric used his symbolic skin as a convenient icebreaker. In no time, he was lifting his shirt sleeves and shirt to reveal the inked images decorating his arms, back, and chest. By the end of the afternoon, I found myself enamored with Eric because his outward appearance so poorly reflected his sensitive personality. The man talked of remodeling his home and surprising his dad with tickets to a basketball game. He exchanged sarcastic jabs at the expense of his brothers, and I laughed at every line, appreciating the constant comedy.

Later in the afternoon, I finally got the opportunity to talk with Ryan's third brother Justin, who stood beside his fiancée and previewed the details of their upcoming wedding. A little quieter than the others, Justin listened more than spoke, but I liked him too, especially his advice on raising a boy.

Overall, I couldn't have scripted a more congenial visit. Why had I feared hostility from the offspring of Grandma Betty and Grandpa Joe? But just as I allowed my nerves to settle and decided to occupy the vacant lawn chair next to Betty, I discovered the arresting truth.

Always one to secrete a good secret, Grandma Betty revealed that when she talked with Mike the night before, he wanted nothing to do with meeting Amanda's chosen couple.

"The oldest brother, Mike?" I asked in disbelief, looking around for his broad profile.

"I'm so happy he decided to show," she admitted. "He's on the phone right now trying to convince his wife to come and meet you. He thinks it will help her with Amanda's decision."

"So is Mike okay with it now that he's met us?" I asked with concern.

"Oh, he's so glad he came. That's why he wants his wife to come, but she's still at work . . ."

Before Betty could finish her sentence, Mike sauntered over, his shoulders puffed up, his mouth holding in a prideful grin. His wife would be here right after her shift ended. He hoped we could stick around that long.

One down. One to go. I thought hastily. (Not that *I* would woo the woman, that's for sure.) No occasion seemed more fitting than now for my ever amiable husband to exhibit his farm-grown charm.

About an hour later, the absent wife appeared, still sporting work apparel, an easy target for Eric's comedic talent. I did not know what to expect from the approaching woman who inwardly despised me—silence maybe, clenched teeth possibly, but certainly not tears. Certainly not acceptance.

Someone had given up the canvas lawn chair next to me, so she sat to my left with no hint of hesitancy, and while at first other people added to our conversation, we eventually talked amongst ourselves, the topics safe, our exchange easy. After a few minutes, the chatty woman paused in mid sentence, stared at Wyatt sitting on my lap, and declared with blurry eyes, "I cannot get over how much he looks like you and your husband. Those blue eyes—you all have them. Now that I've met you, I can see that you belong together."

At first I couldn't respond to the woman's compliment, her very unforeseen seal of approval. I stumbled over a thank you and reiterated how lucky *we* were that Amanda had chosen *us*. The gushing woman, now an open faucet, released more tears and then poured out her own struggles with infertility. As she apologized for her breakdown, she simultaneously shared how she shocked doctors by becoming pregnant with her miracle son. Our chumminess tripled like two veterans realizing they served in the same war, endured the same anguish, then conquered the same enemy.

By the end of the party, when most of the relatives had headed home or gathered inside Ryan's kitchen, I sat outside by myself, a rare moment of solitude. Heaped in speculation, I wondered whether Wyatt would meet Amanda's Uncle Eric or simply hear about him as we looked through a photo album. I didn't know at the time how involved Wyatt would become with his birth family, but I knew I would let Amanda help make that decision. If she invited us back, we would surely come. And this time I would look forward to the opportunity.

*

Gradually, and quite naturally, our visits with Wyatt's birth family climbed from awkward, scheduled meetings to more relaxed, enjoyable outings. As Wyatt grew into a walking, talking animal lover, we met at petting zoos and campgrounds. We fed ducks, spotted deer, and, before our eyes, watched Ryan's passion for the outdoors transfer into Wyatt. With every visit, we also discovered an Amanda who exuded confidence, energy, and compassion, who laughed as her dad told a story that mocked her, and who reddened confessing the details of her latest crush. We enjoyed each other's companionship, and that became more obvious when Amanda's graduation drew nearer. Her large high school only allotted each student a limited amount of tickets to the event; the Schmitts received two.

June 5, 2008—Amanda's Graduation

In the spring of 2008, when the passing of time had allowed frankness and honesty to slip into our reflections, Grandma Betty confessed to me that she had a difficult time enjoying Wyatt's baptism and the party that followed. There we sat, perched on the bleachers in Amanda's high school auditorium waiting for the graduation ceremony to commence, when Betty and I began reminiscing about her views on the adoption experience. I listened with awe as she described the moment the doctors told Amanda, on the day of giving birth, that she was not only pregnant but about to deliver. Betty admitted that she offered to help Amanda if she chose to keep the baby, and when her granddaughter decided to place him with an adoptive couple, Betty struggled with her choice. Eventually, the conversation turned to the day of Wyatt's baptism and how Betty broke down at the church, at our house, and in the car on the way home. Then she shared a most enlightening conversation that she exchanged with Amanda during the drive.

"It's okay, Grandma. You don't have to be sad," Amanda explained.

"I know, honey," Grandma Betty cooed, "I just can't help it. I can't stop crying."

"You know, Grandma," Amanda reassured her, "God gave me Wyatt so I could give him to John and Laura."

"She said that?" I interrupted Betty, a bit dismayed at Amanda's insight.

"That's what she said. You know she loves Wyatt, but she's pretty happy about how all this turned out. Oh, Laura, you wouldn't believe all those binders of pictures we had to look through. We looked at so many different couples." I smirked at the image of Amanda's dad and grandpa paging through portfolios and resisting the urge to make lighthearted comments.

"We wanted Amanda to make the decision on her own, so we didn't tell her who we liked best. Then finally I asked Amanda, 'Did you choose a couple?' I didn't want to pressure her into telling us if she didn't want to, but finally I asked, 'Do you want to tell us who you chose?' Amanda said, 'I chose Laura and John.' I said, 'That's who I chose.' Then Joe said, 'That's who I chose.' Then Ryan said, 'That's who I chose.' It was so funny because we all chose you two!"

"No way," I laughed, shaking my head in disbelief.

"So we took that as a sign and felt a little bit better about the adoption."

As Betty and I shared our differing perspectives of the past, I finally figured out why I relished her company—she reminded me of my own absent mother. Her age, her expressions, her sensitivity, and her pride in her family rekindled a similar connection that I had shared with my mom so many years ago. (I can't say she's the first woman to bring about such nostalgia. Being in the presence of my friends' moms or certain co-workers at school has also triggered a longing I try to keep buried.) But it's situations like these when life reminds me of a giant connect-the-dots template. Whether my actions dictate which dot I will encounter next or whether God has already laid out my design, I still haven't decided, but it seems unrealistic, or perhaps arrogant, to suggest that mere humans could orchestrate such an ideal match. Overall, it's easier and far more humble for me to believe in God's Grace (or that possibly my mother in heaven again petitioned my Maker). What I know for sure is that adoption ushered me into the coveted role of motherhood and labeled both John and me under the demanding, yet thrilling category of parents.

Just as we had hoped, Wyatt enhanced our lives on a daily basis, tapping into our childlike tendencies without much effort. As our new addition sprouted into a wondrous child, we rarely drove for long distances without singing with gusto, "Old McDonald had a farm" with guttural oinks and boisterous woofs. Attending fairs, amusement parks, and the traveling circus fascinated Wyatt, yet at the same time, reintroduced us to the scrumptious smells and tastes of elephant ears, cotton candy, and chicken on a stick. When Wyatt swam in his inflatable, plastic pool or swung on a park swing, he always chimed, "Mama's turn," and without much coaxing, I, too, splashed and swung like a carefree kid.

My Relentless Maternal Urge

By eight o'clock at night, during Wyatt's prolonged bedtime ritual of blessing loved ones, reading books, and recapping the favorite parts of our day, I was quite often struck by my ever-present maternal urge, (which stirred with anxiety at the faintest scent of Johnson's Baby Shampoo.) The same maternal urge that nearly swallowed me whole in my infertile years did not weaken once I met Wyatt; it tripled in force, morphed itself right into a maternal instinct with a constant need to nurture and protect. Deep inside I felt a kinship to any and all adoptive parents—whether they consented to a closed or open adoption, they would someday have to sit down and explain that their child grew in their hearts and not their bellies. They would have to use words like birth parents and adoption. And then, unlike biological parents, they would have to field the toughest of questions.

John and I knew we wouldn't hide the obvious: at a young age, Wyatt would learn that we adopted him and eventually discover Amanda, his favorite visitor, was actually his birth mother. Knowing the bond between them, I doubted he would feel as wounded as simply confused, and over time, I hoped the initial confusion would fade into appreciation. If he questioned Amanda's motives, we had only to admit the truth. Love—she placed him out of love.

So at what magical age would a discussion of this magnitude take place? When my friend Grace admitted that she'd been reading adoption storybooks to her daughter since birth, I felt neglectful. I suddenly valued Grace's "the earlier the better" philosophy. Just after Wyatt turned two, I gathered some of my favorite pictures, created a rhyming storyline, and ordered a photo book entitled, *How Wyatt Became a Little Schmitt*. The pseudo publication looked exactly like any other book in his collection except this one contained pictures of Wyatt, his birth family, and many adopted friends. I was going to wait until Christmas to give it to him, but it surpassed my expectations, so I propped it up as a decoration and waited for him to spot it. Later that afternoon, after spying his photo on the cover, Wyatt pointed then asked, "What's that book, Mommy?"

I offered to read it to him, and he enthusiastically agreed. Unfortunately, the moment didn't unfold as smoothly as I had hoped. In the end, when I reinforced that Wyatt grew in Amanda's tummy rather than Mama's, he immediately corrected me.

"No!" he insisted. "I grew in *Daddy's* tummy." I smirked at his theory.

"Oh, you think so?" I added, and the discussion simply fell away as Wyatt slipped out of my lap and pulled me down to build a train track. Who knows how many times we would have to read that book before Wyatt would truly comprehend his situation, but I viewed the process like I approached potty training. Don't force him. When he's ready, he'll get it.

And like many other milestones, Wyatt began amazing us, transforming from an infant to toddler far faster than we ever expected. From singing the alphabet to scurrying to use the bathroom, Wyatt shed all traces of babyhood and entered boyhood at eye-blinking speed.

About the time Wyatt stopped wearing onesies and began speaking in complete sentences, my maternal urge got downright greedy. The tentacles sprouted again with a pit-in-the-stomach feeling that pleaded adamantly, "Adopt another. Adopt another." It chanted with the rhythm of a heart. "Adopt another. Adopt another." And I couldn't ignore its steady hum. Just before I turned thirty-five years old, my husband asked what I wanted for my birthday.

"I want to adopt another baby," I beamed. "I want to get back in the pool."

But rather than sharing my enthusiasm, he released an intentionally loud sigh, and my singing heart fell bitterly silent.

"We have so much to offer," I began to argue, but one look from my husband, and I knew he was in no mood to debate the issue. We'd become well-versed in the other's view on this touchy topic, and I couldn't deny my husband's logic. When it came down to it, how in the world could lightening strike twice? How could we possibly end up with another Wyatt, another intelligent, healthy child who seemed destined to join *our* family? There were so many outside variables when it came to adoption, so many feelings of inadequacy and helplessness accompanying the process. Did we really have the stamina to reenter the hoop jumping phase? Did we truly possess the patience to wait among other qualified couples? Did we honestly share the resiliency to endure an unexpectedly reluctant birth mother? No, no, and no. We would not adopt another.

Breaking this to myself and my maternal urge would take some precious time, but in the end, I knew I would find contentment. I knew my absence from the adoption pool would be someone else's gain—maybe it would benefit a complete stranger or maybe a dear friend like Amy.

*

As I ponder my path to motherhood, I now conclude some simple truths. Though some assert that patience is the art of hoping, I would also add that hope is the art of believing. Throughout the adoption process, although I cautioned myself to resist Hope, I always ended up surrendering to her power. One look at my adopted son, and I realize I made the right choice by counting on Hope.

PART II

Jen

"The miserable have no other medicine.
But only hope."

~William Shakespeare
Measure for Measure

I was that friend, the one who longed to share both the joys and trials of motherhood with some of my closest friends.

When I arrived at one particular game night, I wasn't sure how the night would unfold. I grew especially uncertain of how Jen would react to my news. She had gotten to that point where asking about her pregnancy hopes sounded borderline nosy rather than concerned. I first met Jen through Laura, but after years of book club discussions, New Year's Eve parties, and girls' game nights, the "friend of a friend" title faded. The more we bonded, the more I envied her knowledge of literature and her ability to transform from a pious Puritan to a scandalous flapper at our annual Halloween parties. With years of community theater behind her, I wondered which character would respond to my news. Would she try for the Best Supporting Actress Award, or this would be the time when her acting skills couldn't pull her through?

By now my friends had already celebrated two births with me. They had gently cradled my fragile newborns and dutifully admired the portraits of my blue and pink swaddled bundles with tiny fingers and toes peeking out. However, I hesitated to announce the news of my third pregnancy, the one that caught even me by surprise. While I wanted to be able to share my excitement, I knew I didn't dare admit to my insecurity about being pregnant again so soon. What right did I have to complain about sleepless nights and fussy newborns when my friends were struggling for what came so easily to me?

~Jenny Kalmon

CHAPTER 6

The Little Details

Before I tell my story, you need to understand something about me. I am a planner. It's not just that I like to have a general idea of what is going to happen; I live by my calendar. To plan my daily wardrobe for an entire month, I write each day's outfit in a notebook (including shoes and jewelry) and iron them one week in advance. Extremely uncomfortable with spontaneity, I start each day with a to-do list, and if I accomplish something significant that wasn't on the list, I will add it just to have the satisfaction of crossing it out. In fact, I make lists of my lists.

What goes hand in hand with these somewhat quirky personality traits—and what drives my husband Kevin crazy—is an inherent need to be in control. Yes, I admit things have to be *my way*. My mother credits astrology for this personality trait, calling it the Leo in me. When things don't go my way, the way that I have planned, I do not adapt well. Flexibility is not really part of my nature, and I view change as a catalyst for stress, not an opportunity for unseen possibilities. I not only sweat the small stuff; I sweat the microscopic stuff. I sweat over every little detail.

With all that said, you might imagine how well I planned for being a parent, how fastidious I was with the details of when and how my motherhood would begin and turn out. Actually, in the past two and a half years, I have experienced three pregnancies. Each one was *unplanned*, none turned out the way I expected, and during *none* of them was I in control.

The Big Picture

Kevin and I were married on June 19, 2004, and the following February, I stopped taking my birth control pills. It wasn't that we were longing for children already or even that we felt we were ready. In fact, we were going through enough life changes for my maximum comfort level. Besides adjusting to our new marriage, we had just purchased and were in the process of renovating our first home. Kevin had secured a new physical education position at a nearby school and was coaching two sports, while I was busy revamping my high school English curriculum, taking two grad classes, and beginning my fifth year of coaching a dance team. No, we certainly had enough on our plates. With a new mortgage, exorbitant student loans that were now in repayment status, and our two measly salaries from low-income school districts, it wasn't the best time financially either.

Nevertheless, there were two major factors that influenced our decision to, if not ultimately *try* to have a baby, at least *not* try *not* to try. One was that these things take a while. I had been on birth control pills for ten years and had heard about the lasting effects they had. I was already thirty years old, so assuming it would take a couple of years to get pregnant, now would be the time to get the ball rolling. Besides that, all our friends were either starting their families or at least trying to get pregnant. I'm not saying that I wanted to get pregnant because it seemed like the "in" thing to do; it was just the natural order of things, and, after all, I *do* like order.

What I experienced next happens so often to so many women, it's almost cliché. Eight months later, I went to see the doctor for a simple sore throat and congestion. Before he prescribed an antibiotic, Dr. K. asked if there was any chance I could be pregnant. Believe it or not, that question took me completely by surprise. I wish I could say that I'd been keeping a close eye on my cycles, that my maternal instincts had begun to kick in, that I had already been *planning* this moment. But, to tell the truth, I had kind of forgotten. Taking that pill was no longer part of my daily routine; since I was no longer actively trying to *control* my non-pregnant status, thoughts of motherhood never really surfaced.

Yet there I was, being asked if there was a possibility I could be pregnant.

"I guess so," I stammered. With those words, something seemed to change in me. All of a sudden, I *wanted* to be pregnant, and I wanted it to be right *now*. That sounds so trivial, like suddenly I wanted to buy a new pair of shoes or to get a puppy. Nothing as momentous as wanting a child can be that spontaneous. In retrospect, I don't think it was. I believe that my subconscious had been gearing up for that moment for a long time, that my maternal instincts *had* begun to kick in. I had just been too busy planning every other little detail of my life to see the big picture.

"Well, let's do a pregnancy test then." Dr. K.'s voice sounded as if it were traveling through dense fog, and I could barely hear him above the pounding of my heart.

I don't even remember taking the test, but I do remember waiting those three minutes in the examination room. I also remember the nurse strolling by the door, presumably to retrieve the test, and then quickly striding by again, glancing at me through the open doorway. I know she gave me a look. She probably wasn't supposed to, but she did. A slightly raised eyebrow. An almost imperceptible grin. Definitely a look. My heart began to race again.

After what seemed like forever, Dr. K. returned and said those magic words: "Congratulations, Mom." So began our journey down the road of *unplanned* parenthood.

Change of Plans

Of course, I can't leave out the one person who has traveled this entire journey with me, who has cruised through every seemingly unsurpassable road block and who has turned every unexpected corner with ease—my husband.

Here is what I've learned after five years of marriage: I am damn lucky to have found someone who puts up with me. Our family and friends would be the first to tell you that Kevin is the easy-going one, the social one, the laid-back one, the fun one. That's okay; somehow we create a perfect balance, and there is no way I could have dealt with the unexpected joys and tragedies I have faced in recent years without him.

Kevin was thrilled with the news that I was pregnant. The next few weeks were filled with talk of baby names and nursery themes. We tried to be careful, not telling anyone until I was further along in case there were complications. At about six weeks, we told our parents, and by eight weeks, we had spread the news to our family and closest friends. Then we hit the magic twelfth week after which couples are usually in the clear as far as a successful pregnancy. It was fun to tell people; I'd be lying if I said I didn't get caught up in it. Plus, I felt great; I didn't have any morning sickness, mood swings, significant weight gain, or food cravings. We even had an early ultrasound picture of our little kidney bean to show off. Yes, Kevin and I definitely loved the idea of being pregnant.

In November, I went in for my fourteen-week check up. I was seeing a new OB-GYN that day. It is the policy of my clinic to have expectant mothers see a different doctor at each check up so that when it comes time to deliver, the patient is familiar with the doctor, no matter who is on call. That day, the doctor seemed, to put it nicely, experienced. By all appearances, he'd been doing this a *long* time, and he seemed a little burned out. We went through the motions. Normal weight gain? Check. Blood pressure? Fine. Measurement? Normal.

"Well, let's get you up on the table," the doctor said, "and listen to that heartbeat." I knew Kevin wanted to be present the first time we heard the heartbeat, but I wasn't going to pass up this opportunity.

I can still feel the cold gel on my stomach and envision the poster of one hundred babies in clay flower pots attached to the ceiling tiles above the examination table. Minutes passed. As I waited anxiously to hear the baby's racing heart beat, I recall the doctor reassuring me, "Sometimes it's difficult to pick up the heartbeat this early in the pregnancy. There is no cause for worry. We'll just do a quick ultrasound to put your mind at ease."

Ultrasound technicians are not supposed to interpret any of their readings to the patient and are experts at keeping a straight face. They are somehow able to set the mood so that you know not even to ask any questions because they will not answer them. What they don't know is that we can still tell when something is wrong. Whether they distract us with small talk or say nothing at all, we still know. As I lay on that table, looking at the unrecognizable shapes and shades of gray on the screen, I tried to make sense of the codes she typed. Feeling the tension build in the room, I knew there was a problem. When it was done, I didn't ask any questions. It wasn't because I knew she wouldn't tell me anything; I just didn't want to hear the answers.

Although I had never seen him before and have never seen him since, I'm glad that I saw that particular doctor on that particular day. There is something to be said for experience. When he came back into the examination room, he gently took my hand, his grandfatherly eyes locked with mine, and he simply said, very softly, "I'm so sorry." I vaguely recall confusing words like "spontaneous abortion," and "D & C," but what was unforgettable was his gentle touch and how he knew just what needed to be done. He paged a nurse who called Kevin at school because I was in no condition to make that phone call. Instead of rushing to his next appointment, he waited with me until he could see I was strong enough to go home. Best of all, he didn't say all those remarks that no woman who has miscarried wants to hear: "You'll still be able to have more children" or worse, "Everything happens for a reason."

This is the point where Kevin became my life support. Not because he was stoic and strong. In fact, if he had tried to convince me that it would all be okay, if he'd insisted on staying positive and just going with the flow as he usually did, I would have lost it. Instead, after rushing home, he held me for a very long time, stooped down with his face burrowed into the crook of my neck, and he cried. I knew he needed me. I'm not saying that I was happy to see him in pain; there is nothing worse than seeing a loved one hurt. I just knew he was the one person who could understand how I felt, and together we grieved.

In the days following our loss, I couldn't bring myself to even think of such menial tasks as cooking and cleaning; they just didn't seem important anymore. I had never understood why family, friends, and neighbors bring food during a time of crisis, but one ring of the doorbell taught me a precious lesson. There were two of my dearest friends, Amy and Laura, at our doorstep, lasagna and garlic bread in hand, hugs at the ready. These two girls (now women) and I had giggled together in the back of our college Shakespeare classes, attended American Idol concerts together hoping for even a brief peek at Clay Aiken, and cajoled our husbands into taking part in outlandish costume parties. When the going gets tough, count on your loved ones to listen to you, cry with you, and to know exactly what you need. Amy and Laura knew that a little bit of Italian cuisine, made with a lot of love, goes a long way.

I realize now that during this first pregnancy, Kevin and I were in love with the idea of being *pregnant,* but we had barely given a thought to the idea of being *parents.* Looking back, I begin to see a pattern of irony. It seems we were always a step behind, not really knowing what we wanted until faced with the unexpected. We didn't realize how much we wanted to be pregnant until I was, and we didn't realize how much we wanted to be parents until we no longer were. So began our journey down the road of *planned* parenthood.

Crossroads

Getting pregnant—what could be easier than that? We had done it once without even trying, I reasoned. But along with my control-freak personality comes a moderate dose of impatience, and after only six months without any success, we decided to consult a doctor. The next eight months were filled with experiences with which so many women are familiar: basal thermometers, increasing doses of Clomid, ovulation tests, blood work, pelvic exams, etcetera. I began to resent my doctor, who not only wasn't fixing the problem but who also seemed barely to recognize me at every monthly appointment. Fighting with the insurance company about which procedures and tests were covered was exhausting. Our sex life became so frustratingly scheduled that I began to worry about the type of environment in which this baby would be conceived. In short, I hated not being in control. I had a well-thought-out plan in my mind, yet forces beyond my control seemed to be working against me. Finally, the doctor referred me to a clinic that specialized in fertility.

Here was the good part: we finally had confidence that these doctors and nurses knew what they were talking about. We saw graphs with statistics and success rates for in vitro fertilization. Procedures were explained to us in minute detail. Doctors and nurses actually asked us questions and had answers for ours. Best of all, we seemed to have their undivided attention. Finally, I didn't feel like just another patient. The bad part? $10,000 for the *possibility* of a child.

We were at a crossroads. One path involved our continuing to try to get pregnant on our own. Even though the doctors said it was unlikely, they didn't say it was completely impossible. After all, it had already happened once. Another path led to in vitro fertilization—countless doctor appointments, painful injections, frozen embryos, further debt, and no guarantees. And the third path? Maybe we should think about adoption.

CHAPTER 7

That Girl

This is where my story turns into a completely implausible, hokey, made-for-TV *Lifetime* movie. If it didn't really happen, I'd hardly believe it myself.

During this emotional stage of my life, my own frustration and uncertainty were put into perspective by a most unusual source—a teenager. Leah Kelly, who had been one of my English students as a freshman, was now a smart, pretty, popular senior, who would seem, to the casual observer, to have it all. She was the kind of person who solved conflict rather than caused it, whose friends ran the gamut of social cliques, and whose dry sense of humor was her most endearing trait once you came to appreciate it. However, Leah's journey had not been an easy one. In ninth grade, she had become caught up in the usual teenage girl drama, her grades suffered, and I feared that her poetry revealed classic signs of depression. After many intense conversations, the guidance counselor discovered that Leah's despair stemmed from strained relationships with both of her parents.

Consequently, for the next two years, Leah attended school-sponsored counseling, and her outlook on life improved. As a junior, she joined my dance team, and the studio became her home away from home, the other dancers her family. What I remember most about Leah during that time was that she never stopped trying, whether it was learning new choreography, establishing new friendships, or maintaining a positive attitude. Yes, she was always *trying*, although at times, she seemed to be trying so hard that I worried what any slight disappointment would do to her delicate psyche.

The one aspect of Leah's life still missing was a best friend, a confidant, someone with whom to share her hopes and dreams, who would need her as much as she needed them. Then, the summer before her senior year, Leah began to date Nick Miller. Nick, though only a sophomore, was the quarterback of the football team, a starting guard for the varsity basketball team, and a member of National Honor Society. *Everyone* knew Nick Miller. And everyone knew Roy and Jackie Miller, involved parents who attended all parent-teacher conferences and every game played by their two sons. The Millers entered Leah's life just when she needed them most. They invited her to their weekly campfires during football season, included her in their family board game nights, and celebrated holiday festivities with her. By that time, I had resigned from coaching but still maintained friendships with many of the girls, including Leah, and I could see a significant transformation in her character. Discontent was finally replaced with genuine happiness (however dependent it was on her new support system). The fun-loving, bubbly, generous girl who had always been hiding inside finally emerged.

After almost a year of dating Nick, during the spring of Leah's senior year, I began to notice small changes in her. Instead of in the midst of a group of giggling girls, I was more likely to see her sitting alone on the tiled floor of the hallway, her head in her arms. She put little time into her appearance. Sloppy sweatshirts drooped over her petite frame. Her blonde hair was thrown into a messy ponytail, and dark circles showed under her hazel eyes. I worried that her parents' fighting had escalated or that she was having problems with Nick, with whom I rarely saw her lately. The few times I pulled her aside to ask what was wrong, she replied with the typical teenage response, "Nothin'. I'm fine."

And then I heard the rumor in the teachers' lounge—Leah Kelly was three months pregnant.

The Grand Plan

Later that day, I noticed Leah standing alone at her locker, staring into it as if she couldn't remember what she was looking for in the first place. Having no idea the right words to say in this situation, I was tempted to turn around and avoid the conversation altogether. Then images of the past year flashed through my mind. A doctor's sincere smile. Kevin gently wiping the tears from my face. My mother's words of encouragement. Leah would need as much support as possible. I took a deep breath and approached her. When she noticed me, the look in her eyes was a combination of "I am so scared" and "Are you disappointed in me?" I wrapped my arms around her.

After a moment, we stepped apart, my hands on her shoulders, and she said timidly, "I was going to call you . . . to talk."

"Any time," I answered.

*

She did call—at all hours of the night—crying, scared, alone. I discovered that, as I'd expected, the news of Leah and Nick's pregnancy came as a devastating shock to their parents. They had first told Leah's mother who was now separated from her father. According to Leah, a fight ensued in which her mother (probably with good intentions) had threatened to tell Nick's parents if he didn't soon do it himself. The argument had then escalated to the point where Leah left to move in with her father. The reaction of Nick's parents was worse than Leah and Nick had feared. Leah told me that they'd basically forced the two teens to break up, forbidding them to continue dating. Several days later, when they had realized that the ultimatum was a bit rash (and probably ineffective—what could it really change at that point?), they had relented. By then it was too late. Nick and Leah had broken up, having said regrettably hurtful words to each other, and the damage seemed irreparable. His parents were now barely on speaking terms with her. Leah confided that she felt as if she had lost her mother, her boyfriend and *best* friend, and a family which had welcomed her with open arms. She was more alone than ever and facing the most frightening time of her life.

During our late-night conversations, my heart ached right along with Leah's. I tried to listen, to help Leah weigh the pros and cons of each option, but I was careful not to offer my own personal opinion on what Leah *should* do. Because, to be totally honest, what I really wanted was to adopt this baby myself, to fill the hole that had been present in my marriage ever since we had lost our baby. Because even though I truly cared about Leah, a part of me screamed at the unfairness of this teenage girl getting pregnant so easily with an unwanted baby when I could not conceive a desperately wanted one. Because even though the important thing was finding the best solution for Leah and the baby, I couldn't help but think that Kevin and I could provide it. And because it was an extremely personal decision and not mine to make.

A few weeks later, I was walking to my classroom before first period when Leah passed me and casually handed me a note. She'd never written to me before, but I assumed it was an update on the never-ending break-up saga or maybe a thank you letter for the late-night advice sessions. What I never expected to read, what brought me to my knees, what changed my life in every way possible was this:

> *I have been thinking a lot about what I am going to do. I know I am not ready to raise my baby and give him everything he needs. I could give him all my love, and it might be enough for him, but I won't be happy. I want him to have more, and I know you and Kevin could give him everything and more. I wanted to tell you this before, but I*

did not want to get your hopes up in case I changed my mind. I am absolutely positive this is what I want to do. I talked to my cousin about it. She has a little boy and she was saying that she would regret giving him up and that she would never want him to call anyone else mom. I thought about this, but I did not feel sad about it. I told her that giving you my baby would make me happier than anything else in the entire world. If my baby were to call anyone else mom, I would want that person to be you. I trust you, and I look up to you so much. A child would be so lucky to have you as a mother, and you deserve that special relationship that a mother and child have. The Millers do not know about this decision yet. I plan on telling them soon though. I don't know how you feel about adopting my baby since you know the parents. It would make me so happy though if you would consider the option. If this is a possibility, I'd like to get together and talk.

The Talk

What does one do when one receives a letter like that? My first and only thought was to find Leah. Fortunately, first hour was my free period, so I did not have to rush to my room and attempt to teach, which would have been nearly impossible. By this time, students were meandering to class. I peered down the hallways, trying to spot Leah in the sea of teenagers. I ran around the four corridors that make up the square of high school classrooms, asking the occasional student if they had seen Leah, and nearly knocking down a freshman or two as I clipped the corners. Checking her locker once more and not finding her, I proceeded to the art room where she had her first period class. No luck. Finally, as I rounded the corner and headed back to my classroom, there she was standing in the doorway. I remember grabbing her arm, pulling her into my room, sitting her down in a desk, looking her straight in the eye, and asking the one question that was pounding repeatedly through my mind: "Are you sure?"

"I'm sure," she answered, with a slight nod. Such a simple response, one teenagers say all the time and hardly ever mean. Looking into her eyes and holding her hand, I let myself believe her.

"What do you think the Millers will say?" I asked. That seemed to be the most potentially significant obstacle at this point. Leah told me they weren't really on speaking terms with her, and I had to keep reminding myself that I'd only heard *her* side of the story. My feelings aside, we would need their support in this decision. Legally, I assumed Nick had certain rights. More importantly, we all needed to be on the same page as far as how this adoption would actually work in a town this size (population 947), where there would be no secrets and where everyone would be aware of, if not in some way involved in, the situation.

The unanswered question still loomed in the air. "What do you think the Millers will say?"

"I don't know," Leah admitted, her eyes filling with apprehension. "I called Jackie yesterday. My dad and I are going meet with them tonight while Nick is at confirmation class." It seemed strange to me that they would meet without Nick, but Leah was not surprised. Nick had basically checked out of the whole scenario; apparently he wouldn't talk about the pregnancy except for a robotic mantra of "whatever's best for the baby."

"You have to call me right away, as soon as you are done," I implored. "I have to know what they say." How would they feel about someone in their own community adopting the baby? What were the implications for Nick, who still had two years left in *this* school? What kind of relationship would they want with the baby? What would they want to be *called*?

I was getting ahead of myself. Leah promised to call me that night about the Millers' reaction, but we had so many other things to talk about *now*. Where did we even begin? First, we went to see the principal, the same man who had set up chairs at my wedding, who had let me cry at his desk when I'd had a particularly bad day, who was like a second father to me.

"Can you get my morning classes covered and excuse Leah from hers?" I asked him, Leah and I peaking our heads into his office. "We need to talk."

One look at us was all it took. "Yep. Use the in-school suspension room." We crossed the corridor and entered the eight by eight foot room. With blank cement walls surrounded a wooden table in the center, it was set up to be as boring and uncomfortable as possible for whatever unruly student had gotten in trouble. Leah took a seat in the one metal folding chair, so I hopped up on the wobbly table, crossed my legs butterfly-style, and met her anxious gaze.

What followed was a surreal conversation. Questions seemed to just bounce off the walls randomly, some seemingly insignificant, some monumental.

"What do your parents think?" I asked.

"They support my decision, but my dad is worried that you'll move out of state or something, and he'll never see the baby."

"We wouldn't do that. We would *want* the baby to know your family."

"My grandma wants to know what religion you are."

The question surprised me. "We're Lutheran."

"Awesome. That's what we are too."

"Do you have a name picked out?" I asked her. I knew one of the early ultrasounds had predicted that the baby was a boy, but she had never mentioned a name to me.

"I always liked Colton, but you don't have to use it."

"I love it!" I did, but I probably would have agreed to Napoleon if that's what she wanted.

"You can choose the middle name," she added.

"Okay. I'll talk to Kevin about it."

"Yeah, Kevin!" Leah exclaimed, her head snapping up, eyes meeting mine. "What's he gonna think?"

What was Kevin going to think? I wondered to myself. *And was it alarming that I was just* now *considering my husband's reaction?*

"Are you kidding?" I smiled at Leah reassuringly, certain that what I said was true. "He'll be thrilled." I contemplated how to broach the next subject. Finally I stammered, "So . . . how do you picture your future . . . with Colton?"

"I don't know. I mean, like, pictures and letters and stuff. I could visit when I come home from school. Would that be okay?"

"Absolutely."

"Can I bring friends over to see him and stuff?"

"Sure."

"I'd call first. I mean, I wouldn't just show up on your doorstep."

I laughed.

"So he's probably going to be blonde," she continued, "since Nick and I are both blonde. Is that okay with you?" *So trivial*, I thought.

"Definitely," I assured her, and then paused. "What if someday . . . ?" I didn't know how to finish.

She seemed to know exactly what I was thinking. "I can always have more kids," she answered my unspoken question. *So profound*, I thought.

"And what if Kevin and I have more kids?" I asked. It was a long shot but not impossible.

"That's good. Colton would have brothers and sisters."

So we talked, and asked, and answered, and laughed until finally we both needed a break and some time to process.

"Well, I think I should call Kevin now," I sighed.

"Yeah, I should go to Social Problems class anyway."

We both stood up and when we hugged, I could feel the bump of her belly against my own, with what I was already beginning to think of as my son inside.

"Leah," I stopped at the door and looked back at her. "Why me?"

She shrugged her shoulders as if to indicate that it was an easy decision, which I knew it wasn't. "Because you never told me what I should do," she said. "Even though I knew what you'd lost, and I knew what you wanted to give, you just listened. It seemed like what a mom would do."

Finally, I cried.

What Now?

I wish I could remember the words I used when I called Kevin at his school. Overhearing some of our late-night phone calls, he was well aware of Leah's predicament, but this news had to come as a shock. I vaguely recall answering his questions: When? Why? Is she sure? Hearing the tremble in his voice, I knew tears were rolling down his cheeks, just as they were mine.

Then came the next logical question. What do we do now? We decided to wait and see how Leah's meeting with the Millers went before we pursued any legal avenues or told anyone else. It only meant a day's delay, but I knew it would be torture for me. I had a new plan to set into motion, and planning, after all, was my forte.

Teaching that afternoon was bizarre. Thank goodness I had been teaching long enough to know *To Kill a Mockingbird* backwards and forwards. Once home, Kevin and I couldn't just sit and do nothing. He proceeded to do what we all do nowadays when we want instant, if not always accurate, information fast—he Googled "adoption" and poured through tons of literature on legalities, cost, open adoptions, and birth parent rights. That was when the problem of cost first entered our minds. We didn't have the $10,000 to $40,000 the websites were telling us we'd need. Nevertheless, the thought of a baby in our house, in our arms, convinced us to find a way.

My job that evening was to make phone calls. The first person I called was my friend Laura. She and her husband had just finalized their domestic adoption that very month, and the process had seemed to go smoothly. As I listened to her encouragement and enthusiasm, I felt my anxiety and worry melt away. By the end of the conversation, I had the number of their agency and had come to believe this adoption was actually possible.

My sister Lynnette, fourteen years my senior, was the next call I made. It was time for the voice of reason.

"Lynnette," I started. "I want to tell you something, and then I want you tell me all the potential problems I'm not thinking of. Tell me what I need to do."

"Okay . . ." she said hesitantly.

When I told her about Leah's proposition, she paused as if in deep thought and then advised me to make sure that this adoption didn't violate any kind of educational policy or code of conduct, either with my own school or even the Department of Public Instruction. See? I hadn't thought of that.

"Okay. You're right. I need to do that." I paused, concerned. "I'll make some calls tomorrow and try to find out."

"I just wonder if you'd have to change teaching positions."

"No, you're right," I agreed, feeling the bubble start to burst.

"Now can I tell you how I *really* feel?" she asked.

"Okay."

"Jen, this is so wonderful. I really hope and pray this works out. I am so happy for you."

Again, just what I needed to hear. My next call was to another of my three sisters, Laurie, my ultimate confidant and supporter. "This is your moment," she told me. "You could look back on this someday as the single moment that changed your life forever."

Finally, at about nine o'clock, Kevin and I went to bed, exhausted but exhilarated. Leah hadn't called yet, which didn't surprise me. I assumed the meeting with Millers would take a while. Checking my cell phone three times to make sure it was on, I placed it on the night stand next to me and fell asleep.

When I woke up at 5:30 a.m. and realized she had never called, I sprang up from the bed and shook Kevin.

"She never called! She never called!" I yelled.

"It's okay," Kevin answered, immediately alert. "You'll see her today. It was probably late when she got home."

I was not reassured. Not caring about the early hour, I called Leah's cell phone. No answer. An hour later, still no answer. When I arrived at school, I immediately looked for her, roaming up and down the halls. She was nowhere to be found. I was frantic. When the bell rang for first period, I went to the office and asked the secretary to check the attendance for Leah's first class. She had been marked absent. My heart sank. The meeting had not gone well. Why else would she not have called? Why else would she not be at school?

I fought the urge to cry or scream and slowly walked back to my classroom. The first thing I saw when I entered was Leah sitting in one of the desks, waiting for me. The second thing I noticed was a bundle of helium balloons hovering above my desk and a vase of white and blue carnations. One of the balloons read, "Congrats New Mom." My jaw dropped, and I swiveled around to face Leah.

"That's why I was late," she said, smiling.

She proceeded to tell me that the meeting with Millers had gone surprisingly well and that they were completely supportive of her decision. I could not have been more relieved, and so was Leah.

"It feels like a huge weight has been lifted off my shoulders," she said. "I made my decision, and it's done. It's done." I hugged her, thinking, *It's far from being done.*

Leah and the Millers had decided to keep the decision confidential, at least for a little while, and I agreed that was for the best. It was only the end of March, three more months of school to go, five months until the August 8 due date. We were dealing with a life-changing experience. None of us wanted the details to travel through the gossip mills, at least not until we were a little more prepared. I put the balloons in my book cabinet for the time being but left the flowers displayed on my desk.

I spent the rest of my free period making more phone calls, which my principal allowed me to make in his office. A lawyer friend of ours had given Kevin the name of a local attorney who handled adoptions, and I called her first. She was straight-forward and no-nonsense, and I left the conversation with complete confidence in her and an appointment to meet later that week. The next call was to the adoption agency. After a few preliminary questions, they said they would send out the first packet of information we'd need to start the adoption process. "Independent adoption," "home study," "termination of parental rights," "finalization hearing" were just some of the unfamiliar terms swimming around in my head, making me feel overwhelmed. Fortunately, both my lawyer, the adoption agency, and a representative at the Department of Public Instruction assured me that a teacher adopting a student's baby was both legally and ethically sound and, in fact, happened more often than one might think. The DPI rep even gave me the names and phone numbers of two other teachers who had gone through the same process with successful adoptions.

By the end of the hour, I had made all my phone calls. Feeling nervous yet elated, I returned to my classroom for more Atticus Finch and Boo Radley.

Nothing in Common

When I got home that night, I knew there was one more person I needed to call—Nick's mom. Eventually, we needed to have a conversation, but I'd always been a bit intimidated by Jackie Miller who, now in her late thirties, was somewhat of a local celebrity. She was arguably the most talented basketball player ever to come through the school and had gone on to play for the University of Notre Dame. I didn't know her well but would certainly recognize her from the display of her accomplishments in the trophy case I passed every day. I, on the other hand, cannot play any sport that involves speed, aim, strength, or a ball. What would I, standing at a proud five feet (if I rounded up), have in common with the nearly six foot athlete, despite an only seven year age difference? What would I say?

Planner that I am, I decided to make a list of topics that I wanted to discuss with her, but even that seemed too daunting a task. As I stared at the blank sheet of paper, the phone rang. Any idea of preparation vanished.

"Hi. Jen? This is Jackie Miller." I couldn't quite identify the emotion I was hearing in her voice.

"Hi," I answered. "I'm glad you called."

"Well, at first I wasn't going to. I kept going back and forth about it. Finally, I was just like, 'Roy, I'm calling.'" Her voice quavered, and I realized she was probably just as nervous as I was.

"So Leah said she talked to you," I prompted.

"Yes, that's why I wanted to call. I just wanted to . . . you know . . . see how you guys felt about her decision." She waited for a reply, but I was at a loss for words, so she continued her jumbled thoughts. "We really wanted Leah to go the adoption route, but . . . you know . . . the idea that our grandchild could be out there somewhere . . . and we wouldn't know him. This seems like a good solution. For you, too. You'll be great parents."

I breathed a sigh of relief. "It really means a lot to hear you say that." I hesitated before broaching the next sensitive subject. "You said, 'grandchild.' Do you want to be a part of his life, his grandparents?" I stopped before telling her that it was what *we* wanted; I didn't want to put her on the spot.

"We would really like that," she answered, and I could hear a slight quiver in her voice. "I know that people probably think we don't care about Leah or the baby because we don't talk about the pregnancy with anyone, even our closest friends, but that couldn't be farther from the truth. Over the past few weeks, Roy and I have done nothing but think about Nick and Leah and the baby, and what it all means for our family. To be totally honest, we love this baby; we already think of him as our grandson. We even debated whether we should raise the baby ourselves. So, yes, we *really* want to be a part of his life, if you're okay with that."

"Definitely," I replied, and I meant it. I knew that it was the healthiest and happiest solution for Colton. How could we go wrong allowing as many loving people into his life as possible? No baby could have too many grandparents, right? The thought made me smile. Then another concern came to me. "How does Nick feel about the adoption?" I asked.

"He is okay. He wants whatever is best for the baby." There was that mantra again. *Whatever is best for the baby.* "Are you sure you're okay with all of us being in the same town?" she asked. "I mean, everyone will know everything. People are always going to think of the baby as Nick's."

Ouch. That one kind of hurt, but I knew exactly how to answer. In my infinite planning, I had rehearsed all these tough questions and prepared responses: "Well," I said, "I guess people will just take their cues from us, and if we are all comfortable with it, then hopefully they will be too." This was actually much easier for me to say than to believe.

"Yeah, you're right," she agreed, but I sensed she was just as apprehensive as I was. "Are you worried Leah will change her mind?" she continued.

Another horrible thought that I tried not to think about. "I don't think she will. She seems sure. We'll just have to trust her," I said with feigned confidence.

"I guess so. It won't be easy."

"No, it won't," I agreed, but this time I had no more reassurances. Time to change the subject. "Are you sure Nick is okay with me being at school?

He has another whole year left after this one. Kevin and I have discussed this, and if it means I need to get a job at a different school, I would."

"I don't think that's necessary. He's a lot stronger than anyone thinks." She paused. "But we do worry about him. His whole life we've tried to keep him on the right path, to protect him from anything that could hurt him. He is such a good kid, but when he told us Leah was pregnant, we were completely devastated. Now I see that our disappointment and the way we handled the situation probably hurt him more than anything. He barely talks to us or to anyone."

Suddenly, I felt deep compassion for this woman who was virtually a stranger to me. She was clearly just as scared as I was. I began to understand why they'd reacted to the unexpected pregnancy the way they had, why they'd distanced themselves from Leah. They wanted what was best for the unborn baby, but they also wanted what was best for their own baby, their son, Nick.

"So, have you called an adoption agency?" Jackie's question interrupted my thoughts. "What happens now?"

"We're working on that. I'll let you know as soon as I find out more."

"Okay. Well, we'll talk soon."

"Thanks for calling, Jackie."

As I hung up the phone, I realized that I did have something in common with Jackie after all. Even though our perspectives were completely different, we were both struggling with the complexities and insecurities of having children. We were both mothers.

CHAPTER 8

Expecting

The next few months tried every last nerve I had. It was early April, Colton's due date was four months away, and there was so much to do. On one hand, we needed to get approved as adoptive parents. In Wisconsin, even if you are pursuing an Independent Adoption (where the birth mother chooses the adoptive parents without help from an agency), you still need to work through an agency, fill out endless questionnaires and applications, get physicals and background checks, participate in excruciatingly invasive interviews, complete the educational requirements, make sure your house is up to code and baby-proof, file the necessary paperwork with the court system, and be scrutinized down to every last detail, all while being completely tapped out financially. To make a long story short, with the help of an adoption loan and several very generous family members, we were able to cover the agency and attorney fees, and two months later, we were approved.

On the other hand, we were expecting a baby! This was supposed to be a time of thrilling anticipation. For the most part, it was, especially when we told our close friends and family. Kevin was a little wary at first; it reminded him of when we'd told people about our first pregnancy and then had to turn around and tell them we'd lost the baby. In fact, Kevin was admittedly reluctant to fully trust Leah's decision at all, to believe that we would truly be parents in just a few months. He was trying to be realistic to protect himself from future pain, and, for once, *I* was the one throwing all caution to the wind. I was already committed one hundred percent and when I told my parents, I did not let myself contemplate the idea that the adoption could fall through.

My mother's reaction was comfortingly and lovingly predictable. When we visited her and my step-father in mid-April, I brought a packet of Christmas pictures she hadn't yet seen. The final photo was a copy of Colton's most recent ultrasound that Leah had given me. Upon seeing it, my mom gasped and looked at me, her eyes filled with tears. Of course, she thought I was pregnant, but when I explained the situation, her response was no less positive than if I were. "Well, that's something our family hasn't done yet," I remember her saying as she cried and hugged me.

I knew it would be a little more difficult trying to explain everything to my dad, not because he would be critical, but because I was daddy's little girl. He would not want me to be set up for heartache. A couple days after visiting my mom, we went to my sister's house to celebrate my father's birthday. Kevin and I gave him and my step-mom a card that read, "Congratulations—you're going to have another grandchild!" On the bottom of the card, I had written, "We are adopting!" so there would be no awkward confusion. Dad didn't know quite what to say—he was never very good with words—but he immediately teared up, held my hand, and simply said, "That's great. That's really great."

Later in the day, he asked me, more privately, "Now you're going to do everything you need to do, right? This will be for good?" I knew he was worried about all the stories he'd heard where birth mothers change their mind ten years later, and children are snatched out of the only home they ever knew. He just didn't want me to get hurt.

"We're doing it the right way, Dad. It'll be legal." He patted my shoulder and took another bite of birthday cake.

In fact, all of our friends and family were absolutely and unconditionally supportive. By now, the word had spread around the school and community too. I thought I would be bombarded with questions from nosy colleagues or that my students, who could be completely naïve, crass teenagers, would blurt out comments during class. I figured I'd face a barrage of, if not audacious comments, at least judgmental stares around town. But surprisingly, people were quietly respectful and seemed to understand that it was an extremely personal matter. Certainly, a few colleagues asked discreetly if what they'd heard was true, but I never encountered negative reactions. Students seemed to acknowledge the significance and acted with uncommon maturity. Even being in school with Nick was not as awkward as I'd imagined it would be. Whenever he passed me in the hall, he politely greeted me just as he'd always done.

Adding to our optimistic outlook was the excitement of being expectant parents. Like any couple who was six months pregnant, we designed a nursery for little Colton. Of course, Kevin really wanted a sports theme. My sisters planned to throw a baby shower for me, so we registered at Target. Having no idea what we needed, we walked through the aisles, staring at bottles, formula, diapers, and strange-looking utensils, wondering how in the world people knew what they needed and what to do with it once they had it. Fortunately, a pregnant woman was shopping in the same aisle for her second little one who was clearly coming soon. She became our personal tour guide, even though she didn't know it. We silently stalked her through the aisles, scanning with our registration gun the same items that she put in her cart next to her toddler.

Yes, everything seemed to be going flawlessly except with the one person who had complete control over everything, who held our future happiness in her hands, or quite literally in her emerging belly.

Out of My Hands

I can't say that Leah ever threatened to, or even hinted at, changing her mind. In fact, she repeatedly assured me that she had no doubts about what she was doing. For a while, she seemed just as excited as I was. She was relieved with having made a decision and felt validated by the positive reaction of her friends and family. Continuing to call me at all hours, she confessed how much she missed Nick. We also discussed Jackie, who was now checking in with her regularly, offering support. Leah was understandably leery of this sudden change, but I believed that Jackie had genuinely good intentions. I had made a concerted effort to keep in touch with the Millers and to reach out to Leah's family as well. Through a morning prayer group, I met Laura's mom Sue, an elementary special education teacher, and witnessed the pain she felt over her estranged relationship with Leah. In late April, Leah invited my mom and me to a Mother's Day banquet at her church where we also met her father and her grandmother.

I even took Leah to her doctor appointments. I knew how lucky I was. How many adoptive mothers get to hear their baby's heartbeat in utero, the stethoscope pressed to their ears, their hands trembling? Leah's closest friends at school even threw a combination baby shower for me/18th birthday party for Leah. All rare opportunities in the world of adoption and ones for which I will be eternally grateful.

As the weeks passed, however, the pressures of school, the more frequent doctor appointments, and the never-ending calls from the adoption agency began to wear Leah's patience thin. She also hated the heartburn, swollen ankles, loss of her thin figure, and ugly maternity clothes that came along with being pregnant. Not to mention missing out on the fun of her senior year. She was scared about the delivery and had no health insurance. College application forms were due along with financial aid requests, all of which she had to fill out on her own. On top of all that, she was worried about her two little brothers in the midst of her parents' divorce.

Knowing Leah's difficulties made it that much harder to ask her to fill out yet another adoption form or to call her to see how she was feeling, if the baby was moving, had she called the adoption agency, etcetera. Eventually she stopped asking me to go to appointments with her. Her late night phone calls ended; in fact, there were no more calls at all. I would try to check in with her every few days, but *I* was always the one making the effort.

Like Jennifer Garner's character in the movie *Juno*, I had good intentions. I was completely enraptured by that baby already, but I was probably very annoying to a seventeen year old at her wit's end. I tried to be upbeat, set my fears aside, and force myself to trust her, but it was difficult. To watch her stomach grow bigger and bigger and yet not know if she was eating healthy or if she was taking her vitamins was torture for me. I wondered if she was getting enough sleep, going to her appointments, changing her mind. Once again, I had to accept that I did not have control over Leah or even the fate of our baby.

At the end of May, Leah graduated high school, and with the summer came even more frustration. I went from seeing my baby's birth mother every day to not seeing her at all. I continued to call Leah every few days just to check in; she usually claimed to be hanging out with friends and kept the conversation short. I knew I had to let her have space, or I risked completely alienating her. So for the next two months, the excitement I should have been feeling in anticipation of Colton's birth was tempered by the constant reminder that Leah was becoming more and more distant and that I was less and less in control.

First Miracle

On July 26, at 5:30 p.m., two weeks before Colton's due date, I received a call from Jackie Miller.

"Jen? It's Jackie. Leah's in the hospital. They are going to induce. She said to tell you to come."

Apparently, Leah had conceded to let Jackie accompany her to that day's check-up. Ignoring the faint twang of jealousy, I listened to Jackie's words replay in my mind. *They are going to induce.*

"We'll be right there!" I shouted and relayed the information to Kevin. His eyes grew wide with anticipation. For the next ten minutes, we frantically tried to figure out what to take. (With two weeks until the due date, we hadn't yet packed a hospital bag). We probably looked like those cartoon characters whose legs spin in circles, yet they don't really go anywhere. At one point, I stopped dead in my tracks, looked at Kevin, and said in a stunned voice, "This is it!"

"I know!" he answered. We allowed ourselves a one-second hug and then resumed our panicky preparations.

On the way to the hospital, Kevin and I called our moms who both said they were dropping everything and would be at the hospital within the hour. The next calls were to the adoption agency and to our lawyer. Once at the hospital, we knew exactly where to go since we had toured the labor and delivery area the previous week. As we rode up in the elevator, I grabbed Kevin's hand.

"I'm freaking out," I said, apparently not very eloquent in times of chaos.

"Me too. Me too," he answered, and I knew he was equally petrified.

As the elevator doors opened, we spotted the same nurse who had given us the tour.

"Hey, guys," she said, smiling. "Are you excited?"

All we could muster were dumbfounded nods and looks of sheer panic.

"Come on. I'll take you to the waiting room." She led us down a short corridor. "That's Leah's room," she said, pointing at a closed wooden door. I stared at it. What was happening behind that door?

"How is she?" I asked as we continued to walk.

"She's doing great. We gave her an epidural for pain. Once the doctor sees her, he'll decide if he needs to give her Pitocin to induce the labor." Not for the first time, I counted my blessings that I wasn't in Leah's place. Unlike many adoptive mothers, it did not bother me that I was not the one going through the actual labor.

Right next to Leah's room was a small waiting room where two teenage boys sat watching *The Simpsons* on the small TV.

"Just wait in here," the nurse said. "We'll keep you posted."

"Hey, Joe," Kevin said to one of the boys as we settled onto the couch. I assumed it was one of his students. "What are you doing here?"

"Hey, Coach," the boy answered, glancing up from the screen. "Our mom's having a baby."

"Oh," Kevin muttered. He looked like he wasn't sure how to respond and was relieved when the boy turned his attention back to Homer.

So far, I had seen no sign of Jackie Miller, and I doubted she was in the room with Leah. Was *anyone* in the room with Leah? My question was answered when Leah's door opened, and her mom walked out.

"Sue!" I yelled to get her attention. I was pleased to see that she was here for Leah and that Leah was allowing her to be.

"Oh, good. You guys are here. I was just going to call you." We hugged.

"How's Leah?" Kevin asked.

"She's two centimeters, and her contractions are about twenty minutes apart." That was probably more information than Kevin really wanted. "I think she's pretty scared, but she's trying to be strong. Ali is with her too." Ali was Leah's best girlfriend. "I'll keep you updated, okay?"

"Okay. We'll be here." We all laughed at the obvious, and Sue returned to Leah's room.

Kevin and I spent the next sixteen hours in that waiting room. Sue was true to her word; she and Ali came out to provide updates at least once an hour. Leah's labor seemed to be at a standstill, but it sounded like they weren't going to induce until the doctor started his shift in the morning. Kevin and I called family and friends and touched base with the Millers who were waiting at home for further news. We passed the time watching TV, playing cards with our moms, and eating McDonalds. I slept for three hours.

At seven o'clock in the morning, the doctor arrived and prescribed Petocin. Finally, at about eleven o'clock, Leah began active labor with Sue, Ali, and her cousin by her side. The rest of us—Leah's father, Jackie Miller, our mothers, Kevin, and I—waited in the hall right outside her door. On July 27, at 11:18 a.m., we heard the sound of Colton Robert's first cry muffled through the doorway, and I collapsed into Kevin's arms.

I have to hand it to Leah; she was a good sport at that point. If it were me, I don't think I would have been too keen on the idea of throngs of people piling into my hospital room after eighteen hours of labor. Nevertheless, she said it was fine for everyone to come in, and that was when I was allowed to put on Colton's very first diaper and t-shirt while Leah watched from her hospital bed. Kevin and I held our son for the first time, surrounded by four of Colton's smiling, teary-eyed grandmothers.

After that, I lost all sense of time. We were escorted, with Colton, into a room next to Leah's where we were told we could spend the night until Colton was released the following day. Everything was a blur. I remember feeding Colton for the first time and Kevin's mom showing me how to burp him. The Millers came to visit, including Nick, who seemed to stare at Colton, somewhat amazed. A few of Leah's friends and some of her family stopped in to say hello on their way to visit Leah. Our mothers headed home for some much-needed rest, and my sister Laurie came to spend the night with us in the hospital. There were a lot of smiles and camera flashes, and before I knew it, it was ten o'clock at night.

Somewhere during that evening, we went in to see Leah. I was nervous, especially after the trials of the past few months. We had a gift for her, a bracelet with her and Colton's birthstones. Surprisingly, she was in really good spirits. A couple of her friends were in the room to lighten the mood, and although Leah looked tired, she was laughing and munching away on a pizza they'd ordered. She and Kevin always got along well just by jokingly picking on each other, so she thought it was hilarious that he had to leave the room because he was getting queasy over the IV needle in her hand. She talked a little about the labor and delivery, telling funny stories about the nurses or bodily functions she couldn't control. It was almost like the past few months had never happened, and we were as close and easy with each other as we had ever been.

After that, though, Leah had a rough night. Somehow she ended up completely alone. So it didn't surprise me when the nurses told me she wanted to see Colton and that she kept him in her room all night. When Sally, the adoption agent, came at nine o'clock the next morning to facilitate the birth plan, Colton was still in Leah's room, and Kevin and I were convinced she'd changed her mind.

When the Moment Comes

As the clock struck noon, we were still waiting for the nurse to bring our son to us. Both Leah and Colton had been officially discharged over an hour earlier, but Leah had requested "just five more minutes" with Colton. Six of us sat in a circle, trying to make the situation less unbearably tense. Each person in the room had a unique perspective. Sally tried to reassure us that it's healthy for the birth mother to spend time with the baby before the transfer. It provides time for the birth mother to hold her child, to say good-bye, to feel as if she's had some kind of closure. "This is a good thing," she kept reminding us, but to me it felt like torture.

For Leah's mother, the moment was bittersweet. Sue truly believed that Leah's decision was the right one for everyone involved, but watching her daughter in those final moments had to be heartbreaking. She darted back and forth, first checking on Leah and then returning to our room, teary-eyed, but assuring us that it shouldn't be much longer. Jackie seemed the most uncomfortable and even more worried than Kevin and I. Her thoughts were probably filled with anxiety and doubt. If Leah changed her mind, what would that mean for Nick? And would she really be included in her grandson's life, as we'd agreed to?

My sister Laurie sat next to me on the edge of the bed. The best part about having Laurie in the room was that she can strike up a conversation with anyone and make even the most apprehensive people feel at ease. Her funny anecdotes about her own hospital stays lightened the mood. Kevin sat on the other side of me, gripping my hand in his as if he thought that if he let go, he would lose me, too. As for me, I was tired of making small talk when my mind was racing, my heart pounding, my ears ringing. Once again, I had no control over the situation. All I wanted was my son.

Suddenly, Sue returned from Leah's room and reported that she was taking Leah home now.

"How is she?" I asked.

"She's okay. She's okay," she repeated, nodding her head. I couldn't tell if it was the actual truth or if she was just trying to convince herself of it. "They'll be bringing Colton in any minute." We hugged her good-bye, another mother who needed to take care of her child. Sally followed her out to check on Leah.

"I'm going to go, too." Jackie stood up, probably sensing that we wanted some privacy and thinking that she needed to get home to Nick. He would need his mom also. After we said our farewells, I faced Kevin and Laurie. Finally, the time had come.

"Let's get the car seat ready," I instructed Kevin as Laurie laid out the tiny going-home outfit we had picked out for Colton. We were all relieved that there was finally something to *do*.

Then I heard someone at the door. When I looked up, there stood a nurse with a wheelchair. A look of confusion crossed my face. All of the nurses were well aware of our situation, including this particular one, whom I'd named Nurse Ratchet for her less-than-friendly bedside manner.

"Um . . . I don't need a wheelchair," I said.

"All new mothers get a wheelchair," she said sternly, and at that moment I could have kissed her.

I was wheeled out of the hospital, Colton in my arms, Laurie and Kevin on either side of me, as we took our son home.

CHAPTER 9

Family Redefined

We were finally a family. It hadn't happened exactly the way I'd planned, but the result was the same. We'd gone through all of the disappointments, the hassles, the worries and now it was time for the pay off. You and me, and baby makes three. The perfect family. It would be smooth sailing now, right?

The first month was a blur. My sister Laurie stayed with us our first night home to think of all the things we were too sleep-deprived to remember or just too inexperienced to know. She started a feeding chart of how much and how often Colton ate. We even kept track of his dirty diapers, "v" for void, "s" for stool. (Thinking back, I believe we kept that chart going for a good three months.) She gave us a quick lesson in how to give Colton a sponge bath and got up with me in the middle of the night when he cried. Careful not to overstep, she always asked if we wanted help, and mostly took care of the laundry, mopping, and dishes, while letting us take care of Colton.

One gift that she brought for me was a calendar to keep track of Colton's first year with stickers to mark important firsts. I used it to also keep a record of Colton's visitors. For the first month of Colton's life, there were only *three days* in which we had no visitors. Friends and family came by to see our bundle of joy, bearing numerous tiny blue outfits, rattles, diapers, and stuffed animals. Of course, another much-needed lasagna accompanied the gifts from Amy and Laura, and my friend Jenny very generously donated three bins of clothes that her three children had outgrown.

Aside from our own loved ones, many of our guests were the friends and family of Leah and Nick. There I was, getting about four hours of sleep a night, still learning the ropes of parenting, yet trying to keep my house tidy and a happy face on for company. I felt bombarded by well-wishers, many of whom I was meeting for the first time. At this point, I began to have my first concerns about open adoption. Was this what our life would be like? Would we ever have a peaceful moment? Would it always feel like so many people were watching? I had to keep reminding myself that I had known exactly what I'd signed up for and had advocated all along. It was time I rethought my definition of family. For me, baby did not make three. Baby made about three hundred. Ours may not have been a typical family, but it was as close to perfect as I was going to get. For Colton's sake, I opened up our home and our lives.

*

My definition of family was tested once again on August 16, the date of the Termination of Parental Rights hearing. Anyone who has adopted knows the significance of that day. For some reason, our TPR was handled differently than others I've heard of. In most instances, the adoptive parents do not attend the hearing. They wait for a phone call from the adoption agency or their lawyer informing them that the parental rights were terminated. In our case, maybe because it was an independent adoption, our attorney told us we would be required to attend the hearing, and, in fact, one of us would have to testify. Our hearing date had been set earlier in the summer, and I had been eagerly awaiting and anxiously dreading the day ever since.

My mother was scheduled to baby-sit Colton, and Leah made plans to meet us at our house and follow us to the courthouse. This seemed perfectly normal to us because Leah was our *family*, but I realize now that it is probably a unique situation for the adoptive parents and the birth mother to go to the TPR hearing together. Leah's parents were not coming with her. In fact, she'd probably told them not to. Nick also would not be there; he'd signed a form a few days earlier, terminating his rights.

When we entered the courtroom, our attorney showed us to our table and pointed Leah to a table across the aisle where Sally from the adoption agency was waiting. We had to sit at separate tables? I felt like we were the big bad prosecutors and Leah was the forlorn, innocent defendant awaiting her doomed sentence. She looked scared to death. I tried to catch her eye and give an encouraging smile.

The hearing itself was very formal. We had decided ahead of time that I would be the one to testify, mostly because I would feel more in control of a completely helpless situation. As I walked to the stand, it seemed to slide farther and farther into the distance, and by the time I reached it, my heart was pounding in my ears.

After asking me to recite my address, birth date, and name of spouse, our attorney began to ask about the adoption circumstances, questions such as:

"When was Colton born? Where has he resided since his birth? Do you wish to adopt Colton?"

And that was that. She had reassured me there wouldn't be any questions to which I didn't know the answers. Pretty easy. I breathed a sigh of relief and returned to my table, smiling at Leah as I sat down.

This wasn't so difficult after all, I thought as Leah was called to the stand. I don't exactly remember all of the questions the judge asked her, but it went something like this:

"What is your name? How do you know Colton? Who is the father on record? Is there any possibility that Nick Miller is not the paternal parent? Do you wish to place Colton up for adoption? Do you realize that all of your parental rights will be terminated? Have you been threatened or bribed in any way? Are you under the influence of alcohol or any other mind-altering drug? Do you understand that your rights will be terminated? Fully terminated? Do you understand? Are you sure? Are you *sure*?"

How Leah ever got through those five minutes, I will never know. Although she spoke quietly, she never cried. She never faltered. When she glanced at me, I nodded with encouragement and support. I just wanted to run up there and save her. It wasn't that I was afraid she would break down and change her mind; in fact, I never believed that would happen. I just wanted them to stop harassing her. To thank her instead of question her. After all, this was a gift she was giving, not a crime she was committing.

When court was adjourned, the gravity of the situation lay heavy on our shoulders. Even though we had just jumped one of the biggest hurdles of the adoption process, I did not feel like celebrating at that moment. I wanted to make sure that Leah was okay, but I could sense that she wanted to be alone for a while. We hugged her goodbye and watched her walk through the bare corridors of the courthouse and out the door. Only then did Kevin and I allow ourselves the indulgence of a hug to celebrate our new status as legal parents.

*

As with any new baby, the novelty of late-night bottles and dirty diapers wears off, the visitors become fewer and fewer, and the new family is finally able to settle into a quiet, comfortable routine. We began to say to ourselves, "I don't even remember what life was like before Colton. What did we even *do*?"

When the new school year began, I temporarily went back to work while Kevin took eight weeks of paternity leave first. Leah started school at a university about half an hour away, and I made sure that we kept in close communication. I was glad that she was making a fresh start somewhere, hoping she would meet new people. She visited Colton about every two weeks, usually with a friend, and she seemed most happy about losing all of her pregnancy weight.

We also grew much closer to the Millers. They had invited their family and friends to their house for a cookout in August so everyone could meet Colton. It was the first time I realized that open adoption is a two-way process. Yes, we adopted a baby from their family, had welcomed Colton with open arms. But they, in return, welcomed us into their family also. It never felt awkward. It never felt like I was being scrutinized or judged. Like I had told Jackie all those months before, everyone followed our lead. If we were comfortable, so were they.

Colton's baptism was in October, and with all my family, Kevin's family, Leah's family, and Nick's family, we packed the church. It was the first time that I truly got a sense of Colton's extensive family. Having six sets of grandparents, aunts, uncles, cousins all in one place, for the love of one child, Colton was very blessed indeed.

*

In mid-October, Kevin went back to school, and I began my twelve weeks of maternity leave. Oh, those were the days! I read books to Colton, hung on his every coo and giggle, saw him roll over for the first time, fed him his first rice cereal. We played; we snuggled. Sometimes neither Colton nor I would get out of our pajamas all day, and my obsessive wardrobe planning was now replaced with the need to get Colton on a strict eating and napping schedule. To begin, I used the computer to plot each feeding and nap, hoping to see a pattern emerge. None did. This chaotic routine worried me. Shouldn't he be eating and napping at regular times? That's what all the books said. So for almost a month, I plotted the line graphs and tried to get Colton to play by my rules. It should have been my first clue that Colton likes to make his own rules. Regardless of the lack of routine, that time together was priceless. Even though he wasn't on a strict schedule, I settled comfortably into the role of mother, and life seemed to be going just as planned.

Colton and I went to visit Leah at school a couple of times which she seemed to appreciate. Time with Leah was like time with any typical eighteen year old co-ed. She was a fun-loving, social girl and was starting to warm up to the possibility of new love interests. There were pictures of Colton hanging in her dorm room, and she was very open about the adoption with her new friends. She seemed perfectly comfortable with him, except maybe when he cried. It was like visiting a younger sister and bringing along her nephew.

Kevin and I also continued to develop our relationship with the Millers, no longer just for the sake of Colton. We liked them; they were easy-going and fun to hang out with. Not to mention they adored Colton. Kevin tagged along with them to several high school football games that fall, and Jackie and I (who shared a passion for reading) swapped books often. While we were home on leave, Jackie would stop by to see Colton almost every Wednesday after work. Sometimes Roy would join her, sometimes even Nick or his younger brother Evan.

We were glad to see Nick become more comfortable around Colton. In the early weeks, every one had watched his interaction with Colton closely, trying to examine the hidden meaning behind each of Nick's actions and facial expressions. I sometimes felt sorry for him; it must have felt like every move he made was being judged. In retrospect, he had behaved like a typical teenage boy around a newborn baby, holding Colton a few times, but a little awkwardly, as if he was afraid he might break. Now, as the months passed, Nick was less reluctant to hold Colton or even play with him. I never had the feeling that Nick thought of himself as Colton's *father*, but there was clearly a familial connection, a sense of wonder. As for us, the Millers no longer felt like company. Plus Jackie, like all of Colton's grandmas, didn't mind receiving about ten pictures of Colton a day via email.

On November 14, my long-term sub called to ask some questions about school. She'd been having problems with some of my students and needed help with the lesson planning. I was happy to talk about work (I rarely spoke to any adults anymore), but school seemed so far removed from my life now that I couldn't really focus. In truth, I didn't really care. Classes, grades, and lesson plans all seemed so remote and insignificant at that point. My life now consisted of preparing bottles, changing diapers, and watching the Food Network.

As soon as I hung up the phone, it rang.

"Hello?" I answered, figuring it was the sub again.

"Jennie? It's Lynnette." *My sister?* I wondered. *At 8:30? On a weeknight?*

"Hey," I answered.

"Jennie? Are you sitting down?" I could hear the gravity in her voice.

"Sitting down? Why? What's wrong?"

"Jennie . . . ." she started. Why did she keep repeating my name? And why "Jennie," my childhood name?

"Jennie, June just called. Dad was out hunting, and he didn't come home. They went to look for him in the woods . . . . Jennie, he's gone. Dad's gone." Lynnette's voice quavered, but her strength carried her words.

"What do you mean?"

"Jennie, he's *gone*."

"What? What? What? What?" I just kept repeated that word over and over, confused, feeling the blood drain from my face. I could hear what she was saying, but I didn't *want* to hear it. Not my *dad*. I knew what she meant by "gone."

"Jennie," Lynnette interrupted my incantation. "Listen. Is Kevin there? Put Kevin on the phone."

I handed the phone to Kevin, who could tell something was wrong. As he talked to Lynnette, I put my head between my knees, afraid I might pass out. I couldn't hear Kevin; my shock muffled all sounds. Although my eyes burned, tears did not come.

Kevin handed the phone back to me.

"Jennie," Lynnette continued. "I'm on my way to Dad's right now. So are Laurie and Toby, and Jodie is flying home. You should come."

"Okay," I answered in a weak, almost inaudible voice.

When I hung up the phone, Kevin held me in his strong embrace, and for a minute I thought I might not ever move. He didn't say anything, thank goodness. What can one possibly say to make it better? Then, as we separated, he asked if he should get Colton ready so they could come with me or if they should stay home and wait for further news. I couldn't figure out what he was asking. I really couldn't comprehend words at that point, but I knew I had to leave right then. I couldn't wait, and I wasn't even sure what to expect when I got to my Dad's. I wasn't even sure what had happened yet.

"You stay. Here. With Colton," I decided in a flat tone.

"I can come as soon as I figure out what to do with Colton. Are you sure you're okay to drive?"

"It's only forty-five minutes," I stated as if that actually answered the question. I grabbed my purse and keys and headed out the door. Still no tears.

While I drove, images of my father flashed through my mind: his smirk when he knew he'd skunked me in a cribbage game, his rough hands over mine as he taught me to cast the fishing line, his silly nicknames for all of his kids. (Mine was, lovingly, Runt.) Could it even be possible that I wouldn't see him again? The word family didn't seem to hold any meaning at all without my father. I imagined the devastated faces that awaited me at his house: my sisters and brother, his second wife June, and my own mother who had been married to him for thirty-three years. The road before me blurred as tears finally welled in my eyes. What was I *thinking*? I needed Kevin *with me*, but I wanted Colton to be secure, away from all the pain and heartache. I had no idea what to expect when I arrived at my dad's house or how long I would be there. Besides, I couldn't be a mother right now; I needed to be a sister, a daughter. So I called the one person who could help, who would watch Colton any time of day or night for as long as we needed. Someone who had also lost her own father so I would not need to explain. I called Jackie Miller.

The next few days, I moved in foggy slow motion. Anyone who has lost a parent knows what I mean. Tears, funeral plans, family, tears, pictures, memories, more plans, and more tears. It doesn't seem real for a very long time. I relied on the support of many friends and family. The night of the funeral, Kevin and I arrived home, exhausted and emotionally drained. When we opened the door, burdened by our suitcases, Colton's overflowing diaper bag, and heavy hearts, the familiar smell of marinara sauce and mozzarella cheese greeted us. A pan of lasagna waited on the counter with a short note from Laura and Amy: "We let ourselves in. Hope you don't mind. Thinking of you."

"You have great friends," Kevin said, giving my hand a squeeze.

"I know," I said, smiling for the first time in days.

Another solid rock during this time was my sister Jodie who had flown in from Rhode Island and was staying at our house for a couple weeks. Kevin had to go back to work, but I was still on maternity leave. I would have gone crazy, home alone with Colton and my memories, had Jodie not been there, sharing my grief, getting through the day minute by minute, and even—in her infinite selflessness—making Colton's first Thanksgiving dinner.

*

Little did I know that losing my father would not be the only shock I received that year. Two weeks after my dad's funeral, I was staring at something I never thought I would see. It was so incomprehensible that I couldn't even wrap my mind around it. There had to be some mistake, yet there I was holding the plastic stick in my shaking hand, staring at two impossibly clear blue lines.

And the Other Shoe Drops

Yes, I was pregnant. *Pregnant*. But *how?* The same way everyone else gets pregnant, I guess. The thought had never really crossed my mind to go back on birth control after Colton was born, not after all those months of trying, and all the doctors telling me it was highly unlikely I'd get pregnant again without some kind of assistance. My cycles were irregular so I'd stopped paying any attention.

However, only a couple weeks after my father died, I started thinking it had been an awfully long time since my last period. In fact, flipping through the calendar, I calculated it had been almost sixty days. Still, I figured the reason was the emotional stress I was going through wreaking havoc on my hormones. Without even mentioning it to Kevin, I bought a pregnancy test. Figuring they were all the same, I went with the generic brand. Plus, this box had a bonus test in it. That afternoon, home alone, I took the test. My first reaction upon seeing two blue lines was that it was a false positive; I should have followed the directions and taken it first thing in the morning. So the next morning, I took the second test. Again, positive.

I felt slightly uneasy, but I convinced myself it was another false positive. I should have gone with the high-quality, expensive brand to begin with. After another trip to the drug store, I waited until the next morning to take the third test, still not saying a word to Kevin. Telling him would have made it too real. Now with three positive tests, there was no denying the fact any longer. I was going to have a baby. Again. And, again, it was not planned.

I waited a whole day before telling Kevin, partly because I wasn't sure how to tell him or what his reaction would be, but mostly because I was struggling with my own reaction. I *wanted* to feel overjoyed, but if I'm being painfully honest, I was too shocked and scared to be happy. I was struggling with grief over my father's death, and Colton was not even four months old yet. To anyone who has desperately wished to be pregnant and not been able to conceive, I know those reasons seem shallow. And those were my *good* reasons. The other thoughts that ran through my mind are almost too shameful to admit, but the fact of the matter is that I was worried about what everyone *else* would think.

First of all, what about Leah? How would I ever tell her? She and I had discussed the possibility of my having more children, but at the time it seemed completely implausible. Would this take away from the incomparable gift that she had given us? Would it lessen it somehow? Would she worry that we would love this baby more than Colton? And what about the Millers? What would they think? They were such an integral part of our lives, but how would they treat this baby, one that was not biologically related to them? What would our friends think? My colleagues? The community? Would they think we shouldn't have adopted in the first place, if we could conceive a child on our own? These questions, unfortunately, created such a dark cloud in my mind that I wasn't allowing myself to rejoice in this newest blessing.

Sadly, I didn't plan any creative way to tell Kevin, to surprise him, to celebrate. I walked into our bedroom that night, turned off the TV show he was watching, stood several feet away at the edge of the bed, and said, "I'm pregnant."

"Are you kidding?" he asked.

"No. I took three tests. I'm definitely pregnant."

Kevin stared at me, open-mouthed for a few seconds, then sprang out of the bed, pulled me into a huge bear hug, lifted me off the ground, twirled me around, and yelled, "Yes!"

Shocked by his enthusiasm, I was momentarily pulled out of my gloom. I couldn't help but smile as he set me back down on the floor, firing questions. "How long have you known? Why didn't you tell me? How far along are you? Do you think it will be a girl or a boy? What should we name it?"

"Wow," I said in an understated tone. "You're really happy."

"Of course. Aren't you?" he asked, and then I saw the light click on in his mind. "I know this isn't great timing, with your dad and all, but maybe that means it's the *best* time. Your dad's probably behind this whole thing." I know he meant this as reassurance, a silver lining in the black cloud of my father's death, but I wasn't buying it. At that moment, I would have rather had my father back.

I just shook my head and sighed, exasperated. As I hugged Kevin again, I mentally geared up for the long haul ahead, a trip that I did not want to take but one that was taking me along for the ride, whether I liked it or not.

*

We decided, okay *I* decided, that we shouldn't tell anyone yet, for a couple reasons. One, we had to tell Leah before she heard it from anyone else, and I wanted to tell her in person. Now that she was busy with school, we didn't see her as often, and our visits were frequently postponed and rescheduled. More significantly, I'd had my first ultrasound, and the doctors had found an abnormality with the shape of my uterus. They had told me there was no cause to worry, at least not yet, but it could potentially mean that the baby would have restricted room to grow. They would do another ultrasound at sixteen weeks, and I was determined to wait until we had more definite answers for people.

Christmas that year was bittersweet. We were kindly invited to both Leah's family Christmas and the Millers' Christmas, so Colton was surrounded by doting relatives who pinched his cheeks and told us how happy they were for us. I couldn't help but wonder what they would think if they knew that as we opened their gifts, shared their meals, and seemed the perfect family, we were actually keeping a significant secret from them.

It was even more difficult with my own family. We planned our Christmas party the same as every year, everyone putting on brave faces and cheery smiles, but never forgetting it was our first Christmas without Dad and only six weeks since we'd lost him. The worst moment came when it was time to open gifts, our gift-passer-outer painfully absent. How easy it would have been for me to provide some wonderful news amidst all the sadness, to announce that we were pregnant. But I just couldn't do it. I was anxious about the pregnancy and angry with God or fate or whoever had taken my babies' grandfather away. I tried to make Colton's first Christmas as happy as possible but selfishly kept my news to myself. Even New Year's Eve was surreal. We celebrated with our usual group, and I knew that my closest friends—Laura, Amy, Jenny, Erin—would be overjoyed at the news. Instead of telling them, I played cards, laughed at everyone's jokes, and pretended to sip champagne.

This secret remained between me and Kevin until February when I finally relented to his continual requests to share the news with our family. The latest ultrasound had turned up nothing unusual; in fact, the doctor could not even see the original abnormality that had showed up the first time, so I really had no good excuse for keeping the secret any longer. Besides, Kevin was bursting at the seams, and I felt guilty for the dark cloud I'd placed over this pregnancy.

We called our parents and our siblings and shared the good news. Of course, everyone was thrilled, and for a while at least, I allowed myself to get swept up into the happiness too and admonished myself for being such a drag.

By this time, I was back in school working eight hour days, grading papers at night while still trying to spend time with Colton, and struggling with the fatigue of being sixteen weeks pregnant. With my small stature, the weight gain was minimal, and thanks to heavy winter sweaters, I was able to hide my pregnancy at work. We still had not told anyone except our closest family, a decision I defended by reminding Kevin that we needed to tell Leah first, and in person. In truth, I didn't want to tell anyone. At that point, I had accepted the fact that I was *pregnant*, that my body was changing, that I was tired all the time, that this would change my life in ways I wasn't sure I wanted. However, I hadn't yet accepted that I was going to be a *mother* again. One of the biggest reasons I struggled with that idea was Colton. Not because he was adopted and would be "different" than the rest of our family, but because my love for him was so strong that I could not fathom loving another child as much as I loved him. Even at Colton's adoption finalization hearing, which took place that month, I was still concealing my baby bump under a sweater while Kevin and I took pictures with the judge, two very happy and proud parents of *one* child.

Finally, in March, Leah came to visit, and we tactfully told her the news. The smile on her face flickered for a moment, and her eyebrows furrowed in surprise as she tried to come to terms with that news. I could tell she wasn't sure how to react at first, but then she smiled and began to ask us all kinds of questions. Had we told the Millers yet? No. Was it a boy or girl? We didn't know yet. Did we have any names picked out? Not yet. She hoped it was a girl, she said, since we already had a boy. She was all smiles and cheer, but I could tell it would take her some time to get used to the idea. In fact, she called me the next day.

"Hey, it's Leah."

"What's up?"

"Well, um, I can't stop thinking about you being pregnant. I don't know . . . ." I was surprised at how forthright she was being.

"Are you mad?" It sounded so teenager-ish when I said it, but that's what I was truly wondering.

"No, I'm not *mad* . . . ."

"Do you remember when we talked about this at school that one time?" I thought maybe reminding her of her previous opinions might help. "You thought it would be nice for Colton to have a brother or sister."

"Yeah, but . . . what if you love this baby more than Colton?" I couldn't believe her candor. It wasn't that I was offended by the question; I was proud of her for having the courage to ask it. Strangely, it was the exact opposite of what I was worried about.

"Oh, Leah, that won't happen," I assured her. "Remember when you were pregnant and we were planning the adoption? I was sometimes worried about what you were thinking or how things might turn out, but I just trusted you because you seemed really sure. And it all worked out. Now, you'll just have to trust me when I tell you that this will too. Believe me, this does not take away from the gift you've given us. We will always be grateful, and we will always love Colton. No matter what."

"I guess I know that. I just have to keep telling myself."

"I'm glad you called. I could tell that you weren't quite sure what to say last night."

"Yeah, I do feel better though. Actually, I'm kind of glad you're pregnant. Giving birth sucks, and now you'll have to go through it too. It's only fair." We both laughed.

*

We confided in Millers almost immediately after telling Leah, and they had a different type of delayed reaction. When we first told them the news, they were sincerely happy for us. They asked lots of questions and seemed genuinely worried about the early ultrasound. I didn't voice my concerns about how they would feel about the baby, if they would treat him differently than Colton. After all, to Colton they were Grandma and Grandpa. How would that work with the new baby? I figured we'd cross that bridge when we came to it. A few weeks later, while we sat around an early spring campfire in their back yard, Jackie brought up the subject again.

"Hey, Jen. Roy and I were thinking. We figured since you guys adopted Colton, we'd like to 'adopt' this baby, you know, be his or her grandparents, just like we are to Colton." I looked at her through teary eyes and smiled. I should have known they would consider the baby one of their family.

"Wow," I said, "that'd be great." I could feel at least one of my many worries melt away.

As the weeks passed, Kevin and I gradually told more people, first our close friends, then colleagues, until eventually the word was out. There was no need to hide my increasingly growing belly anymore, but I still tried to, wearing really big sweatshirts and lots of layers, because—and I hate to admit this—I did not enjoy being pregnant. Some women say they love it; they've never felt better. Not me. And I didn't really have any excuses. I was never sick, and although my ankles were swollen, it wasn't unbearable. The back pain was only minimal. Yet I hated pregnancy all the same. My body seemed to have a mind of its own, and I just didn't feel like *myself*. At our first Lamaze class, we all had to share one thing we disliked about being pregnant and one thing we liked. I was not afraid to admit that there was *nothing* I liked about being pregnant, not to mention that I absolutely dreaded the thought of labor.

Having had enough of surprises, we found out the sex of the baby as soon as possible. We were having another boy, which was what we were hoping for. Picking out a name was one of the few highlights of the whole pregnancy. It was something we hadn't been able to do with Colton, so Kevin and I bantered back and forth, vetoing names we didn't like, writing down the few that we could both agree on, even ranking them. In the end, we decided on Kayden Paul. We just liked the name Kayden, spelling it that way after my sister Jodie's middle name of Kay. Paul was in honor of my dad; it had been his middle name.

As more people heard the news, I became increasingly aggravated by their inane responses. If I heard one more story about someone who "never thought she could get pregnant, tried for years, finally adopted, and then—boom—got pregnant," I would throw up. Or my favorite: "See, you just had to relax. As soon as you stopped stressing about it, it happened." Ugh. I resisted the urge to slap them and smiled as if their insight was truly remarkable. Actually, I'd never felt more stressed in my life. At least no one was ignorant enough to say something like, "Oh, that's wonderful. Now you'll be able to have one of your *own*," which is another common response adoptive parents hear in the same situation. The worst was when people commented on our infertility. "So did you think you couldn't get pregnant?" As if we had any less right to adopt just because we could conceive a child of our own. Didn't these people know how many families had both biological and adopted children, *on purpose*? I usually just smiled, said something like, "It was a surprise to us too," and found a way to cut the conversation short. No doubt about it, I was a crabby pregnant woman, as Kevin will attest. Being pregnant became my excuse to complain about everything: *It's too hot in the house; I can't lean over the tub so you'll have to give Colton his bath; I should get to watch what I want on TV. Have sex? Forget it.*

By the time June rolled around, I was sick and tired of being pregnant, and I was only seven months along. I hated not being able sleep on my back, even though I never slept on my back in the first place. I hated how not one pair of pants fit anymore, except one set of ratty pajama bottoms. Also, I could feel waves of pressure throughout my belly, which I assumed was Kayden changing positions, although I never really felt any kicks. The people at work said they were called Braxton Hicks contractions and that they could last the whole pregnancy. Great.

I came home on the last day of school, looking forward to my relaxing though probably very uncomfortable summer. At least I would get to see Colton all day every day, and there were no papers to grade. As I lounged on the couch watching *Ellen*, I could feel the waves of pressure again, and I put my hand on my belly to see if I could feel any movement. It occurred to me that maybe I should see how often these Braxton Hicks things were coming, since they seemed to be more frequent that day. Watching the clock, I calculated that every four to five minutes, I felt another wave of pressure that lasted anywhere from ten to thirty seconds. *Should this be something to worry about?* I wondered.

"Do you think I should call the doctor?" I asked Kevin, explaining about the pressure.

"I don't know," he said, looking worried.

"Well, I don't know either." God, he was no help.

We'd only had one Lamaze class so far, and all I'd really learned was how to give Kevin a massage. I decided it didn't hurt to call the hospital, even if I sounded like a moron.

When I explained my symptoms to the nurse, she didn't seem too concerned. She told me again about the Braxton Hicks.

"And you're feeling the baby move?" she asked.

"No," I said. "I told the doctor that the last time I was in."

"How long has it been since you've felt movement?"

"Well, I can't always tell if it's movement. I feel a lot of pressure."

"How about a good strong kick?"

"I never feel that. I haven't felt a kick for at least a month."

"Can you hold for a moment, please?"

"Sure." My worries intensified.

The nurse came back on the line. "Why don't you just go ahead and come in, and we'll check it out. Since it's after 5:00, you'll come in the Emergency Room entrance, and we'll have someone waiting to bring you up to our floor."

"Okay," I said and hung up. I stared at the phone for a second, and then panic sank in. "Kevin!" I yelled.

He came running into the kitchen.

"They want me to come in."

"Is it serious? Should I go with you or stay here with Colton?" he asked.

I'd made this mistake before. "Call someone to watch Colton. I want you to come with me. It shouldn't take long; I'm sure they'll just do an ultrasound."

We called some friends to watch Colton and headed to the hospital. I would not return home for ten days.

CHAPTER 10

Second Miracle

When I got to the hospital, they discovered I had high blood pressure and that I was going into early labor. Those Braxton Hicks had been actual contractions. They hooked me up to all kinds of wires and did another ultrasound. The baby seemed to be fine, but they needed to send me to another hospital about an hour away with a Neonatal Intensive Care Unit (NICU), just in case I went into active labor. I was whisked away in an ambulance. In the meantime, Kevin went home to pack some clothes, called the Millers (who immediately agreed to pick up Colton from our house and take care of him for as long as we need them to), and then drove at insanely high speeds to meet me at the hospital.

Riding in the ambulance was a hoot, even though I was scared out of my mind. It helped that the two EMT's were good-looking young guys, each with a crazy sense of humor. They tried to set my mind at ease. "Don't worry," one of them told me. "We'll get you there. We've never had to deliver a baby in here, and we don't plan to start now."

"That makes three of us," I agreed, with a weak giggle. I lay on the gurney and watched the minute hand on the clock above the ambulance doors. My contractions were two minutes apart.

The next two days were horrible. I received two steroid shots to help with Kayden's lung development, in case he was born premature, and was then put on some kind of IV drip to stop the labor. Whatever it was, it made me so hot my face looked like a tomato, and I had to remain lying on my side for forty-eight hours, which meant a catheter was necessary. My contractions were monitored and eventually slowed to about one every hour. At that point, none of the doctors seemed too concerned. They said early labor was not uncommon. After forty-eight hours, they would discontinue the IV, and if I didn't go into active labor, I'd be sent home. I might have to deal with these minor contractions until the end of my pregnancy. The ultra-sounds seemed normal, although one showed that Kayden was pretty small for his gestational age. No surprise when they looked at me. I wasn't really scared; mostly I was just bored and hot.

By the second night, anxiety replaced boredom. I had nothing to do but wait and worry. My mom arrived, and she and Kevin did their best to cheer me up, bringing me magazines and books and offering to play cards. Despite their best efforts, I was completely miserable. Physically, I wasn't in much pain except for the subtle contractions, the dull ache in my hip from lying on my side, and the intense heat I felt. Emotionally, I was at a low point. Part of me was hoping I'd just go into labor, get the whole thing over with. Then again, how early was too early for Kayden? His due date was August 1, almost two months away, putting me at thirty-two weeks. I was understandably scared and confused, but one emotion was stronger than the rest, and I couldn't quite put my finger on it. It was that emotion which left a lump of uneasiness in the pit of my stomach, that made the TV screen blur with my unshed tears. It wasn't until there was a quiet knock on the door that I finally understood what I was feeling.

Into my room, carried by his Grandpa Roy, came the one and only person who at that point could put a smile on my face—Colton Robert. Somehow the Millers had known exactly what would make me feel better. They'd called Kevin to see if they could bring Colton to visit, and, of course, Kevin had agreed. One look into Colton's innocent hazel eyes, and tears streamed down my face. I held out my arms, and Roy placed Colton into my embrace. At that moment, I realized the emotion I'd been feeling was loneliness; I had been homesick for my son. As I held Colton tightly in my arms, a sense of gratitude and relief washed over me. Thank God that even though I was completely helpless, at least I knew that Colton was with family, with people who loved him.

At nine o'clock the next morning, they unhooked the IV, and we all waited to see what would happen. I felt remarkably better without that drug coursing through my veins, my energy was renewed, and I could finally get up and walk around. Dr. M. examined me a couple hours later and determined, after another blood test, that I was not going into labor and could go home. He just wanted to do one last ultrasound.

That ultrasound was one of the worst moments of my life. Watching the silent technician as she stared at the screen and punched buttons was like déjà vu. I knew something was wrong. When she called in another technician, an older, more-experienced looking one, I began to panic, and I could see in Kevin's eyes that he felt the same way. The two technicians whispered to each other; the only words I caught were "blood flow." Finally, I couldn't stand it any longer.

"Is something wrong?" I asked.

"Oh, we're just checking on some of these (blah, blah, blah) and see this here is the (blah, blah, blah)." I was being fed a bunch of medical jargon to pacify me. It wasn't working.

Finally, the older technician said, "Okay, I'm going to share this information with Dr. M., and then he can discuss his thoughts with you." He patted my knee, as if to reassure me, and whisked out of the room.

We found our way back to our room where my mom was packing up my belongings, assuming I was heading home.

"We have to wait and talk to the doctor one more time," I informed her. "I think maybe something was wrong on the ultrasound."

"Well, let's not jump to conclusions," she said. "We'll wait to see what the doctor has to say."

As if on cue, Dr. M. knocked on the door and came in. I really liked Dr. M., even though I'd only known him for a few days. He was very friendly and kind, yet spoke in a no-nonsense kind of way. You could tell he had a lot of medical expertise, but he also knew how to take care of the patients, including their anxieties.

"Okay," he said, pulling up a chair next to my bed. "Change of plans." I looked at Kevin and back at the doctor. "Your placenta has decided to make a complete turn-around in the last twenty-four hours. We've never seen such a quick change. You see, the blood," and he began to demonstrate with hand gestures, "should pump into the placenta and back out again, but there seems to be some kind of blockage, and your blood is not getting through to the baby."

"That sounds bad," I said, my eyes wide.

"It's not good. We need to act fast. Think of it this way. Your baby is sliding down a hill, and we need to reach down and pluck him off before he reaches the bottom." No kidding, that's what he said, yet coming from him, it sounded perfectly reasonable.

"Get him off the hill!" I pleaded.

"Right. We need to get the baby out. You'll need to decide if you want vaginal birth or C-section. Vaginal birth would be less risky for you with an easier recovery, but it could be traumatic for the baby. With a C-section, there is always risk for infection, and the recovery for you is much longer, but it will be less traumatic for the baby. You can have a couple minutes to talk it over with Kevin."

"No, I already know," I said, knowing Kevin would agree with my immediate decision. "Do whatever's best for the baby." As soon as the words were out of my mouth, I could hear them echo in my ears, in Nick's voice. *Whatever's best for the baby.* Now I understood.

"Okay," Dr. M. said, and I could tell he agreed with my decision. "I'll be doing the surgery, and they'll be coming in shortly to prep you."

"How long will she be in the hospital?" Kevin asked. He was already anticipating the child care plans for Colton.

"Four to seven days, depending on recovery," Dr. M. answered.

"Does this have anything to do with the shape of my uterus?" I asked, seemingly out of the blue.

Dr. M. laughed. "No. By the way, have you picked out a name?"

"Yep, Kayden Paul," I said.

"Oh, no, not Paul. Don't you know what Paul means?"

"No, what?"

"Well, I know because Paul's my name. It means runt. You don't want Kayden to be a runt!" he said, laughing as he left the room.

"Oh, yes, I do," I answered under my breath, smiling up toward heaven.

*

On June 9, 2008, Kayden Paul was born at 11:10 a.m., almost the exact time of day as his brother. He weighed three pounds, two ounces.

After the C-section, they wheeled me, bed and all, into the NICU to see Kayden for the first time. I was not prepared for what I saw. Kayden was in an incubator with a respiration tube, colored wires connecting him to monitors. I had never seen a baby so small. When Kevin put his arm in the incubator, his hand was the entire length of Kayden's body, crown to rump. I looked at Kayden's tiny face. His eyelids were almost translucent, and as I touched his tiny hand with my finger, I was overcome with guilt. This was my fault. Even though I had loved Kayden from the moment I knew he existed, I had not always embraced that love. Resentful of the pregnancy, I had not allowed others to love him from the beginning, keeping his very existence a secret. I had not asked enough questions about the ultrasounds, the lack of movement, the early labor. I had not let myself bond with him, be his mother. This was my fault. Tears again welled in my eyes.

Please God, I prayed silently. *Please give strength to my son.* I was overcome with love for this child, my child. All my worries about not loving him as much as Colton seemed utterly ridiculous. Like every other parent with more than one child, I could love them both—equally and unconditionally—because I was their *mother.*

*

While I was recovering in the hospital, Kevin spent half his time there and half his time at home, getting our house ready for another baby and checking in with Colton. (My sisters were now baby-sitting at our house.) It was a difficult time for me. First and foremost, I was worried about Kayden. His prognosis was actually very good, but to see him so small and helpless was unbearable. Second, the pain from the C-section prevented me from even holding Kayden comfortably, let alone walking upright. Finally, I missed Colton terribly and was afraid I'd be in this hospital bed when he took his first steps. My melancholy was eased, though, by visits from friends and family members, including Amy and Laura, who burst into my hospital room one day with baskets of preemie clothes.

"What? No lasagna?" I kidded them, and we all laughed.

Whereas I was discharged after ten days, Kayden was in the NICU for thirty-three days, during which time he grew to over five pounds, learned to breathe and eat on his own, and developed into a healthy "newborn" baby. Kevin and I came to visit him every day, our friends and family helping to baby-sit Colton and donate gas money.

Had it not been summer, with good roads, both of us off of work, plenty of time to recover and get the house ready for Kayden, I'm not sure how we would have managed. I could not have planned the timing better myself.

Speaking of timing, once Kayden was born and the doctors ran more blood tests, they determined his due date was actually later than we'd thought. The new due date was August 8, the exact same due date of his older brother.

As for guilt, I struggled with it. My head told me that Kayden's premature birth couldn't have been my fault. I took vitamins, went to my doctor appointments, did all the pre-natal care I was supposed to do. Yet my heart still ached when I thought about all the time I had lost with Kayden, even before he was born. When I looked into his big brown eyes, eyes just like mine, I realized that I had taken for granted the most precious gift that anyone can be given—a child. It reminded me of what we had told Leah and Nick when we adopted Colton. We had said that the only way we could ever thank them for their gift was to show that same kind of unconditional love and generosity to Colton. It was the same with Kayden. All I could do to make up for our lost time was make the most of every priceless moment we now had together and to never take my family for granted again.

A Snapshot of Open Adoption

"So how's the weather down there?" I asked Leah, my cell phone cutting in and out as Kevin and I drove down the leaf-covered back roads to the Millers' house.

"About eighty degrees today. I went to the beach earlier," she said light-heartedly. After her finals in May, Leah had tagged along with a friend who was visiting relatives in a distant southern state. Her friend returned home in August; Leah, on the other hand, decided to take a break from school (and the overwhelming tuition fees), got a job at a restaurant, and settled into her new community as if she'd lived there her whole life. New friends, so much to do, a real fresh start.

"Oh, the pictures of Colton came in the mail today," she added. "I like the ones with him and my dad when he came to visit you. And the one of Colton in his little pool is too cute!" As always, it was easy to talk to Leah about Colton. During her weekly phone calls, I filled her in on his latest developments, how he was fearless when it came to climbing, how he was obsessed with sports already, saying "ball" every time he saw anything round. I was sure that Leah missed him, but the majority of our conversations were about her new apartment or her plans for the weekend.

"How's Kayden?" Leah asked, dutifully.

"Really good. We have to keep Colton at a safe distance though. He likes to throw toys at Kayden." We both laughed, and Kevin chuckled behind the steering wheel.

"Well, I better go. Corey's picking me up for work in a few minutes." Corey was Leah's new boyfriend, her first real boyfriend since Nick. There had been other guys, but it always seemed like she was trying to force herself to move on. She'd met Corey at work a few months earlier, and they had become fast friends. The friendship had blossomed into the kind of relationship I'd always wished Leah could find. She rarely mentioned Nick anymore. The wounds between them had healed, and during the course of many phone calls, they had re-established a healthy friendship. I was glad for that too, for Colton's sake.

"Okay, I'll talk to you next week," I said and clicked off my phone just as we pulled into the Millers' driveway.

Finding a parking spot on game nights was tricky. The driveway was lined with cars and SUVs, parents of the other football players, all there for the traditional tailgate party at the Millers' house before Nick's home games. Kevin pulled Colton from his car seat, swinging our double-sized diaper bag over his shoulder. On the other side of the backseat, I unbuckled Kayden and grabbed the two bags of Doritos I'd brought. That was about as fancy as I could manage nowadays when it came to a dish to pass.

As we entered the backyard, I heard Colton say, "Ball!" pointing to Nick and his brother Evan who were tossing a football back and forth. As soon as Kevin lowered Colton to the ground, he toddled over to the big boys.

"Hey, buddy," Nick said, handing him the ball. I paused for a moment, watching Nick interact with Colton. It always fascinated and amazed me. For a seventeen year old, Nick was handling the situation so maturely and even, I could say, lovingly. He played with Colton the same as he played with his little cousins, and Colton would point to pictures of Nick and say his name, just as he did our other family members. Questions would come someday, and we would figure out a way to explain just how Nick and Leah fit into our family. But they definitely *were* family.

I turned my attention to Roy, who stood by the grill, flipping burgers.

"Hi, Roy," I said as Kayden began to fuss in my arms. I looked around for Kevin, but he had temporarily disappeared.

"I think he wants Grandpa," Roy said, closing the grill and taking Kayden from me. "I swear you get bigger every day!" he said, holding Kayden in the air.

"I'll go give these to Jackie," I told him, motioning to the chips and walking through the sliding door into the house.

The kitchen was full of people clad in the blue and white school colors, discussing the various plays they expected to see that night.

"Hey, Jen," Jackie said, taking the chips from me. "Where are the boys?"

"Outside, hanging out with Roy, Nick, and Evan. Hey, I brought those books you wanted to borrow. They're in the diaper bag."

About an hour later, the party ended abruptly as everyone headed to the game. Kevin and I had decided to take the boys until half time, as usual. It was still warm enough for Kayden, and Colton loved to watch the uniformed teenagers tackle each other on the field, at least for a few minutes before insisting I chase him around under the bleachers.

As we stood on the sidelines next the Millers, my thoughts were not on the game. In fact, I couldn't even see the game, blocked by the tall spectators in front of me. Instead, I glanced at Kevin who was discussing the last play with Roy, and prayed yet another silent thank you for my husband, who had been my source of strength and love every step of this journey. Wrapped in a blanket, tight in his Snuggli, curled into Kevin's chest, was my smallest miracle, my little Kayden Paul. Next to them was my other miracle child, Colton, sitting high on Jackie's shoulders, pointing to the scoreboard lights. And behind us was the whole town, cheering on their team, our adoption old news by now.

My family may not have happened the way I'd planned, but what I came to realize is that we don't always get to *control* the obstacles—and miracles—that life has in store for us. It was only when I lost control that I gained everything.

PART III

Amy

"And Hope enchanted, smiled, and waved her golden hair."

~William Collins

I was that friend, the one cuddling the cooing infant, entertaining the busy toddler, and shushing the chatty preschooler in a crowded church pew barely acknowledging how very blessed I really was.

When Amy and her husband Richard first joined my church, I would find them in the section to my left and wonder if they could hear my children. Amy would never admit it if she had; she's far too polite, much too kind. At my firstborn's baby shower, hosted by Laura, I still recall the hope and dream Amy shared for my baby-to-be: generosity. She printed it cheerfully on a tiny pastel blue slip of paper, the word underlined and punctuated by two exclamation marks. Generosity. This word describes my friend Amy precisely. Gracefully and generously, she embraced each of our children as they arrived, showering them with gifts and affection while she endured her own pain quietly. Amy, through the process of adoption, would finally find out how generosity would return to her.

For a full year, I never put much thought into how Amy felt at Sunday mass, surrounded by fertile Catholics and their sometimes large families. Most Sunday mornings found me rushing around the house deliberating whether my son's jeans without holes were more appropriate church attire than the less casual khakis with holes. When that problem resolved itself, I next debated with my daughter about the merits of wearing a jumper and tights rather than a sleeveless sundress and sandals in below zero weather. Although we usually attended the latest service possible, it seemed that we were always in a race against the clock. Peaceful and serene most definitely would not describe the mood I exuded upon arriving to church toting a bag overstuffed with diapers, tiny trucks, and board books. As we slid into the pew with no time to spare, my primary goal was not to reflect on the readings of the day, but to keep everyone as busy and quiet as possible. If I caught Amy looking my way, watching my toddlers, I wanted to reassure her that she'd be a mom someday soon. But I couldn't lie, especially in a church.

~Jenny Kalmon

CHAPTER 11

I Don't Know Nuthin' 'Bout Birthin' No Babies

The first and last time I truly believed I was pregnant I was eight years old. Cause of pregnancy? Boy germs. I had been sitting on my bed with my neighbor, Charlie Fitzpatrick, and everyone who still sleeps in footy pajamas knows when a boy and a girl sit on the same bed, babies are made. Always a worried child, I agonized over telling my parents and taking care of a baby. Even though tending to my dolls and stuffed animals was my full time job when not in school, I felt completely unprepared for the trials of motherhood. I always shied away from the strange *Baby Alive* dolls owned by my more affluent friends, proof positive that I was not ready for two a.m. feedings and dirty diapers.

Thankfully, my best friend Beth Kendall (who had much more liberal parents than I) showed me her disturbingly graphic children's book *How Babies are Made*. Since there was only transference of germs and no sperms, I was safe. Although I look back and laugh at my naiveté, relatively speaking, I remained somewhat unsure of how exactly someone became pregnant into my later adulthood. Being the youngest of six children in a family where all of my brothers and sisters procreated with ease, I never thought I would need to know the science of baby making. The fear of becoming pregnant (during the 70's and 80's we all saw the difficulties of teen parents played out in the high drama of *Afterschool Specials*) and the even worse hellish repercussions (deeply instilled in the third pew at St. Cecilia's Catholic Church) of engaging in premarital sex kept me spending my money on Pac man instead of on pregnancy tests. Ironically, the fear of *not* getting pregnant would eventually consume over a decade of my life.

I had never been one who actually longed for the act of giving birth. Seeing enough reenactments on TV and at the movies cured me of any romantic notions: Scarlett O'Hara's giving birth to her son in burning Atlanta while her maid insisted she didn't "know nuthin' bout birthin' no babies," the horrendous birth and subsequent death of the lizard/human baby in *V*, and Sigourney Weaver's alien baby bursting out of her chest. The screaming, the sweating, the pushing—it's just not a good look for me. Even the thought of *being* pregnant seemed a little strange: fetuses floating around in a woman's uterus, and eyes, brains, intestines (strangely to me—magically to most) developing inside the mother's body. And don't even get me started on how they make their entrance into the world. I am 39 years old, and I don't really know what being dilated means. Not really, and for God's sake never show me.

*

I met my husband, Richard, when I was seventeen years old. We pulled up to the same stoplight and looked over at each other. A girl with big eighties hair, a Guess miniskirt, and an Esprit sweatshirt fell in love with a boy in a maroon polo shirt with a prepped collar, baseball cap on backwards, piercingly beautiful and kind blue eyes with Guns 'n Roses blaring from his black Camaro. That night we obviously weren't seeking our future spouses, but, thanks to fate, we found them. The way we met was how we approached creating a family. Neither of us wanted to make the official proclamation: "Hear ye, hear ye, on this day, in the year of our Lord 1991, Richard and Amy will begin copulating with the single aim of conception. Henceforward, let it be known that the Bowmans are officially ***Trying***." We lived by the credo *things will happen when they are meant to happen*.

As we were busy letting our lives happen in our twenties and early thirties, we didn't often glance at our biological clock but at times heard its faint ticking. However, unlike the grandchildren frame on my parents' wall with one square left vacant for "Amy's babies," we didn't feel anything was empty about our lives. It simply wasn't the right time for children, and I was a person who, at least in theory, thrived on doing things right and at the right time. As we were struggling to make ends meet when we first married, we knew we weren't ready to have kids. When I went back to school to get my degree, it wasn't time. When we lived in a trailer house next door to a Peeping Tom, we really knew it wasn't time. Then, I started my teaching career, and Richard began working his way up in his company. We bought and renovated an old four bedroom farmhouse with a huge yard, purchased a reliable car we could trust, and we even owned a gigantic Saint Bernard, ready to protect our child like they do in old fashioned pictures. We had been married for nine years, and it was officially time for Amy's babies.

So, we began trying. In our minds, it would only take one time. After all, reproduction is one of the most basic functions we have. Just look around the next time you are at your local Wal-Mart. It obviously doesn't take a rocket scientist to conceive. That (as we would soon discover) was where we were wrong, and, unfortunately, as an English teacher, I knew more Shakespeare than science.

For awhile we chalked up our inability to get pregnant to bad timing. We enjoyed a happy, healthy sex life, but we were creatures of habit. Maybe babies weren't conceived exclusively on weekend mornings. We hit the snooze on my biological clock and tried not to dwell on the fact that we were at a time in our lives where we should have been nurturing a baby instead of watching *Battlestar Galactica* marathons in our basement. We busied ourselves with other projects. I went back to school and earned my master's degree and Richard tackled huge remodeling jobs on our house. To admit that something was wrong would have meant we would have to start investigating and solving the problem. Instead, we changed perspectives. After all, we weren't exactly trying; the more official decree was that we were more officially not *not* trying.

Coincidentally, my friend Laura and her husband were also trying (officially trying), also with no luck, to get pregnant. Unlike us, they weren't going to wait for years to magically become parents, so they actively sought out answers and a medical prognosis. In my mind, there was no sense in both of us going to the doctor, so I shook Laura down for advice and insight into her medical tests and treatments. She told me stories of having sex every day for a month and still not getting pregnant. Well, there was no way I was doing that. Then Laura graphically described the barrage of tests they had to undergo from running dye through her fallopian tubes to carefully examining John's "swimmers."

After listening to details of the various atrocities the Schmitts had to endure, I decided unless our prayers to the Diaper Genie were answered, I would treat my infertility myself. After all, I had always been taught that if I put my mind to something and worked hard enough, anything was possible. After doing some reading on infertility, I quickly determined my weight was the culprit, so I joined Weight Watchers and lost over sixty pounds. Taking up running, I became more fit than I was when I graduated high school 15 years before. I was perfectly healthy and thoroughly happy. Now, a baby would come.

But it didn't.

So, reluctantly, we visited the doctor. Some may wonder why I had actively tried to conceive for five years before going to a doctor. A hypochondriac from a young age, I had been plagued my entire life with the fear there was something medically wrong with me. I had (in my mind) by the fourth grade suffered from a heart attack, a brain tumor, and various strokes. As an adult, I suffered agonizing gallbladder attacks for years (where I would regularly tell my husband "good-bye" in moving speeches only an English teacher versed in romantic literature could deliver) before finally consulting a doctor because I was afraid of acknowledging that something wasn't right and that something would have to be done about it. The test for a faulty gallbladder was only a simple blood test; for infertility, I knew the stirrups were coming out. No woman enjoys gynecological exams, but I feel I am a more private person than most. I don't even like people sitting next to me on a couch much less a person peering into and prodding my private parts. During my first Pap test, I fainted. Plus, I'm a nervous sweater. I sweat in places where I don't even think there are sweat glands, but regardless of my fears, I stocked up on deodorant and scheduled an appointment.

Madame's Ovaries

In the doctor's office, Richard and I quickly scanned the white paper with **Fertility Checklist** boldly printed on top. The most important "to do" list of our lives started with blood tests and a cervical mucus test (was nothing sacred?), proceeded to an ultrasound, a hysteroscopy, an endometrial biopsy, a hysterosalpingogram, and ended with a laparoscopy, a surgery where an incision would be made into my belly button so a camera could investigate my reproductive organs. My doctor must have sensed my sweat glands kicking into gear as I shifted from the *this might not be too bad* mode to *holy crap* mode; he quickly assured me that since the laparoscopy was the last item on the list, we probably wouldn't get to it. Our baby would most likely be conceived before half of the "oscopys" would be performed. After taking his time to thoroughly discuss the physical aspect of the list, our doctor explained how the mental aspect could become overwhelming as well. He told us he had worked with couples whose sex lives and even marriages were destroyed due to the stress and pressure of trying to conceive. Richard and I looked at each other with the smile that said, *oh, he doesn't know us.* Adversity solidified us. We were sent home with a prescription for prenatal vitamins and a stack of graphs to keep track of my basal body temperature. This was going to be a breeze.

Or so it seemed. Let me explain how a breeze turned into a daily hurricane. Each day I woke up to the realization that my bladder was bursting, but I had to ignore this intense need and move slowly to grab the thermometer. If I couldn't easily grab it without moving too much, I would punch Richard in the arm and make violent hand gestures to which he had been trained to decipher as, "Honey, please hand me the thermometer." He would get up, look all over, and eventually find it behind the night stand, under the bed, or in the middle of the book I had been reading the night before, and Richard would hand it to me in an agitated manner. (As I was supposed to remain in a "half-asleep" state, his abrupt wake up from his full asleep state meant that he was now officially up for the day.) I would press the button, insert it into my mouth, and wait for it to beep. My first thermometer never beeped, so, in accordance with my chronic hypochondria, I took that as a sign that my internal temperature was always in a state of flux. (I realized six months later that the thermometer was simply malfunctioning.) I would have that infuriating thermometer in my mouth for ten minutes waiting for it to beep all the while moving my eyebrows in Morse Code to my poor husband to show my frustration. Finally, I would just give up, write down whatever the temperature read at that second, and rush to the bathroom.

Being an extremely unorganized person, I didn't record this vital data in a special notebook or even on the same piece of paper but on receipts, bookmarks, price tags, pages of the TV Guide—anything I had available. When it came time to plot my graph, I would gather all of these temperatures (those I could find), most with no dates or even days of the week. Needless to say, the final product had more ups and downs than a teeter totter at the local playground (where I would never go to because we didn't have kids). So, with head hung low, at the end of the first three months, I turned in my temperature charts. I vowed to be more diligent after a slight scolding from my doctor about not taking this step seriously and was prescribed the infertility cure-all—Clomid. We were now no longer not **not** trying; now we were getting pregnant.

We bought our first baby name books, began lollygagging in the infant sections in the stores, and imagined the scenario that would produce our child. Our lovemaking during the now clearly identified fertile days was to be beautiful and meaningful. The stuff of romance novels. And believe you me, I read enough Danielle Steel in my high school days to show me what beautiful was. Heart to heart, mind to mind, all the love we could muster to create the product of our intense respect, adoration, and devotion of each other. The lone flame from our unity candle illuminated our bedroom reminding us of the commitment we made to each other on our wedding day to bring forth children from our union. I wouldn't let my mind wander to the research papers I still had to correct that night, that new outfit I was eyeing at Kohl's, and definitely not on the fact that *American Idol* was going to be on in eight minutes. No. To avoid our baby being born a Damien or one of the *Children of the Corn*, he or she had to be created in the perfect mindset, perfect setting, and perfect moment. That's what was going to make our baby, nothing less than a preparation for a Tony Award winning Broadway play. Maybe not performances deserving standing ovations, but definitely ones left with two satisfied customers. I don't know how those Broadway people do it, but by the end of our week long "production" (with a dress rehearsal and encore performance thrown on either end for good measure), we were more than ready for closing night.

And the reviews? Not good. We were not pregnant. Then, when I found out that while I was on Clomid I had to be examined each month while I was having my period in order to search for ovarian cysts, the sweating began in torrents. I would rather have cysts exploding inside of me like a frenzy of fireworks than to subject myself and my doctor to that. Ah, the indignities. I was beginning to experience the dark underbelly of the beauty and the miracle of creating life.

Besides the mortification of monthly examinations, it was upsetting to see my own disappointment begin to be reflected in my doctor's eyes. In a crazy way, I felt that I was letting him down by not getting pregnant. When I handed him my chart full of sex day circles, I felt as if I were handing in an essay or an assignment to be graded. I am the type of person that if I even received an A-, I would agonize over it for weeks. Now, I was earning F's. Since I was earning failing grades anyway, I began cheating, adding circles here and there outside of the fertile week so that we wouldn't look so pathetic when it was obvious the only sex we were having was for procreation. It got to the point where I was adding circles even during the ovulation time because our Broadway productions had quickly turned into *National Geographic* specials.

Heart of Darkness

With the monthly disappointment came shame. I lied to coworkers as to why I was absent so often. We bought books on infertility that stayed hidden in our closet when we weren't poring through them trying to find the hidden, magical answer to our problem. We retreated into ourselves and questioned what our lives and our marriage would be like without children. We wondered what we had done to deserve to remain childless. I'll admit, I was a horrible teenager, but I felt I had more than been paid back for that by having to put up with 125 hormonal high school students every day. Richard had been rambunctious as a youth, but he grew up into a model citizen: generous, helpful, and kind. Laura claimed that people went through various trials in their lives because they had something to learn. What had Richard and I to learn? Patience? Humility? That life wasn't always fair? That my menstrual flow was fodder for social conversation?

We looked hard at our lives and Richard came to the grand conclusion that our infertility had absolutely nothing to do with drops in basal body temperatures or ovulation obstacles. According to my husband, we were infertile because we were not regular churchgoers. Out of our close group of friends, only one, Jenny, had babies. In his eyes, the only difference between us was she went to church and we didn't. (Of course, the fact that she was younger and didn't have fertility abnormalities didn't figure into it at all.) God was the answer. We felt good about getting back into the church, but as much as it served to give us some hope that a family was in our future, it was also a place filled with babies and children.

I never thought I would be the weepy type of person who would well up when seeing other people with babies, but after months of increasingly high dosages of Clomid, weepy I became. We desperately scrutinized each child to see if he had a cowlick in the back of his head or if she had ponytails so tight that her eyes were bulging. Then we would say to each other with a sigh and a wistful smile, "That's what our child would look like."

Although on some deep level I was happy for friends and coworkers who became pregnant (at least that's what I had to tell myself in order to think I wasn't a completely selfish, awful person), the news ate at my stomach like an ulcer, especially if, in my opinion, they hadn't paid their dues to the fertility gods. In other words, if they had been trying for a lesser amount of time than Richard and I, they had not paid their dues. My feelings of loathing and jealousy weren't only saved for my friends and family, but for the world at large. I don't know if America's obsession with celebrities' "baby bumps" began at this time or if I was only then sensitive to it, but even watching *E! News* after dinner was enough to send me running to a psychiatrist. Celebrities who previously were infamous for being caught without underwear, for having torrid affairs, or for public intoxication were suddenly raised to a Madonna status because they became pregnant. J-Lo, Halle Berry, Nicole Richie, and even Britney Spears' little 16 year old sister could become pregnant. What, these stars were perfect beings with nothing to learn about life? At least I knew enough to wear underpants in public.

As the six months allowed for the Clomid trial came to a close, we revisited the fertility workup checklist. All that remained was the last item, the surgery that nine months previously I said I would never do. After all I had been through in the past year, it seemed as if the only thing I'd never do is actually get pregnant, and so Richard and I decided to go ahead with the procedure. Because this was surgery, and because I always plan for the worst possible scenario (death), we finally told our families about our infertility.

The Importance of Being Earnest

We are private people to begin with, and exceedingly private about our private parts, so telling people was no easy task. *Hi. I can't perform a basic human function; I'm lucky I can even breathe! Please start contemplating my sex life. Hey, every time you call me, please wonder if you are "interrupting" something. Why don't you, with your vast knowledge of baby making, start giving me advice? Tell me to relax and then it will happen. Tell me that sometimes it just takes time. When the time is right, the baby will come.* Then, my paranoid inner voice really took over as I imagined my husband's family thinking, *We knew you were never good enough for Richard.*

First, we told Richard's family. We invited them over for dinner, and during dessert, I kicked Richard under the table which was the signal to make the announcement. With no segue of any kind, Richard blurted, "Amy and I can't have a baby, so she is going to have surgery to figure out why." All eyes quickly moved to me; I felt they were all thinking about my inside parts and Richard's outside parts. The sweat started to drip as Richard continued (with what seemed to me excruciating slowness) a description of what had led us to this point. After a stunned silence, they basically said, "Well, good luck with that" and quickly left. Obviously, embarrassment is not only reserved for the infertile, and nobody wants to hear about sperm tests over tapioca pudding.

After telling my family and having the news of our defectiveness spread to all of our siblings, our greatest secret was finally out in the open. Our private problem had become fuel for their gossip. (Or at least that is how I perceived it.) In retrospect, I know that most of our family members were genuinely concerned for us and saddened by our inability to fulfill our grandchildren collage frame obligation. However, at the time I thought they were thinking, "What kind of a person can't have babies?" In actuality, those were the thoughts I had about myself.

Endometriosis, My Dear Watson

Two days later, I had my surgery. Prognosis—endometriosis. To put it scientifically, my egg scooper-uppers were fused to the inside of me. All of the Clomid in the world, all of the temperature taking with my defective thermometer, all of the earth-shattering sex could never in a million years have gotten me pregnant. The doctor removed the endometriosis, but since the scar tissue was caused by menstrual blood, it would grow back each month. To slow down the re-growth and to allow my insides time to heal, my doctor put me into menopause for six months.

Six months of wasted time. Six months of hormone shots that left me limping in pain. Six months of hot flashes so intense I went to bed holding a fan instead of my husband. Although being artificially thrust into menopause in your thirties probably isn't on any woman's wish list, the experience did have an upside. This leg of our infertility journey rejuvenated me spiritually. Hormonally I was years older, but I felt ten years younger because finally all the pressure was off. I took a break from the temperature taking, a break from the Clomid, a break from mandatory sex, a break from my monthly appointments, and a break from disappointment. It was a chance to regroup. I took this opportunity to increase my exercise. Even though all the websites I read claimed Lupron shots caused weight gain, I lost weight, and, without the moodiness from my monthly cycle, my husband had a respite from my monthly wrath.

After my last injection, I felt like my normal self. Even though another birthday had come and gone, I was happy, healthy and optimistic. There was a definite reason why we didn't get pregnant, and that reason no longer existed. Armed with a new basal body thermometer and a notebook for keeping track of my daily temperature, I was ready, once again, to conceive the child of our love. I now had as good of a chance as Britney Spears' little sister of getting pregnant.

Now that our infertility was out in the open, the conception experts came out as strong as the pundits during presidential elections. My sister-in-law offered to research what to do to heighten chances of getting pregnant, friends cautiously asked if I should be doing so much running and if I shouldn't eat more full fat foods, and, of course, everyone inquired if we had anything to report.

Love's Labor's Lost

All of that *helpful* advice didn't do us any good because in a month I was back in the stirrups. I think my doctor knew by this time I was a lost cause but still believed there was a slight chance that six more months on Clomid might work a miracle. He was done with advice, and he seemed to look at me as the resident teachable moment since he had begun working with job shadowing medical students. I was the pop quiz. As I sat there bleeding and sweating each month, my doctor asked his students, "How old do you think this woman is?" Although cursed with infertility, I was blessed with a young appearance, and invariably they would say I was in my 20's or early 30's. He took glee in the misconception and informed them that I was much older. 36. The doctor would explain, "You see, that is why a doctor should always refresh himself with a patient's vital statistics. When treating a woman with infertility in her 20's, you can take your time. But with a woman Amy's age, you need to be much more aggressive." He would pat my knee, the students would look at me with pity, and I would sit there sweating so much that I looked like I just cleaned a Brawny mess with my paper towel gown.

As we came to our final month on Clomid, our desperation reached a fevered pitch. Surgery, pills, numerous invasive procedures, temperature taking, ovulation tests, and appointments: it had all come down to this last cycle. Gone were the romantic trysts—sex had become only a means to an end. The pressure mounted, and everyone knows pressure is no aphrodisiac. Basically, my attempt at foreplay consisted of telling Richard *for God's sake, just do it and get it over with.* Now that would have been a romantic conception memory! What devil child would have been born under that kind of duress?

Now, all areas of our lives were unfulfilled. Just as we gradually checked off items on the fertility checklist, we created a new checklist of our own.

No baby? Check.

Annoyed at friends and family members for meddling? Check.

Relationship reduced to a sexual act producing a child? Check.

Our sex lives, as well as our self-esteem, destroyed? Check.

We thought back to the warning our doctor gave us that this would be a difficult process.

Knowledge that even our relationship could take a beating? Check.
We were officially finished trying.

I visited my doctor's office for the last time. He resignedly referred us to the same fertility specialist as Jen and Kevin and wished us luck. Hopefully, the specialist would find some easy-to-fix, overlooked problem besides my endometriosis and tell us our chances of success if we decided to try in vitro. We prepared ourselves for a battery of tests, and my husband was even going to have a fancy sperm test. We were high-brow barren now. This *was* rocket science.

When Richard and I arrived at our appointment, we were nervous but the atmosphere of this clinic was amazing. The receptionist was friendly, the doctor was competent, and the nurses were kind; they all sported the right kind of attitude. Not humor, pity, nor disappointment. Even Barry Manilow music was playing in the background, "It's a miracle, miracle, a true blue spectacle." To us, in this lyric, Barry was predicting a boy. The office's business manager gave us a steep estimate of the cost for the tests and in vitro. *Well*, Richard and I thought, *we were in it this far; there was no turning back now.* We had given everything: our dignity and our privacy, so we might as well give every last cent. My uterus was fast becoming a money pit.

After the tests, our new doctor assured us that we had a good chance to get pregnant through in vitro. All that was left for us to do was to make a decision.

CHAPTER 12

Choosing the Best Ending

Well, evidently the Bowmans again were not going to do things the normal way. While I appreciate the wisdom we gained and the battle stories we were able to share by often taking the road less traveled, for at least one of life's big moments I would have loved to have traveled down the interstate in heavy traffic. I yearned for destinations boldly printed on signs every half mile instead of taking the barely identifiable path through the woods where we could so easily end up lost. Unfortunately for us, there wasn't just one road less traveled, to us there were three. As we stood at the crossroads, we looked at our options.

A beautifully manicured street called *Normal Way* was the one we desired to travel. Sounds of laughing, singing children filled the air, men stood at their barbeque grills slapping each other on the backs, women sat in various stages of pregnancy knitting baby blankets. Every house had a swing set and every car had at least one car seat. Kool-Aid flowed from water fountains and popsicles hung from trees. Of course, this way was barricaded, local traffic only.

Another way was *Adoption Alley*. Birth moms stood on every corner judging the residents, each mailbox was overflowing with paperwork, but there were kids in this alley, kids of all sizes and colors who looked nothing like their parents. Every once in awhile a birth mom would leave her post and rush off with a child while the other parents looked on in fear.

In Vitro Street was filled with frenzied activity. Volvos sped frantically from clinic to clinic, telephone poles were shaped like hypodermic needles, and the kids on that street were perfect: *Stepford Children* perfect.

Finally there was *No Kids Court*—barren, empty, and quiet. Tumbleweeds crossed the road.

None of those paths besides *Normal Way* were what we desired, but it was our destiny to travel one of them. Perhaps, as Robert Frost insisted, taking the road less traveled would make "all the difference." But which path would we choose to make sure the difference was positive (i.e. well adjusted, kind, happy child) instead of negative (i.e. future serial killer)?

When I was a little girl, I was enthralled with the books that had alternate endings based on decisions I made. Invariably, I would end up choosing all the options and peeking to see which ending I favored. If only this decision could be made so I could peek at the future result. What would our lives be like if we traveled down one of these roads? Do Richard and Amy remain childless? Go to page 90. Do Amy and Richard choose in vitro? Go to page 63. Do Amy and Richard choose adoption? Go to page 52.

Pg. 90

> *Richard and Amy came to terms with the fact that they couldn't have children of their own. They spent the rest of their lives sending pictures of their pets on Christmas cards and remodeling their home. They had the money and time to travel, and they took advantage of that often. Perpetually tan with a house cluttered with souvenirs, the couple seemed to enjoy their lives. However, as they spent the last years of their lives in a nursing home, they harbored only one major regret—they never shared the love they had to give with a child.*

Remaining childless was a real option for us. The fact that we hadn't more quickly pursued answers to our infertility was a clue that children were not our top priority. Always awkward around babies, I harbored an irrational fear I wouldn't adequately support their necks and their heads would fall off. I was not the rowdy, get down on the floor, roughhousing kind of aunt but more of the craft-making, quietly reading together or playing games type of aunt. Richard, although not the rowdy type either, was a kid favorite. He exuded a sense of interest in little people; kids liked to talk to him about everything from rugs that felt spiny to obviously embellished sporting conquests. We both enjoyed being around children, but we could enjoy being around them without actually having to take them home.

We began astutely observing families and parenting styles. Some parents were way too indulgent and lax as we saw their children running around like maniacs in stores and restaurants. Other parents were overly strict, and we cringed when saw them slap and belittle their kids. Although it was probably unfair to judge parents in the snapshot episodes we witnessed, we knew we would hate our lives if we ended up being in either extreme. We were critical enough of our own actions and felt guilt about our many mistakes, and I cannot imagine any worse guilt than being a bad parent. As a teacher, I have seen numerous children who were headed into a lifetime of heartache and trouble because they haven't been taught responsibility, compassion, or sometimes even decency. Of course, not all parents are bad parents. Our friends and relatives had the magic formula for raising outstanding, funny, respectful kids who have grown into spectacular adults. If only our child could be born with a money and time back guarantee, we would feel much more confident about the undertaking.

Plus, I admit it. I was selfish. After being responsible only for ourselves for the twenty years we had been together, Richard and I enjoyed our free time. We liked going to the movies on a whim, taking overnight excursions, sleeping in on weekends, and taking naps when we were tired. We liked our quiet house and would much rather watch *Die Hard* than *Dora*. Did that make us bad people?

Besides, we already worried constantly about our own lives and the current state of the world: the economy, rising gas and food prices, war, cancer, terrorists, global warming, and even the fate of contestants on *American Idol*. Did I really have enough worry to add another person into the mix?

Did we have to be parents to be happy?

We knew the answer to that was no. Although we longed to share our lives with children and at times felt a lack of purpose, mostly our lives were pretty great. We earned enough money not to worry about how we were going to pay the bills. We had fulfilling jobs, a strong marriage, and excellent friends. What if having a child was the worst decision we ever made and ruined everything?

pg. 63

> *Richard and Amy underwent the grueling process of shots, exams, and bed rest. They spent their entire home equity loan on the chance to have a biological child, and whatever the outcome, they would be making payments on this procedure for many years to come. They had no money to try other options. Amy and Richard anxiously waited for the doctor to enter the examining room to tell them if the procedure worked.*

In vitro fertilization was the option we thought we would most likely choose. Even though it would cost every cent we could mortgage, at least we would, most likely, become pregnant. I would have nine months of memorable pregnancy moments worthy of any birth movie montage: Take a moment and play these episodes in your head to Paul Anka's hit song *You're Having My Baby*.

I take Richard to the very spot he first told me he loved me when we were eighteen years old and tell him he is going to be a father. He lifts me up, swings me around, and at that very moment a shooting star rushes past.

We laugh when we see the ultrasound for the first time because we know each other so well we can easily imagine what sort of a baby we have created.

Richard and I are lying in bed. Richard is reading the paper and using my big belly as a place to put his coffee cup.

Richard goes to the store at 2 a.m. to buy pickles and ice cream and Dots and Whoppers and cheesecake . . . and flowers.

Richard lovingly kisses me and my belly good-bye every morning.

In the delivery room, the doctor holds up a tiny perfect baby and asks "Dad" to cut the chord while I, who look stunning after twelve hours of labor (after all, I am the director of this imaginary drama) look on. Richard takes our baby into his arms for the first time and brings him to me, and we both have tears in our eyes.

For whatever reason, as silly as they are, experiencing these moments was important to me. I know that a more honest scene would also feature hemorrhoids, stretch marks, morning sickness, and "cankles," but at least the result would be a baby to love, a baby whose traits would reflect both of us and (excuse the corniness) be our love brought to life. I longed to have a child whose eyes I would look into years in the future and see his father in them. What a miracle life is. Even though this miracle wouldn't be created through natural methods (being conceived in a Petri dish was a far cry from the music and candlelight dream), perhaps it would be even more miraculous for that fact.

Plus, after years of almost monthly doctor's visits, it seemed strange to cut the doctor out of our lives. The *doctor* became such a part of our baby making experience that we half expected our little one to exhibit some of his traits, to exit my womb in a white lab coat and with a stethoscope instead of an umbilical cord. With all of our testing, monitoring, and medicating, it seemed foolish not to take the natural next medical step. The fertility specialist appeared confident and competent; my eggs and Richard's sperm would be in good hands, and we could maybe even convince him to dim the lights and sing a little old school Bon Jovi while he administered the injection.

After reading books on in vitro (understanding about 50% of what was said) and being assured that we were good candidates, we consulted with the fertility nurse about the implications of the process besides the obvious pain of the shots and the high cost. She asked us how we would feel if I was implanted with the fertilized eggs and a reduction had to be made. Some eggs might have to be eliminated for the sake of the remaining eggs. Also, what would we do with our remaining eggs that weren't implanted? I guess I never gave a thought to the leftovers. We would have to sign a document stating who would get the eggs in a divorce situation or if Richard and I both died. The eggs would have to be included in a will. Sorry nieces and nephews, instead of money, cars, property, or jewelry, how would you like to become the proud owners of your aunt and uncle's sperm and eggs? What a great inheritance!

If we didn't want to keep the eggs, we would have to dispose of them ourselves because the clinic would not. Obviously, this was a serious ethical issue. Richard and I had to struggle over one question. Did life begin at conception? Were these fertilized eggs babies? Was it selfish of us to sacrifice six or more possible babies to have one or two? Could we live with ourselves knowing that we had to destroy life in order to create life?

Ironically, the church (remember, our pregnancy through prayer technique?) was the blaring alarm clock disrupting our dream of having a biological child. The Catholic Church has a strong stance against in vitro fertilization (which ranks right up there with stem cell research)—do it and incur God's wrath big time. Each week it seemed the congregation would fervently pray for babies only to be born "naturally." We heard a story of a couple who became pregnant through in vitro and the priest refused to baptize the baby. Now, I have never been one to follow all the church's teachings: I took birth control (will I really go to hell for that if I was infertile anyway?), I broke the commandments, I didn't always go to church; heck, I even watched *and* read *The Davinci Code*, but for some reason, based on my gut feelings, I guess I believed life began at conception and to destroy fertilized eggs would be wrong.

Of course, I was being optimistic thinking I would have enough viable eggs to open a farmer's market, when, in reality, many women have the procedure and the doctor would only retrieve one or two eggs. Both could be implanted, and twins! The perfect end to our saga. If we had more eggs, I vowed that I could go through with in vitro in good conscience only if I used them all. As I gave it more thought, I wondered what I would do if I had three, four, or even six remaining eggs? I would have to undergo the entire procedure one, two, or even three more times. We would have to rob banks to support our growing family and the family sitting in our refrigerator waiting to be born. Plus, I was already 37 and had spent the last ten years of my life trying to get pregnant; did I really want to devote the next decade to doing the same—possibly with devastating results—not to mention the whole burning in hell afterlife downer?

There were other medical options. I could have had artificial insemination. The church frowned on that as well, but a frown was better than a flaming hot pitchfork in your eye. This procedure included shots and many medical appointments, and the success rate was low but increased with each try (up to three). The doctor didn't think this method would be as successful as in vitro since it relied more on chance than science, but it was still a course of action we could have pursued.

All we knew for sure was we had to make a decision quickly. Once I turned 38 (in one year), the chances of having a healthy baby steeply declined. We were running out of time.

Pg. 52

Richard and Amy experienced the grueling adoption process. They were interviewed, background checked, properly schooled, and put in the pool. Their fate was now entirely in the hands of some hypothetical young woman who they were told might base her decision on the color of the adoptive mother's hair, on the make of their car, or on the cuteness of their pet. The Bowmans were close to forty, and they worried they would never be picked. If something didn't happen soon, they figured they might as well go into an adopt-a-grandchild program. However, they dutifully created their profile and waited for the phone to ring.

We always thought adoption was a cool thing *other* people did. When I was young, always a philanthropist, I thought one day I might adopt some underprivileged kid as a way to round out my own biological family. In my wildest dreams, I never imagined it would be my only choice, and when the choice becomes more desperation than inspiration, it becomes a little less cool. Then, Laura and John decided to adopt. Adopt *domestically*. Gasp if you must; I know Richard and I did when we heard the news. Obviously John and Laura never watched the *Lifetime* network where kids were stolen by their biological parents, or where adoptive parents spent thousands towards the welfare of the mother and her baby only to have her change her mind at the end. We didn't want our friends heartbroken and broke, but they had made up their minds. Plus, everyone knew they would have to wait years for a baby, and in the end the baby would most likely have something wrong with it. That's why (according to our vast knowledge—via cable television—of the pitfalls of domestic adoption) the vast majority of people adopt internationally. Shockingly to us, Laura didn't waste her time hemming and hawing over the pros and cons or getting caught up in the minutiae of every possible outcome, but she investigated the facts and committed quickly.

We were amazed with how fast they finished the process. They wrote their autobiography, were interviewed, and created a portfolio in what seemed like only a few weeks. Richard and I celebrated with them when they were officially in the adoption pool, all indulging in a cake that looked like an ocean. At this time we were still trying to battle our infertility medically. Although we were interested in the process the Schmitts were going through, we never really thought it would be the route for us.

The Missing Piece

A couple months later while engrossed in an episode of *Survivor* (the childless couple's secret luxury: reality TV), I received a call from Laura.

Bordering on giddy, Laura almost yelled into the phone, "You are never going to believe this. We have a baby. Right now. We are driving home with him right now. His name is Wyatt." The tribe had spoken. Holy cow. Laura, a mother. All of the usual "they have a baby and we don't" feelings flooded me when I heard the news, but in addition to the odd mix of happiness, sadness, excitement, jealousy, and self-hatred for the jealousy, I experienced one more emotion: hope.

Maybe it was time we looked into this adoption business.

Wyatt not only ended up being the miracle of John and Laura's lives, but ours as well. We instantly fell in love with their bundle in blue. Did this creature who loved dogs, balls, and M&M's know that his godparents were in a deep struggle trying to create a family of their own? Did he know that this couple needed a little guy like him to show them how awesome kids could be and what they were missing? We lived vicariously through the Schmitts' parenting experiences. Eagerly we would recount Wyatt's childhood triumphs to any family and friends who would listen, and soon our favorite expression at our house was "That Wyatt" which would lead into a discussion of all his crazy antics. I relished his chewed up pretzel kisses, melted when he brought me books to read and sat on my lap, and laughed when he did his strange unadulterated happy dance. Richard's adoration for Wyatt was downright silly. Seeing my husband's patience as he chased an endless supply of poorly thrown balls, picked up crayon after crayon when Wyatt played his favorite Crayola dump game, and his tenderness as he changed Wyatt's diapers and clothes was proof that the childless route was never going to work for us. We wanted a Wyatt of our own.

Then, as if God knew the Bowmans had to be seriously led to decisions we made, Jen and Kevin announced they too were adopting a son. Richard and I couldn't believe they had fallen into, what seemed like to us, a perfect scenario. I thought of pregnant students in my school and wondered if perhaps one of them would consider choosing me to parent her child. What were the chances Jen's situation would be repeated in my school district only fifteen miles away? On the other hand, what were the chances I would be a part of a group of friends with such a high occurrence of infertility, where the one person able to get pregnant was looked at as the anomaly? In our case, statistics and percentages had about as much validity as Milli Vanilli.

Through the Looking Glass

Following our friends' examples, Richard and I visited the same adoption agency as John and Laura and Jen and Kevin. We learned how the process worked and had many of our questions answered. After hearing about our recent appointments with the fertility clinic, Sally, the social worker, thought we should wait before committing to adoption. She sensed we were still on the fence with in vitro; she was right. I wasn't ready to put the hope of having a biological child to rest, but Richard was ready to put an end to trying and start doing.

We struggled. We talked about our options. During car rides, before work, after work, during dinner, and during commercials we talked, dissecting every pro and con. The bottom line for Richard was he didn't want me to go through any more medical treatments. I knew he felt bad that I had to bear the brunt of the pain, discomfort, and humiliation of most of the infertility tests and treatments. The bottom line for me was that I desperately didn't want to let Richard down. We talked about why we wanted children and how important it was that we have biological children. Was it to carry on our legacy which in reality consisted of watching TV and having outlandish Halloween parties? It wasn't like we were Nobel Prize winners or supermodels.

How would we feel if our adoptive child wasn't bright? Wasn't healthy? Didn't look at all like us? Couldn't bond with us? Wasn't it more important to have a child to love and to share our lives, regardless of these concerns? We honestly didn't know the answers to those questions. If we attempted in vitro, would I be strong enough to undergo the shots and the discomfort? If we tried to adopt, could I handle the rejection? In either case, was I strong enough to deal with more disappointment?

To see if I was strong enough, I did what any normal person would do—I ran a marathon.

Nothing gives you time to mull over life's difficult decisions like miles of senselessly pounding your joints. I thought that if I could survive running 26.2 miles, I could handle whatever was coming our way as we continued our struggle to have a family. During those hours of the race, I knew I would have to dig deep into my soul, push aside all the trivial aspects of my life, and in so doing, I would certainly find the answers for which I'd been looking.

Unfortunately, I discovered that during the first half of the marathon I was so high on endorphins I didn't think of anything except what pose I would want to strike as I cruised across the finish line, and the second half of the marathon I thought nothing except how I wished death would take me immediately. I crossed the finish line (striking my *please God let me stop running now* pose) and still didn't have anything resembling an answer.

All I knew was that I was strong enough for whatever our future held.

CHAPTER 13

And Down the Rabbit Hole

We spent the next couple months agonizing over the "how would you feel ifs" and "could you live with this" and "what if this happened?" Potentially dealing with a difficult birth mother, waiting for years and never getting picked, and experiencing the heartbreak of a changed mind were better than the life and death choices that would have to be made if we went ahead with in vitro. Finally, we had made our decision—we would build our family through adoption.

So began the paperwork journey that would eventually, we hoped, lead us to our baby. We put away our infertility books and pregnancy tests and took out our W2's and insurance cards to provide our basic biographical and financial information. Then, we went in for a preliminary interview which was basically a rundown on what to expect from the adoption process and to be followed by individual interviews. Richard and I were thrilled to be assigned to John and Laura's social worker, Tina. She had worked magic once, and, after meeting her, we were filled with confidence that she could do the same for us. She was like a coach psyching us up for the biggest game of our lives.

Next, we were asked to write essays giving insight into our relationships with each of our family members. Now the psychoanalyzing began. What were these nebulous adoption approvers looking for? What were the red flags? Richard and I both come from large families, and we don't have perfect relationships with each of our siblings. Our families were more like the Bundys than the Bradys. Everyone has a few skeletons in their closets, but ours didn't even have the common sense to stay hidden; they were dancing in our front yards. We also had to write about each other, how we met, and the admirable and the not so admirable qualities about each other.

Then, we filled out a questionnaire about ourselves and our spouses regarding marital roles, how we reacted when angry, what we thought were appropriate punishments for children, and a description of relationships with our own parents. The responses were there for us, we just had to check the boxes that applied. The red flags were easy to see here. Obviously, strapping children down, verbally abusing them, or withholding the necessities of life from them was not appropriate. But what if I happened to be a little bit of a yeller? Did I yell once a day? Once a week? Once a month? How often did we disagree? How did we usually resolve disagreements? Do most couples always listen to each other and make compromises? Obviously so, because stomping off to the bedroom, slamming the door, and waiting for your husband to slide a letter of apology under the door before you would resume the conversation wasn't an option on the yellow checklist.

Some of these questions, although seemingly ridiculous, did make us reflect on how we acted and on behaviors we wanted to change to be better role models for our children. If the questionnaire was this intense, how were our interviews going to be? How much was Richard going to divulge about me and my crazy ways? Although I had been trying to act in ways that would encourage Richard check the flattering boxes about me, such as always trying to rationally discuss instead of going ballistic when he left the cap off the shampoo bottle, being understanding when he was late coming home from work instead of the stubborn, irrational, yeller that the packet was trying to weed out, I knew that a few days of being the model human being was not going to make up for the 37 years of the real, flawed, me.

As the day approached for our individual interviews, we tried to brainstorm what Tina would be asking. Of course, with my pessimistic view, I thought she would want us to divulge the worst aspects of each other. We rehearsed our answers like in a job interview where they ask what your worst quality is, and you admit to being a perfectionist or a workaholic. In this situation, we pondered whether Tina would buy that I loved my husband too much and that Richard sometimes displayed too much patience. Laura was convinced that she would try to find something to make me cry since Tina was a crier. I remember Tina explaining how I would probably cry when I met our baby's birth mother or that I might cry when discussing our infertility. I worried that being quick to tears was mandatory to becoming an adoptive parent because unless she was going to show me the ending of *The Titanic*, that wasn't going to happen.

As a good omen for our interview, we woke to severe weather warnings recommending everyone stay home unless it was an emergency because the wind chill was 60 below. A reprieve, I thought. We called Tina to allow her to cancel (I, of course, feverishly praying that she would put it off and Richard hoping to get it over with), but she wasn't bothered by the cold weather at all and wanted to keep the appointment. We dressed in our "respectable parent" attire and left for the agency. We fought half of the way there because we (running late as usual) didn't gas up before we left, and

Richard was certain we could make it without stopping for fuel. I reminded him of the weather advisory and insisted we could die within minutes if we were stranded. With tensions running high, and our behavior deteriorating into the negative check boxes peppered with the exceedingly mature "and you can tell Tina I said that" we made it to the appointment on "E," alive and on time, but definitely frazzled.

The interviews were not the grilling we had dreaded but were basically a recap of what we had written in our essays. We didn't have to defend ourselves, rat out our spouses, or even cry a river of tears. Tina impressed upon each of us the importance of being good parents. With tears in her eyes, she described how our kids would become the center of our hearts, and we had to do our very best to raise them to be caring and loving people. I wondered if some of her clients had been trying to have a baby for so long that serious thought had not been given to what would happen after the seeming unattainable miracle arrived. Her speech made us believe that we were, undoubtedly, going to become blessed with a child, and when we did, we had better be people worthy of the gift.

Our next task was to decide what kind of a child we wanted. We couldn't request a sex, but everything else seemed open to choice: race, physical limitations, the mental health of the birth mother, the circumstances under which the baby was conceived, and the type and amount of drugs the birth mother might have taken during pregnancy. Of course, we wanted a baby who was healthy, a birth mom who was scholarly and had just gotten carried away with her boyfriend on prom night, with both baby and mother given excellent prenatal care the day after conception, but we had to be realistic. Although we quickly checked the boxes under Tina's guidance, she insisted we give these questions careful consideration because while it would be easy and politically correct for us to say we will take whatever child needs a home, ultimately we knew what resources we had to give a child. Since we would take a child of any ethnicity, Tina thought we could be picked quickly and set the appointment for our home visit for the next weekend. There would be no time to relish in the relief that we had passed our interviews; a new stress was only a short week away.

For some reason, I could clean my house 24 hours a day 7 days a week, and it still would be messy. With crafts covering every wall, Weight Watcher recipes bursting out of drawers, clothes waiting for a much larger closet, dishes for every holiday crowding my cupboards, and, just in general, the minutiae of our lives (receipts, bills, postcards) marching through our house, we knew we had to go on a marathon cleaning spree. Six days later, when Tina arrived, our house smelled so much like Pledge we couldn't even have a conversation because our noses were all plugged with the overpowering lemony scent. It was probably the shortest home study in the history of the adoption agency.

Great Expectations

Finally, all we needed to do was to complete a profile of our lives that displayed what we had to offer a child. Thus began the project that almost killed me. As I have said before, I always strive for the A+. In fact, that isn't even good enough. A++ is my goal. I needed to create a profile to crush the other profiles where we were showcased as the most loving and caring people in the world. (Was *crushing the competition* a good motherly trait?) As I looked through the profile examples, I saw how people showed exotic vacations, meticulous new houses, beautiful pets, and families that would put the Waltons to shame. What did we have? Realistically, our lives consisted of hours of sitting on the couch asking each other what we want to do, being excited about *Lost* and *American Idol*, and talking baby talk to our one-eyed St. Bernard, Bailey. Not exactly "crushing" material. On further introspection, though, we realized that while our day to day lives might not be the material for a raucous comedy or a gripping drama, the Bowmans definitely had moments of excitement and uniqueness. It was all in the packaging. Once again we followed the Schmitts lead and incorporated a theme in our profile, something both Richard and I loved—games.

Each two-page spread incorporated a board game. For *Scrabble*, I used words to describe our relationship, for *Monopoly* I highlighted various rooms in our home, for *Life* I described our hobbies and careers. I agonized over every photo to make sure we looked young enough, interesting enough, and worthy enough. Plus, time was limited. Tina was encouraging us to finish our profile quickly because some birth moms would be coming in to look at profiles the next week, and she didn't want us to miss any opportunities. Initially, I stayed up for 48 hours straight working on it, called in sick to work, and drove all over the state to take pictures of family members and friends. Richard came down with the flu and was absolutely no help, but he was still willing to put on whatever clothes I told him to and to strike whatever pose (even out in below zero temperatures) needed to make this the perfect profile. For an entire week I didn't come to bed until 3:00 in the morning. I lugged the supplies to school to work on it there and returned home and feverishly continued working. When I finally finished what I crazily considered my masterpiece, it was 3:30 in the morning. Hopped up on Diet Pepsi and pretzels, I finally hit the wall and was completely delirious from lack of sleep.

I went to bed, told Richard I had it done, and feverishly prayed we would never get a child. *And for God's sake*, I thought, *don't touch me*; I didn't want a biological child either. I had just spent about ten days working on a promise of what we would provide our baby. I promised everything. On paper we seemed to be the perfect parents: lives constantly filled with fun and caring for others, family functions that were anything but dysfunctional, and friends who would give us their vital organs if we only asked. In my momentary loss of sanity, I wished I hadn't done such a good job because I didn't think I was ready for the grade. This time it wouldn't be an A, it would be a B for baby. If I couldn't even get a scrapbook done in a timely fashion without taking time off work and losing my mind, how would I stand up to the stress of motherhood?

Luckily, upon completion of our profile in mid-February, we went on a short trip to Mexico to relax and regroup. On the white beach listening to the ocean waves, Richard and I fully expected to get a call from Tina saying we had to come back and pick up our baby. When that didn't happen, I have to admit I was a little relieved. We had been in full blown baby mode for years, and it was nice just to be anxiously *waiting* instead of anxiously *doing*. We had no idea how intense the adoption wait would be until I received a phone call in March.

The agency had a young mother who was due in a few weeks, and she was going to look at our profile as well as those of several other couples. The game was on. The social worker said we should know in a few days. We discussed baby names and planned the nursery. Every time the phone rang, I jumped out of my skin. Every time I called my husband, he jumped out of his skin. After all, this was the most important phone call of our lives. I made bets with myself. If I ran nine miles that day instead of six, we would get the baby. If I made Richard's favorite meal, we would get the baby. If I cleaned the entire house, we would get the baby. I guess I should never go to Vegas because my bets didn't pan out. When we finally received the call from the adoption agency, we were disappointed and somewhat shocked to learn that our profile wasn't even one the birth mom took home to contemplate. My A++ project was an F? Maybe this wasn't going to be as easy for us as it seemed to be for John and Laura.

The Lord of All Rings

Our disappointment didn't last long. A few weeks later, during my seventh hour American Literature class, my phone rang. Again, it was the adoption agency. Showing the great parenting quality of responsibility, I left my class unattended and ran into an empty classroom next door to take the call. This time it was a social worker, Chelsea (who would be working with us instead of Tina), calling to say that we had been picked. There would be no waiting for a decision; the decision had been made. My heart stopped, but I continued the conversation as if I were taking a call from an insurance company. The young woman was due in the beginning of June. The baby was an African-American boy. Would we be willing to meet with the mother the following week? There it was—the phone call that was going to change everything. In that moment I didn't react the way I thought I would. I didn't do cartwheels down the hallway; I didn't yell at the top of my lungs; I didn't even shed a tear of any kind. I was in complete shock. I staggered back to my classroom, looked around, and wanted to ask my students if they thought I would be a good parent. I tried to feel maternal. The remaining ten minutes of class will go down in history as the nicest I've ever been to my students. When the bell rang, I called Laura (instead of my husband, the father-to-be), and she urged me to come to her house right away so we could go baby shopping. On my way to Laura's, I waited for the tears of excitement and joy to overtake me. Still I was paralyzed with trepidation. What was wrong with me? Maybe after sharing the news with Richard, my maternal floodgates would open.

I wanted to make this a *moment* for Richard, and with all of my dreaming of getting this news, I never developed a substantive plan for telling him. I didn't have time for a large production since he would be home in just a couple of hours, but I still wanted it to be special and memorable. With Laura that afternoon, I bought a shirt at a baby store that proudly stated *Boy*, bought balloons and a figurine of a mother and father holding a newborn. After rushing home, I brought our St. Bernard, Bailey, in the house and tied a big yellow bow around her neck with a note that asked, *Are you ready, Dad?* Minutes later, Richard walked into the house, and Bailey bounded to him. Richard read the note and gave me a look of shock that mirrored my own. Then he saw my shirt and said one word.

"Really?"

I filled him in on the details, and he quickly sat down. A few moments later, I saw the excitement in his eyes, and I knew everything was going to be all right. Somehow, we would be ready when our baby came home.

Our Pride, Their Prejudice

We were going to be parents. On top of that, we were going to be parents in a multiracial family. Not only were we going to have to make sure our son had feelings of belonging within his family but within the community as well. We lived in a primarily white city; would we be strong and wise enough to school our son on the ways to overcome prejudice? What if prejudice came from within his own family? A consummate worrier, I began to obsess over the obstacles our son would face. Like any other mother, I would never want to see my son's heart break. Knowing it would happen due to girls and general disappointment was one thing, but quite another if it was due to irrational, hateful ignorance.

On top of the worry about prejudice, we were even more worried about our ability to become good parents in two months. I, who hadn't changed a diaper in about 26 years, and Richard, who thought the most important aspect of child rearing was collecting boxes to make cardboard forts, had a short time to learn everything there was to know about child-rearing, or at least enough to get us through the first week. We had nothing ready for a baby; our house was not baby proof or at times even adult proof. A vague sense of being pushed into something before I was ready began to fill me. I began to have a recurring dream of not being able to find our baby as if he were our car keys or a favorite winter hat. I knew the only way to get past this fear was to be as prepared as possible. The next day after work I went shopping for necessities for the baby. I bought four wicker baskets and a dress for myself for his christening. This baby was in big trouble.

Thursday at Starbucks

Our nervousness at becoming parents was momentarily assuaged by the nervousness of the upcoming meeting with the mother of our child. This would be the interview of a lifetime. We couldn't get much information from the social worker except that Tamyka was 19, just finishing high school, and taking excellent care of herself and the baby. She had the support of her family, and the birth father wanted nothing to do with the child. Basically, for us, a perfect scenario. We were meeting Tamyka the following Thursday in Milwaukee at a Starbucks. Richard and I couldn't wrap our brains around how we were supposed to approach this occasion. What should we wear? What should we say? What was she going to think of us? What were we going to have in common? We were old enough to be her parents. Talk of the weather, the Packers, and her favorite classes seemed weird. This moment was big and had no room for small talk.

I felt I was under more pressure than Richard. In my heart I knew that the birth mother was going to want to feel some sort of connection with the adoptive mom. I know if it were me, I would look into the woman's eyes, the mother to my son, and expect to see compassion, kindness, love, and strength. I would have to feel that she was somewhat like me. I would have to trust her. I know that I have these qualities, but being somewhat shy, I don't make a strong first impression. Richard, on the other hand, loved to talk to people and could make anyone feel at ease, so maybe with my cute plaid pants and Richard's personality, we might make it through this meeting.

Arriving in Milwaukee early, we walked around a shopping district, practically the only white people in the area. In our minds, this experience was the first part of our education on how to make sure we would always do right by our son. This was what our son would feel like immersed in a Caucasian community. Vowing to regularly take him to places where he was not the minority, we sincerely hoped that Tamyka would want us to visit her often in Milwaukee and that her family would want us to be part of their lives.

After some shopping, we waited in the parking lot for half an hour getting pumped up for our meeting. We reviewed what we were not going to do (refer to the baby as ours or dwell too much on the baby), what we would do (ask her about her family and hobbies and thank her for considering us), and debated on what we might do (hug her and take a picture of the three of us). We reflected on the events that brought us to this Starbucks' parking lot, just minutes away from meeting the mother of our son. It was truly a bizarre sensation. We had no idea what she might look like. Short or tall? Thin or heavy set? Tattooed? Pierced? Then, there was her personality. Sweet? Tough? Shy? Funny? Sitting and watching the customers coming in and out of the nearby grocery store, we considered each person as if she might be Tamyka and just kept saying, "We'd be alright with that." After about twenty minutes of this ludicrous exercise, it was time to meet the girl who would be making us a family.

With a quick kiss and hug to calm our nerves, we entered the coffee shop and pondered where to sit. Acting like this coffee shop was our own living room, Richard moved some of the furniture around so that we would be right there, front and center, when she walked in and somewhat away from the other customers. Every car that pulled into the parking lot stopped our hearts as we tried to determine if these were the people we were waiting for. Finally a Mercedes pulled into the lot, and we had a strong feeling that it must be our social worker and Tamyka. Sure enough, a young pregnant woman stepped out of the vehicle. Our immediate response was relief. A petite, smartly dressed girl emerged. Our hearts were racing in the few seconds it took her to enter the coffee shop. When they entered, Richard and I rose and both hugged her and shook the social worker's hand. From that moment, I transformed from the mild mannered Amy Bowman into a crazy person with a smile so big it could engulf Rhode Island. I was trying hard to be one of those women from whom you can feel the warmth and sunshine emanating from her soul (or in my case, my mouth). We wanted her to feel instantly comfortable with us. Richard and I looked to Chelsea to transition from our greeting to the rest of our conversation, but she just sat there watching us trying not to intrude on this important moment. So, I took the reins. Me, the quiet one who dreaded conversations with people I didn't know suddenly had to turn into Oprah Winfrey. But I acted more like her most famous interviewee, Tom Cruise. Thank God there was no couch or I would have been jumping on it to show how excited I was to meet her.

Asking her questions, we tried to feel out how solid she was in her decision to place her baby for adoption and kept a mental tally of anything she said that made us worry. We inquired about her hobbies, her favorite subjects in school, and her family. She said she loved school (Richard and I gave each other mental high fives), she loved her teachers (mental Lambeau Leaps), and she tried to stay out of the usual teenage drama. I told her that her mom must be very proud of her for making such a courageous decision. Tamyka said her mom would support her either way. Alarm bell #1. Then, she gave us the ultrasound of our son. He was curled up, sucking his thumb, and oblivious to the hubbub he was causing. Tamyka told us we could be in the delivery room if we wanted to be. Smiley Monster said that would be great, but in reality I was just a little freaked out. I wouldn't want to be in the delivery room if I was the one having the baby, but we'd cross that birth canal when we came to it. An awkward silence ensued.

Tamyka tried to fill the space by asking us what we did for a living. Richard and I had the feeling she didn't look through our profile very carefully. Alarm bell #2. We asked her how she envisioned the adoption. Would she want to keep in touch with us and the baby? She offhandedly said that she would just want a couple of pictures. Alarm bell #3. Tamyka told us she picked us because "y'all seem like nice people." This sweet statement somewhat muted the alarm bells, but we still had a feeling she didn't fully realize what she had signed up for. She seemed disconnected from the life growing inside of her, which would be fine if she remained disconnected. What would happen when the baby became real to her? Would she still choose to place him for adoption? After our half hour of stilted conversation, the social worker ended our meeting and said they'd be in touch. We had Chelsea take a picture of the three of us in that Starbucks: Smiley Monster and husband with their manic desperation for a baby apparent by the way they had their arms around a shy young girl with a protruding stomach. We exchanged phone numbers and addresses, hugged again and said we'd call Tamyka soon.

Chelsea called us about fifteen minutes later and told us the meeting went really well and that Tamyka felt good about us. With immense relief, Richard and I decided it was time to test the waters to see our families' reactions to our news, so we stuck our pinkie toes in and called my sister Peggy. A liberal, open minded person, we knew the water would feel fine as far as she was concerned. Instantly excited and dismissing our concerns about our son's acceptance into the family, Peggy's overwhelming happiness for us made us feel like this was the family we were meant to have. I looked at the ultrasound and tried to assure myself that everything was going to work out and there was nothing to worry about. But worry I did.

Midnight Drearies

As the first few days went by, a strange phenomenon ensued. During the day, I anxiously planned for the baby, but as darkness fell, I would get what I call *the worries*. One moment I could be laughing, retelling stories of the day, paying bills, gazing at the ultrasound with excitement, but when the sun went down, I would look over at Richard with an expression that yelled, "Help! What are we doing?" Undoubtedly, a chapter of our lives was closing, and we had no idea what the rest of our story would entail. Fear overwhelmed me. Were these really my last days of unplanned shopping trips? Were these my last days of lounging around, taking naps and leisurely bubble baths? Were these really the last swear words I would be able to utter because in a few weeks I would have to be a role model? Richard and I began going to movies at least once a weekend knowing our freewheeling days were over. Every time we went to a restaurant we said, "Well, this will be our last time dining out alone." It was almost like we were counting down the last days of our lives. Instead of being told we were being given the precious gift of a baby, it was as if a doctor told us we were given a terminal disease. I was utterly terrified, until the sun came up the next day.

The Gift of a Grandson

Besides my parenting worries, we still hadn't told any other members of our family about the baby, and we were already defensive about what their reactions might be. We had some legitimate reasons to worry. Both sets of parents grew up in a time when racial tension was at its peak. Some of our relatives have been known to make off-color comments about other races. Would they be able to put their prejudices aside to wholeheartedly welcome our son into the family? The weekend following our meeting with Tamyka, we decided to find out. I bought two kids' books called *What Grandmas and Grandpas Do Best* highlighting various special activities that grandparents and grandchildren enjoy together. In the front cover of each I pasted a library card and on it wrote *Baby Boy Bowman due June 2008* and included a copy of the ultrasound. I put the books in cute blue bags.

My parents came to visit and I presented them with the package. My mom opened the book, looked at the ultrasound and asked the obvious question, "You're pregnant?" She jumped up with spryness that belied her 77 years and gave both Richard and me a hug. I explained that no, we were not pregnant (and felt the familiar stab at my heart) but we were chosen by a birth mother, and we were going to be parents in just about six weeks. We said he was African-American and waited for her reaction. I was not surprised when she said, "He's black? Who cares?" The excitement my family displayed buoyed us and made us more confident and excited. It was going to be okay after all.

That night, we drove to Richard's parents' house. While their reaction was somewhat guarded, Richard and I knew they would be happy for us once they understood the magnitude of Tamyka's sacrifice, that she was giving us hope where before there had only been despair.

CHAPTER 14

The Adoption Express

As the few short remaining weeks before our child was born flew by, I waited for my maternal instinct to kick in. I remember asking Jen if she had felt like a mother the moment she was shown Colton's ultrasound, and she wholeheartedly said she had. Even Kevin cried when he saw it. Obsessing too much on the adage *Be careful what you wish for; you might get it*, I feared that since the baby wasn't ours biologically, there was a chance we wouldn't "click." There would be this 20 inch bald person in our house looking at me and me looking at him—both of us thinking—"this is *so* not going to work out." I knew I had every capability of being a parent, but did I have what it took to be a mommy? I had a long way to go in two short months, but it was a journey I had to take to be sure this wasn't going to be the biggest mistake of our lives.

I compare this mental expedition to a physical journey. This was no leisurely hike across Europe gazing at glorious castles and lounging in exotic locations. This was an intense, one-way mission traveled on the supersonic Adoption Express.

First, we prepared for the journey. Even though in Laura and John's adoption, Tina told them not to even buy a crib, our social worker made no mention of being overly cautious. Transforming our guest bedroom into a nursery made this child seem more like reality instead of a dream. We splashed a coat of bright green paint on the walls, decorated with vintage toys, bought a beautiful crib, fixed up an old wardrobe that was mine when I was a little girl, and created a room ready for our little prince. With every item we bought, I felt my maternal instinct (that I was worried was nonexistent) go up a notch. Making a checklist of items needed for a new baby helped calm my obsessive compulsive side. It was as if everything I could check off took me one step closer to mommyhood. Imagining his likes and dislikes, I picked out clothes, blankets, and books: he would look fantastic in greens and yellows, he would adore books about puppies, and he was going to love making mud pies with his mom and dad. As I sat rocking in his nursery, I looked around at the homey touches: a hand stitched blanket, the Playskool phone with instructions to call Wyatt and Grandma, the picture frame that held the image of Richard, a pregnant Tamyka, and me with the saying "Loved From the Start," and I felt an ache in my arms for the first time. I was ready to hold our son.

Next, we had to take care of our baggage—primarily, our concerns about our family's reaction and our imagined societal reaction to our multiracial family. For the most part, we had faith in our families. We knew we wouldn't have to worry about blatant racism, but what would we do if someone made a racist remark or an off-color joke? Would we always have to be on guard? Then, on the next visit to my mom, I received a present that put my fears to rest. She had knit for the baby a doll with blue trousers, yellow suspenders, a red hat—and black skin. I knew with this simple, heartfelt gift, our baby was going to be loved and accepted.

As far as society, there wasn't much we could control. Richard and I had long talks about what our lives might be like. We braced ourselves for inappropriate comments and curious looks. I knew I would have to toughen up. I stepped up the miles, hoping that under the influence of my runner's high, I would reach some sort of epiphany to quiet my inner turmoil. During my hours on the road, I tried to picture his face, imagine his tiny hands as they reached for me, and envision him sleeping in his father's arms or riding on Richard's shoulders smiling wide and easy instead of focusing on how other people might react to him and our family. These images assured me that although our family might be different, it was going to be extraordinary. Richard and I have always lived by the credo "be the change you wish to see in the world," and we were ready to do so. Our baggage was checked.

Next, we had to name our destination. After much deliberation, we decided to name our son *Atticus* after the beloved character in *To Kill a Mockingbird*. It was strong name with a special connotation. The novel's themes as shown through the courage of Atticus Finch are to never judge a person until you have walked in his shoes and to always protect the innocent. We hoped our son would live his life with the same strength and fortitude of my favorite literary character.

If Atticus was our destination, Tamyka was our pilot, and we had complete faith in our safe arrival. We were so proud of Atticus' birth mom's strength and determination. Even though she was eight months pregnant, she still had plans to attend her senior prom, and though she was due the day after her graduation, Tamyka had no doubt that she would be able to walk across the stage to get her diploma and attend a party or two before the next day when she would deliver our son. At times the pessimist in me worried that her confidence in her decision to place her child for adoption and her seeming emotional distance from her son was too good to be true. Was she simply bottling up her true feelings? I voiced my concerns to Richard that perhaps the baby wasn't a reality to her, just as he wasn't a reality to me at first. If all it took to turn him into a real person for me was a few trips to Target, what would the bonding that takes place in the later stages of pregnancy do for Tamyka?

We wanted to be sure she was making the right decision because we wanted her in our lives after Atticus was born. Before we knew anyone who adopted, we envisioned birth mothers in a negative light. They gave up their babies; what kind of people could do such a thing? Then, we met Wyatt's birth mother, Amanda: a beautiful, caring, intelligent girl who became almost like a daughter to John and Laura. We thought Tamyka would be an Amanda whom we would get to know and welcome into our family. We protected her as if she already was family. If anyone had a negative comment to say about her or suggested she would change her mind, we became disgusted and insisted Tamyka was solid.

During the first week of May, Tamyka called us for the first time. I asked her how everything was going, and she said really well except that she was having trouble getting to her doctor appointments because she didn't have a car. Her mom would cosign for one, but she was too busy to do so.

Silence.

In my urgency to fill the dead phone line, I said that we would be happy to cosign for a loan, but that we couldn't because of the strong rule against giving money or favors to a birth mother. I said I'd ask Chelsea, and that we'd call her back later. In the back of my mind, my usually pessimistic mind, an alarm bell went off.

When I told Richard about the call, my ever optimistic husband questioned if she actually asked us to cosign for a loan or even for us to do anything about her car dilemma, or if I had rushed in with this option. I admitted that it was all me, and perhaps the car issue was small talk instead of the reason for the call. We called Chelsea, and she said we definitely couldn't cosign for a car, but that the agency could get her a free bus pass. In fact, she had offered this to Tamyka before, but she had turned it down, further evidence of Tamyka's pride and self-sufficiency. What a girl. Richard called her back and after chatting about prom and school, he told her what Chelsea said. Tamyka seemed very agreeable and ended the call by telling Richard about a teddy bear she had made for the baby and how she was going to put a picture of herself at prom on the bear. The sweetness was coming out; we had nothing to worry about.

Things Fall Apart

Then the turbulence began. The following week, Tamyka had an appointment with Chelsea to discuss the birth plan which spells out what exactly happens at the hospital, and it would be the first actual signed document stating her intentions to place her baby for adoption. When Chelsea called to tell us Tamyka was sick and had to cancel, she told us not to worry because she had rescheduled the appointment for right away the next week. In my mind, at prom she had met up with the birth father, resplendent in his white tux and glowing smile; they made amends, were planning on getting married, keeping the baby, and moving into a duplex. For someone who had nothing to worry about, I was worrying a great deal.

Our social worker was the flight attendant on the Adoption Express. She welcomed us aboard, voiced safety concerns, and tried to ensure smooth sailing. While she served warm cookies and Diet Pepsi, smiled, looked nice, and fully expected us to reach our destination, she was also the one well versed in flight disasters. Her job was to explain the worst possible scenario without having people refuse to get on board. She assured us that Atticus' birth father hadn't attended the prom; in fact, he was in prison. Our sweet, strong, intelligent birth mother dating a man who was sent to prison? It was tragic the way Tamyka must have been taken in by such a hardened criminal, we thought. Knowing that our son's birth father was incarcerated was a little unsettling. What was his crime? We hoped that little Atticus' genes didn't come from a violent person. We patiently waited for another week to pass until Tamyka's next appointment.

Another cancellation, another rescheduling. Tamyka was still sick. We felt so sorry for her. How terrible to be sick and have the stress of finishing the school year, all just weeks from delivering a baby and placing him for adoption. I thought we should call Tamyka, but Chelsea didn't think we should pressure her. As long as she was rescheduling the appointments, we were fine.

Mother's Day arrived. This was the first one I would be able to celebrate, but I didn't feel like celebrating. At church that day, the priest offered a blessing for all the mothers in the congregation. When he asked everyone to stand, Richard urged me to join in because in just a few short weeks I would be a mother. Atticus might not be in my belly, but he was in our hearts. I was his mom. Somehow, though, it just didn't seem right. With Tamyka's cancelled appointments, and how she didn't follow through on her promise to send prom pictures, doubt kept me seated in the pew. Tears trickled down my cheeks. Richard pulled me close to him and whispered in my ear that everything was going to be all right and that I was a mom. I began thinking how Tamyka must have been feeling on that day. Perhaps she was sad too, mourning her imminent loss. I decided that I would call her the next day. What did we have to lose?

So I called her. Tamyka answered the phone and gone was the loquacious girl we had talked to a few weeks ago. I told her it was me, and she said "hi." I asked her how she was feeling and she said "better." I asked her how prom was and she said "fine." I told her we were thinking about her, especially on

Mother's Day, and she said "oh." Classic angry, disinterested teen-speak. For all of Tamyka's one word answers, her unspoken message was clear: *I am having second thoughts.*

The next day, we learned that she had missed another appointment with Chelsea but hadn't called to reschedule. Our always friendly, informational stewardess said that some mothers pull away at this point and don't make a birth plan. We remembered Jen experiencing some of these same issues with Leah, and their adoption still went through. Richard and I began to think that perhaps Tamyka was planning to deliver the baby and then call us. Maybe she just didn't want the pressure of having us at the hospital. We begged Chelsea to call Tamyka to see what was going on, but she refused. Then she dropped a real bombshell. Very matter of fact, as if she were telling us the lunch special, she said we might never hear from Tamyka again. She could have changed her mind, and sometimes birth moms will just sever all contact with the adoptive parents and the adoption agency. This scenario seemed unimaginable to me.

We still had three weeks until the due date, so we tried to hang on to a thread of hope. I feverishly looked at our adoption website and to my horror discovered three other couples had been matched during the time we were waiting for Atticus. As selfish and foolish as this sounds, I felt jealousy and anger towards these couples who were going to be parents to babies that could have been ours. If Tamyka was not going to go through with this adoption, how long would we wait until we put ourselves back into the pool of prospective parents? Chelsea couldn't give any advice; she said it was up to us. But how could we just turn our backs on little Atticus? There was still a chance this adoption could go through. We desperately tried to call Tamyka, but her phone was disconnected. As the days passed with no word from her, we fastened our seatbelts, crossed our fingers, and waited for the due date.

Surprisingly, on the Sunday before Atticus was due, the phone rang. It was Tamyka. I sank to my knees in relief as I heard her tremulous, desperate voice say, "I'm worried. This is my son. I want to know him." It broke my heart to realize she was only now trying to come to terms with her decision. I anxiously tried to assure her she would know him; we would make every effort to let her see him and to update her on his life. I told her how important it was to us for Atticus to know his birth mom. Then, she asked if she would be able to pick him up on weekends and holidays and said she would maybe like to take him home with her when she came for a home visit with Chelsea.

The plane was plummeting, and Richard and I braced for a crash landing. The questions she asked showed she envisioned this not as an adoption but a shared custody. I tried to assure her as much as I could without making promises. As desperately as we wanted a child, I wasn't about to lie to this young girl to get him. Tamyka's apprehension seemed somewhat calmed, and she told me that she would have her mother call us when she went into labor.

She wanted us there with her at the delivery. Tamyka was going to hold tough. We were back on course.

Immediately, we contacted Chelsea to describe our conversation. She promised to have a serious discussion with Tamyka about the reality of adoption when she came in for her appointment. Even though we heard the doubt in Chelsea's voice, Richard and I had renewed faith. After all, Tamyka had called us. We focused on her wish for us to be there when Atticus arrived. We were circling for a landing.

In that final week, I went crazy making final preparations for our new arrival. Reading that birth moms often feel sad leaving the hospital empty handed, Richard and I went to Build-a-Bear to create matching bears for Tamyka and Atticus. We placed the hearts in each bear and our Professor of Bearology told us to make a wish and to kiss each heart before they were sewn into them. Richard wished happiness for Atticus, and I wished that Tamyka would have the strength to bless us with this baby. Where our faith in Tamyka might have been wavering, our faith in Build-a-Bear was strong. I made daily trips to Target to scour the baby department for items I might have forgotten. I prepared a basket to give to Tamyka filled with chocolate Hugs and Kisses, cookies, flowers, and a cute baby album to assure her that we would send pictures. I created a memory book for her to fill out with advice for Atticus, family memories, and her wishes for him. I packed the diaper bag and printed off the directions to the hospital. Then we heard—again Tamyka didn't keep her appointment with Chelsea. We figured we were so close to our destination that that didn't even matter. This plane was coming down if I had to land it myself.

Tamyka's due date arrived. I put Richard on strict orders to stay close to home and to have his cell phone with him at all times. Every time the phone rang I practically lost my mind, but it was always just a family member or friend calling to see if we had heard anything yet. My shopping and nesting reached a manic level. I tried to remain positive, but I couldn't help thinking that the odds might not be in our favor. I read that one in three adoptions fall through, so if Laura's and Jen's were successful, did that make ours the unlucky third?

One day past the due date.

We were calm; first babies were usually late. As a way to close the deal, we decided to create a playground in our back yard. We pulled sod, brought in loads and loads of mulch, and filled the area with slides, climbers, a swing set, a castle, and even a rocket ship. Even though in our rational minds we knew Atticus would be too little to play on these for at least a year, it was like Kevin Costner's character in *A Field of Dreams*. If we build the playground, Atticus will come. There was no way this grand gesture could be ignored. Our sweat, aching backs, and strained muscles were a final plea for our son.

As the days went by and we built our shrine, doubt set in again. Chelsea told us doctors usually won't let pregnancies go past a week, especially if the patient is on state funded medical care.

Maybe her due date was wrong. Maybe she had had the baby and wanted to spend her time in the hospital privately saying goodbye to her son and then later would call us to pick him up. Maybe something was wrong with the baby.

Maybe she had the gestation period of an elephant.

Throughout this time we continued to call Chelsea, and in each conversation she sounded bleak. Our flight attendant was showing us the emergency exit, but we didn't want to go. I began calling the hospital and asking to be connected to Tamyka's room in the hope that she was indeed checked in, but each time they said she hadn't been admitted. Had we missed her, or could we keep our dream going? Our son was out there somewhere, waiting for us.

The phone calls from friends and family changed in tone from excited and inquisitive to morose and disappointed. They opened with a somber, "How are you doing?" We insisted that we were still waiting for the phone call. Our hearts said she was going to call. Our brains said she might call. Our guts, churning with dread, told us the truth. She would never call. Chelsea suggested we choose a date to end our waiting and then assume Tamyka had changed her mind. We begged her to go to Tamyka's house to check on her, but she said it would be too confrontational. She had our phone numbers; if she wanted to talk to us, she would. To us, if Chelsea had a good relationship with Tamyka, it wouldn't be confrontational, it would be showing concern. If Chelsea didn't even know Tamyka enough to go to her house, did she know her enough to be sure adoption was the right choice for her? Couldn't she at least clandestinely drive by to see if she could learn anything? Couldn't she try to find something out from the hospital, off the record? What if Tamyka had had the baby and initially thought she would keep him but changed her mind after a few sleepless nights? With no contact from any of us, she would think in her teenage mind that we were "mad" at her for not calling us and wouldn't take Atticus after the fact.

My adoption friends rallied around us. Grace could relate to the pain Richard and I were feeling. Ginger, remembering her own difficult journey, gave us hope that somehow a family was in our future. Jen, who was still in the hospital recovering from her c-section and caring for her premature son, said if she could drive, she would camp out at the adoption agency until someone found something out about Atticus. Laura called Tina to try to get some answers and to ask how this could have possibly happened to us. Our building anger and frustration was directed entirely, albeit completely misguidedly, at our flight attendant, who was still serving us pretzels as the plane was engulfed in flames.

Paradise Lost

June fifteenth was our seventeenth anniversary and Father's Day. Thirteen days after the due date. The date that we officially decided to give up on our baby. I hid Richard's Father's Day gift which I had so joyously bought and wrapped so many weeks before. There was no Atticus to fill the *Daddy and Me* frame, no Atticus to wear the *I Love My Daddy* sleeper, no Atticus to teach about life with the books on raising strong sons. After the Mother's Day fiasco at church, I refused to go to church and have another meltdown when, for another year, I had to look at my husband sitting, head down, while all of the fathers stood to receive their blessing as their blessings slept on their shoulders, held their hands, or sat on their laps. We half-heartedly finished the playground which we christened *The Land of Pretending*, went to a movie (*Kung Fu Panda* in a theater filled with laughing children), and drowned our sorrow in cheesecake.

Then, we made the calls to our families and friends saying what they had known for days, we weren't going to get our baby. Their disappointment, coupled with the anger and disbelief at our lack of closure, not only increased our sadness, but made us feel like colossal idiots. Any faith our families had in the domestic adoption process, which we assured them was nothing like the urban myths they had all heard, was gone. Tamyka turned out to be exactly as they all expected, but we continued to stand up for her, saying she was young, and that she loved her baby. How could we begrudge her that?

But a part of us did. When we took off our rose colored glasses, we realized that Tamyka was no paragon, nor was she the devil incarnate. She was a person who had to make the toughest decision of her life. We only wished that she would have had the fortitude to call Chelsea, write us a note, or at least have her mother let us know what had happened. Even for a nineteen year old girl, to leave us completely in the dark was cold. In order to have some sort of closure on our end, I sent her a letter congratulating her on the birth of her son, telling her we weren't mad about her decision to parent, and wishing her and her child, our Atticus, a happy life. We never received a response.

Our emotions bounced from sadness to anger. When well meaning friends said this baby wasn't meant to be ours, we couldn't agree. Of course he was meant to be ours. Atticus had his name on the wall over his crib and engraved in bricks declaring *Atticus' Garden* amongst red geraniums I had planted for him. People said our baby was still out there. Where? At that time, the adoption agency wasn't working with any birth mothers. Three couples had been picked while we were waiting for our son, and since then many couples were added: cute, energetic, successful, loving, young couples. More competition. We thought of Jen and Kevin and their beautiful son Colton. Everything worked out so perfectly for them. We thought of John, Laura, and Wyatt, and how literally overnight they had become parents. What were the chances we would have such an extraordinary story? Luck like that just was never in the Bowman cards. A full house was not in our deck.

Even though we had traveled nowhere in our two month whirlwind from being picked to having a failed adoption and had experienced such profound sadness and disappointment, the trip was not for nothing. Remembering again Laura's view of what we had to learn, we had actually learned a lot. In those two months we came to love a child, and it made us grow as prospective parents. If we were ever lucky enough to be picked again, we wouldn't be ambivalent about it. We wouldn't second guess what other people might think. We would just be grateful and accept him with every fiber of our beings. Through experiencing the loss of Atticus, we would be able to somewhat empathize with the loss a birth mother must feel when she hands her baby into another woman's arms and be more sensitive to her needs. We learned our lives wouldn't be fulfilled without having a child to love, and we knew that we had to risk another heartbreak if we wanted to have a family, but how could we endure another disappointment?

After searching our hearts, we decided we would give it one more shot. We called the adoption agency, got back into the pool, and then Richard and I sat in our newly erected swings in our empty, quiet playground and hoped.

CHAPTER 15

The Summer of our Discontent

When I pictured my summer of 2007, I saw days filled with Atticus and me visiting Daddy at work, going to Grandma's, and quiet evenings on the porch swing after hot days. Tired days, sweaty days, happy days. Family days. It was a dream. In reality, it might have been three months full of raging diaper rash, power outages due to summer storms, and humidity that made baby and mommy stick together. A mixture of it all would still have been heaven.

Instead, it was back to the usual routine with a few exceptions. Since I was planning on having a child at home, I missed out on my usual summer school job which gave us our summer "fun money." This was depressing considering we could have used that money to pay for the lawyer bills that managed to arrive even if our baby didn't. The freedoms I had so valued and thought I would miss, like day long shopping sessions and leisurely naps, seemed empty. I trained for another marathon, as if each punishing workout would pound out the devastation that had seeped into my bones. Again I thought, if I can do something as hard as this, I am worthy of a second chance.

At least three times a day I checked the adoption website to see if anyone was being placed. It was a slow summer—more couples were added, but the agency wasn't working with any birth mothers. We forced ourselves to think positively. We were picked pretty quickly the first time, so maybe we'd have another baby by the end of summer. Unfortunately, there were no babies.

Summer turned into fall, and school started again. I dreaded going back to field the questions of "what happened" all over again. I had sent out an e-mail to the entire school briefly telling what happened in order to ward off the astonished "what are you doing here" looks I was trying to avoid. I just wanted to put the debacle behind us. I wished I had a shirt that read, "Please ignore me." The only saving grace was that I had, thankfully, resisted the urge

160

the previous school year to tell my students that I was going to be on maternity leave in the fall.

One result of letting so many people know what had happened was the knowledge that our pain of not having children was not exclusive to us. One of my fellow teachers who also suffered from infertility explained how she prayed about her situation, and God told her that her kids at school were to be her children. It moved me so much that someone could have such faith. When I thought about the roster I had for students, I was glad God hadn't given me the same message.

But what was the message we were supposed to get from this heartbreaking experience? We considered in vitro again, even though I had just turned the magic number of reduced success, 38. Plus, we would have to pay for the battery of tests again since over a year had passed, but at least our lives wouldn't be in the power of some hormonal teenager. We were back to where we were the previous year, entertaining all of the "what ifs" again. They had moved back into the Bowman household like termites gnawing away at our peace of mind. I felt like Dorothy in *The Wizard of Oz* who was just waiting to be swept away to a place where my dreams would come true.

The Son also Rises

Then came the tornado. On the most depressing day of the year, September 11, our lives changed forever. When I heard my cell phone ring while I was in study hall and saw that it was Tina, I thought, *this is it*. When she told me I had better sit down, which I knew from Laura's experience was Tina-speak for "your baby's here," I had a feeling of déjà vu from a few months before when Chelsea had called with the same news. The only difference was that this baby was already born and ready to be picked up. And, just like Dorothy, we stepped from our black and white world into one of Technicolor wonder.

A young woman had given birth to a baby boy that morning (in the same hospital Wyatt had been born two years before), and she had chosen us to be his parents. Ana was in her mid-twenties, already had two children, and could not afford a third. The baby's biological father was out of the picture. Tina thought Ana was solid in her decision. Ana had been told what had happened with Atticus, and Tina told her she had to be "really sure" if she was going to choose us. Could we come down on Saturday to pick him up? Ana thought it would be too painful to meet us, so Tina said to come after she had checked out of the hospital. I took a moment to digest what had just happened, and just like the previous spring, I told my best friends at work and called Laura to tell her the news. Even though I had only one day to get ready for a six week sub, my mind couldn't comprehend lesson plans or anything else. Only, *this is it. I'm a Mom!* How was I going to tell Richard for the second time that he was already a father? I decided to recreate how I told him the first time, but this time there would be a happy ending.

I rushed home and barely got in the door when the phone rang. Again, it was Tina. She had talked Ana into meeting us, and could we come to the hospital the next morning? My 37 hours to create six weeks of lesson plans, prepare my room for a sub, clean my entire house, write the birth mom a letter, buy her a gift, pack for us and the baby, and not to mention become emotionally ready to turn into a mom had now been reduced to 14 hours. My brain could barely keep up.

I quickly brought Bailey in, tied a note around her neck with the message "In the presence of Love, miracles happen" and I added "this one is for keeps." I donned on the same old "boy" shirt and tried to calm my racing nerves as I waited for my husband to come home. When Richard came in, read the note, and saw my shirt, all he could say was, "No way." Elatedly, I told him, "Richard, our baby is already born. We are going to meet him tomorrow." I think initially you could have knocked him over with a hiccup, but once the realization set in, a smile I had never seen before crept over his face. The smile of a dad.

We decided not to tell anyone besides Laura and John about our astonishing news in case something went wrong. Anyway, we didn't have time for phone calls. I made a list of what had to be done. We quickly ate dinner, dashed to the store, and bought a modest sapphire (the baby's birthstone) necklace for Ana and two little girl's necklaces with three hearts symbolizing all three siblings for Ana's daughters. I resurrected some of Tamyka's coming-home-from-the-hospital basket, replaced all of the chocolates I ate in my depression, and bought flowers.

By the time we arrived home at about 10:00, we sat down to brainstorm a list of names. Could we still name him Atticus? No, that would imply that Atticus never was, and even in all of our excitement, our love for that little boy wasn't forgotten. We both grabbed a baby name book and wrote down the possibilities. Then, we read our lists, crossed off the names that were definitely out, and looked at what was left: Finnegan, Casey, and Riley. We would wait to meet him to make the final decision.

We cleaned our house, packed our overnight bag, and installed the car seat. After one hour of sleep we dressed and took a picture of ourselves to document our last moments before becoming parents. The snapshot showed Richard and me holding a yellow bear, our first gift to our son, and our faces were lit with the first glow of parenthood.

In our frenzy to get ready, we kept imagining the moment of meeting our son and Ana. How should we act when we met her? What if she didn't like me? What if I didn't radiate enough warmth? How would we react if she fell apart? Remembering the stories of the intense emotion of Jen's and Laura's hospital meetings with Colton's and Wyatt's birth moms, we were extremely nervous. I packed *two* bottles of deodorant in preparation for sweating like I've never sweat before.

We left early so I could stop at school to prepare my sub for the day. I intended to keep the reason for my absence a secret, but when my plan to be gone from school before my first hour started didn't happen, I told my class I would see them in six weeks because my husband and I were going to go pick up our baby. They clapped and hooted and hollered—it was a sendoff like we were going off to win a state basketball championship.

We drove to the hospital and played every possible scenario in our heads. Should we bring the basket in right away? Should we take pictures? When should we give her the gift? What should we do if Ana starts crying? What will the first moments with our son be like?

As we pulled into the parking ramp, Tina called. Our stomachs sank as we recalled stories I had read on the Internet about couples getting to the hospital and then being called to turn around and go home because the birth mom changed her mind. Lucky for us, Tina just called to see where we were and said she would meet us in the lobby. When we met up with her, we sat down, and Tina outlined what would happen. Ana was upstairs waiting, and she wanted to place the baby in my arms. We would visit for a short while and then Ana would go home since she was already discharged.

Second to the Right, and Straight on Till Morning

We went up the same elevator John and Laura were in two years ago to meet Wyatt; the coincidence was surreal. As we got out of the elevator, a fog seemed to settle over me. I slowed down, lagging behind Tina and Richard as my mind tried to process what was about to happen. It couldn't; some events are just too big for thought. Experiencing tunnel vision, I barely noticed on the periphery a few nurses who obviously wanted to see the gathering of the new family. Finally, I saw a woman holding a little bundle with dark hair. All of the emotions that I had built up came out in that moment, and I began to shake all over. Ana placed the baby, our son, in my arms and Richard quickly ushered me over to a chair probably worrying that my shaking would give him a concussion or that my legs would go out from under me.

As much as we imagined and waited for what will always be known as *The Moment*, there are no words to express the feeling of having that baby in my arms, eyes wide open, alert, neck straining to get a look at his new parents just as we couldn't get enough of looking at him, drinking him in. To quote Dr. Seuss, our hearts "grew three sizes that day." He was astonishingly beautiful with his tiny mouth, pursed lips, steely grip, and luminous dark eyes. I cried (Tina, in her infinite wisdom, was right about the crying after all) at the wonder of it all—the baby, the generosity and tremendous heart of Ana, the miracle of the moment. Gratitude enveloped me. We tried to say thank-you, but these words seemed so small. How do you say thank you to someone who is doing something so brave that you could never do in a million years? Ana told us this was the nicest thing she had ever done, and we could tell holding on to this thought was giving her strength. Ana explained how she couldn't afford another child, and she had to take care of the two she already had at home.

After a few minutes, Tina ushered the baby, Richard, and me into a room next door while she talked with Ana. It was ironic that now, when we had finally finished waiting for our baby to arrive, the room we were put into was a *waiting* room. We took turns holding our little boy and wallowed in our happiness. We fed him his tiny bottle, whispered reassuring words as he studied us, and snapped a few photos of these first minutes alone. Tina came back in and said Ana had cried, but she was ready to let him go. Ana walked in, watched us with the baby, and showed me how to burp him. Then, after another minute, she asked, looking into my eyes, "Are you going to be okay?" With the burping? With the baby? With our entire lives changing in a moment? We answered "yes," and then she said she was going to go. We thanked her again, she promised to send pictures of her and the girls, and Ana courageously walked out the door.

Richard and I looked at each other in amazement. We had gotten off easy. No speeches needed to be made, and although tears had been shed, they were mostly mine and Tina's. We marveled at Ana's strength. We knew, though, underneath her tough exterior her heart was breaking just as ours were made whole. Adoption creates such a dichotomy of emotions. I voiced my concerns saying it was sad that in order for Richard and me to be given everything, Ana had to lose everything. Tina, the voice of reason, reminded us that Ana still had her other two children, and that she was providing for all three of them by making this decision.

Tina left with a promise to come back later, and we were checked into a hospital room. We talked about how we were going to introduce this little guy to the rest of the family, and had only told my sister Peggy, again making her the secret keeper by proxy of distance since she lives in Indiana. She was, of course, ecstatic and demanded that we check in with her hourly. Later, the nurse came in and insisted our baby needed a name. After a moment's deliberation, we chose Riley which means valiant. There was no one braver than our son who had just been born the day before and had been given to two complete strangers who didn't know much about caring for a baby. Riley Richard Bowman.

The next day, after calling my other sisters with our miraculous news and surprising my niece and her daughter with our new family member, we made the trip home. Richard and I couldn't stop looking at Riley in his blue and purple striped knit hat. How brave, how valiant. When we approached our driveway we saw a Welcome Baby balloon by our mailbox, and I knew the Schmitts had stopped by. Flowers and a basket full of baby goodies were waiting by our door. *Welcome home, Riley.*

Our first night home I fell completely in love with my son. Overwhelmed with emotion, I rocked Riley, sang to him, and told him stories. I was his mother, and it seemed like he knew it by the way he looked at me with such trust. When he went to sleep in his bassinet for the first time that night, I missed Riley so much I wrote him a letter telling him how much he meant to me. This was the same girl who three months before thought she'd prefer *Battlestar Galactica* to motherhood. All of the fears and doubts I harbored drifted away and disappeared in a baby's breath.

The next day we took Riley to meet all of his grandparents. We knocked on their doors and asked, "Are there any grandparents who live here?" When we walked in with Riley, they were completely shocked. After being convinced Riley was really ours and not just some kid we were babysitting for the afternoon, our parents welcomed our little boy with their entire hearts. As both sets of grandparents had also been great-grandparents for a few years, I know their "surprise" grandson is a special gift in their lives.

We had our beautiful baby, a birth mother who seemed solid, and 30 days to wait for the TPR hearing. We spent that time introducing him to more friends and family members and adjusting to parenthood. Through the fog of the sleepless, we opened our door to a stream of visitors: Grace with baked ziti, Jen with chili, Ginger with chicken and dumplings, and Laura with hamburger soup. Richard and I were so grateful for these friends who knew from experience that even though I wasn't recovering from giving birth, I was still an overwhelmed new mother who didn't have the energy to put dinner on the table. Jenny brought us baby books and a calming influence: here was a veteran mother who assured us we would sleep again, someday. Our house was the image of a new family—a couch transformed into a makeshift bed, baby bottles in the sink waiting to be washed, *What to Expect the First Year* on the end table ready to be referenced, and a beautiful baby, sleeping in his bassinet, unaware of the chaos around him. It all seemed too easy, too perfect, and not the way the Bowmans actually do business. Where was the drama? Where was the shocking twist?

To Have and Have Not

The shock came when we were only a week into parenthood. Tina called. Riley's birth father, Carlos, was going to contest the adoption.

When Tina told me, I couldn't process the bad news. I said "okay," and then I repeated what she said, "He's contesting it?" This was the birth father, the "out of the picture, nothing to worry about" man. Well, he *was* in the picture, and we began to worry. Tina and our lawyer assured us that he didn't have a case. At best he could slow down the proceedings and make it more costly, but the end result was Riley wasn't going to be taken away from us. Often, they explained, birth fathers make a big deal when first notified, but they rarely followed through with trying to regain custody once they make their initial displeasure known.

The follow through came in a heartfelt letter we received a few days later. Riley's birth father wanted to see his son and to meet us before he would consider signing away his rights. The drama that we missed in Ana was going to come to fruition through Carlos. We frantically called Tina, who tried to reassure us, but in those few days waiting for the meeting, I don't think Riley left our arms for more than a few hours. There was no way we were going to let him go.

Richard and I had no idea what to expect. Because of our fear of losing Riley, we were on the defensive and anticipated the worst. Deep down, we knew it was a good thing that Carlos wanted to meet his son, that one day Riley would be happy to hear that both parents knew him, loved him, and wanted what was best for him. We decided that all we could do was to show how much we loved little Riley.

Another trip, another meeting with a person who could give us everything or take it all away. Richard and I reminded ourselves not to refer to Riley as ours and to try to remain as open minded as possible. At the adoption agency, we waited nervously while Riley basked in the attention of the two social workers. At the exact meeting time, in walked Carlos, his two kids, and a roommate. Strength in numbers. We stood with smiles on our faces all the way around: all nervous, all defensive, all terrified.

After introductions, Tina invited us all to sit down. We immediately asked if Carlos wanted to hold his son, and he looked at us with Riley's brown eyes and Riley's round face and nodded with tears in his eyes. Carlos sat, cradled Riley in his arms, and looked at him with amazement and desperation, as if he wanted to memorize every aspect of his little boy. Riley looked back. I felt that in that moment Riley had a sense of their connection; it was palpable. All I could feel was sadness for Carlos. Would this be the first and last time he saw his son?

Riley was passed around to Carlos' daughter and son, neither of them wanting to relinquish their brother for the next pair of arms. The children, 10 and 15, understandably were not in favor of the adoption. They looked and found similar physical characteristics (hairlines in the shape of "M's" and beautiful, inquisitive brown eyes) and were enamored with Riley. We had made a copy of our profile to give to the family, and Richard paged through it with the kids to break the ice. After half an hour, Carlos asked if he could talk to Richard and me privately. Here it was, the moment of truth. Everyone else left the room.

Carlos began telling us about his family and how he ended up in an unfortunate financial circumstance. He said that we probably made more money in one day than he made in a month, which hit me like a bullet. More than anything, I didn't want the decision to place Riley for adoption to be about money. Carlos had visited a lawyer to see how much it would be to contest the adoption, and he vowed he would find a way to do it if he didn't feel right about us. He wanted to be assured that we would allow him to be a part of Riley's life, and that we would teach Riley to speak Spanish since he was part Puerto Rican.

With tears streaming down his face, he spoke directly to Riley, telling him how much he loved him and how he knew in his heart he was doing what was best for him. Carlos told Riley he was born his son, but now (he looked at Richard and me) he was "our" son. All of ours. He wanted Riley to have a better life than he did with opportunities that he would never be able to give him. Riley, our valiant one, listened. Carlos explained to us how important children were in his family and how his mother always told him that you couldn't give up on your kids. Carlos' way of not giving up was *by* giving him up. He said he had come to this meeting prepared to fight to keep his son, but after meeting us and seeing how much we loved Riley, he was going to do what he knew in his heart was right—he was going to sign the papers.

The Truth of Our Story

Carlos gave Riley back to us and left to speak privately with the social workers. Alone in the room, Richard and I hugged Riley and broke down as relief flooded over us. We were completely, emotionally drained. Being witness to such pain, strength, and goodness was something I don't think we'll ever experience again. Both of Riley's birth parents amazed us with their selflessness, and we see it as our honor to always assure Riley that he comes from tremendous people who love him very much. That moment, we decided to give Riley a second middle name, *Manuel*, Carlos' middle name, which means "God is with us." Dr. Martin Luther King, Jr. once said, "Faith is taking the first step even when you don't see the whole staircase." God was certainly in that tiny adoption office that day watching over all of us and guiding us up that staircase.

The papers were ready to be signed, and Carlos insisted we watch him sign them so that we wouldn't have to worry any longer. Then, Riley was passed around again. The arms were tighter this time in knowledge that the meeting was almost over and they didn't know when or if they'd ever hold Riley again. It was time to say good-bye, even though the Rosales family probably wanted at least three more pass-arounds. We hugged each other and promised to keep in touch and to take care of "our" son.

*

The morning of Riley's TPR hearing, at the time when I knew his birth mother was in court giving up her parental rights, I rocked my beautiful son and held him extra close. His brown eyes locked with mine, and I breathed in his baby smell. Kissing his forehead, I promised him his father and I would love him enough for all of us: Ana, Carlos, his brother and sisters, and the rest of his biological family that he might not ever know. Our hearts would always be filled with them. We are all a part of Riley, just as he is a part of all of us, and I wouldn't want our family to be any other way.

*

A few weeks later I was given my first real chance to celebrate my new status as a mother in the time honored tradition of the baby shower. Hosted by Laura at Grace's house, the party had a literary theme, so my friends gave Riley either books or magazine subscriptions. Besides the standard children "must-reads," Riley received, from my fertile friend Jenny, books showcasing Spanish words (Carlos would be so proud), and nearly every other book I unwrapped were tales about adoption where animals find families in unexpected places.

Sitting in Grace's living room that day, I couldn't help but reflect on the incredible adoption stories shared by the women around me. While each of our stories was unique, all tales proclaimed the similar theme of how, ultimately, hope won out. Looking at Laura and Jen, I thought of our interwoven characters and connected plot lines—would I have even considered adoption if those two hadn't? (Only fellow English teachers would be so kind as to provide such extensive foreshadowing for their friend.) Then, contemplating Grace's story rife with conflicts unique to foster care adoption and Ginger's almost unbelievable tale set in exotic Russia, I couldn't help but acknowledge the old adage that sometimes truth truly is stranger than fiction.

That night, gazing at my sleeping son in the midst of his crayon-colored dreams, I thought, *here is the truth of our story*—our enchanting Riley, full of endless smiles, who made us a family.

PART IV

Ginger

"Hope doesn't come from calculating
whether the good news is winning out over the bad.
It's simply a choice to take action."

~Anna Lappe

I was that friend, the one who would wait years to sit beside my friends watching our children play.

Imaginary friends—I thought only preschoolers had them. When I first became pregnant, I envisioned my friends and myself having babies and raising our families together. In my mind, my friends and I would gaze at our babies chewing their own board books as we discussed the latest book club pick. We would push toddlers in strollers side by side on warm summer mornings as we chatted animatedly. We would sit together clutching cameras at our children's first kindergarten performance. I never imagined that one of these playmates would come from halfway around the world and with such an unbelievable story of her arrival.

I can easily picture Ginger purposefully and gracefully rushing down my elementary school hallway bearing her violin. For years, I'd seen her travel up and down our halls, briefly inhabit a classroom to conduct her music lesson, then rush back out to go to another class in another school. Occasionally, we would acknowledge one another as we crossed paths, but neither of us knew each other by name. It wasn't until a few years later that I would become familiar with this exuberant Greek storyteller trapped in a refined musician's body. When I became friends with Ginger, I also found the playmate for my firstborn that I'd always hoped for.

~Jenny Kalmon

CHAPTER 16

Bikes in the Driveway

On our wedding day, I was twenty-nine and Dick was fifty-one. Two years before reciting our vows we discussed the idea of marriage and a family. Dick had already raised three children from his previous marriage who were ready to start planning families of their own. Still, there he was standing in the House of Ludington courtyard with me in front of our minister and our nearest friends and relatives, fully aware of what was in store for him, while his friends were preparing for retirement and investing in golf course condominiums and motor homes. *What was he thinking?*

I was thinking, *this man was perfect father material.* A technology education teacher, he could fix practically anything, and he could cook. His penchant for duct-tape and the Weather Channel were also a plus. What was not to like? He was the man I wanted to father my child. He took care of everything. Without Dick, my car tires would never be rotated, and I'd be driving with expired license plates.

Luckily, Dick followed through with his promise, and though I don't want to share all the gory details of how I got pregnant, suffice it to say it involved too many day trips to a clinic forty-five minutes away.

"Don't worry, I'll get you pregnant," the fertility specialist said with a twinkle in his eye. "We try to mimic nature here, giving you the same probability of conceiving that you would have in the back of a '57 Chevy." A rather unsavory image, yes, but we were desperate.

Like Dick, the doctor also kept his promise. I knew I was pregnant right away. I ran out and bought *What to Eat When You're Expecting*. I spent hours going over my menu for the week, buying organic vegetables and eating eggs and broccoli until I smelled like a natural spring. After six weeks I couldn't contain it any longer and had to tell people. On a Friday after school, we threw our suitcases into the Jeep and headed for the Upper Peninsula of Michigan to share the news with my parents. I tried to be coy and clever in my delivery, but I'm not mature enough to pull that off. Instead, I went with a straight-forward approach and screamed, "I'm pregnant!"

Just as I reached the end of my first trimester, I miscarried. It makes it sound so routine, like I just dropped something, or missed a catch. However, our Little Peanut had actually *died*. I knew it when my breasts stopped hurting. I knew it when my belly wasn't bloated anymore. I knew it when I frantically placed a cell phone call to my gynecologist's office while traveling between elementary schools where I taught fifth and sixth grade orchestra. I knew it when I heard the receptionist transfer my call to the nurse's station. I knew it when I knew it, and then I went to the hospital for an ultrasound.

I remember chugging two 20-ounce bottles of water before heading over to the imaging wing of the hospital. I remember telling the receptionist that if my appointment didn't come up soon I was going to pee all over the floor. I remember her handing me a cup and telling me to only "fill it half way," not even meeting my eye and talking through pursed lips. I remember going into the bathroom, tossing the cup in the tall stainless steel trash can filled with stiff and crumpled paper toweling, falling onto the toilet seat, and completely emptying my bladder. I remember asking *why,* and then I formed my own hypothesis.

This was punishment for bad behavior in my youth, I reasoned. About one month before heading off to my freshman year of college, my period was two weeks late; and yes, I had good reason to worry.

During that time I was plagued by dreams of being the only pregnant student at the small private college I would be attending in the fall. I had no idea how I would tell my parents, and I prayed if I were pregnant I would miscarry. I decided that my parents would most likely kick me out of the house, and I may have to live in a refrigerator box in downtown Escanaba behind Mueller's Pizza with my viola as my only comfort. I prayed, *"Please God, don't let me be pregnant. I'll go to church every Sunday, and I'll never have sex again."* Did I consider having an abortion? Yes, I did.

Finally, on a humid August morning before I was supposed to take my grandmother on her Saturday morning errands, my period started. I vowed never to have sex again. Okay, so I vowed never to have sex again without *protection.*

Fifteen years later, as I sat in the ultra sound waiting area, I knew this miscarriage was some sort of divine retribution; I had gotten my pathetic wish. As I lay on the examining table with that clear gooey gel on my belly, I prayed again, *"Please God, let Peanut live."* The technician ran a probe over my lower abdomen pressing it into my bladder. I watched her face in the dim light trying to discern hope in her expression. "I suppose you can't tell me what you see, huh?"

"Sorry, no I can't," she said. I looked at the wall and swallowed. "Good luck with everything," she half-smiled as I left.

I don't remember walking from radiology to my doctor's office. I don't remember what I said to Dick who met me in Dr. Carlson's waiting room. I don't remember feeling anything but disconnected, as if I was having an out-of-body experience. I felt as if I were behind the lens of a camera, filming someone else. *Was this really happening to me?*

I sat on the edge of my seat with my purse in my lap and my sweaty hands in the pockets of my trench coat. Dick sat leaning forward with his elbows resting on his knees. We didn't wait long before a nurse called us in to the examining room. We waited on the narrow chrome and orange vinyl chairs set so close that they touched and waited until Dr. Carlson came in. My wonderful doctor has a perfunctory yet friendly way about him, and as he swung the door open, I noticed he was looking at the floor. He sat on the padded seat of his swivel stool with a sigh and said, "You want me to be honest, right?" We nodded. I inhaled deeply through my mouth.

"Right now we should see a baby bopping around, and we don't see any movement which means . . ."

I didn't hear or just don't remember the rest. Would it matter anyway? A baby *bopping* around. I imagined a bean-sized baby floating in warm darkness, silent and still.

"I'd recommend a D & C at this point because you're at the first trimester," he said, almost apologetically.

I nodded, "I think I'll do that."

"Okay. We'll go ahead and schedule that right now. I'm sorry to give you bad news."

Dick and I left the examining room and walked into the waiting room. I made my appointment with tears in my eyes and snot running out of my nose. The receptionist didn't bat an eye. She snipped, "What do you need?"

"I have to schedule a D & C."

"Our first available appointment with out-patient would be May 12," she said while staring at her computer monitor and snapping her gum.

"Okay."

She reached up to the counter from her swivel chair and handed me an appointment card. *A funeral invitation*, I thought. I happen to be pro-choice, but this was my baby, and it was my choice to be a mom. I turned from the crabby receptionist, and Dick and I walked through the waiting room toward the stairs. I glanced at the pregnant women sitting with magazines on their bellies and the mothers with delicate newborns in car seat carriers. None of them looked up at me. Perhaps they feared that my condition was contagious. These women seemed so nonchalant with their bulging diaper bags and gurgling newborns. Didn't they realize how lucky they were?

Because we arrived at the hospital in our own vehicles, we drove home in tandem. I pulled into the garage and got out of my car. I left the house that morning thinking I was a mother. That morning I had hope. Dick slid out of his truck and walked over to me. He put his arms around me and we hugged and cried in front of our garbage cans.

We staggered into our dimly lit kitchen and I headed straight to our bedroom where I sank onto the edge of our bed. Dick lowered himself next to me, put his arm around my shoulders, and offered, "Honey, God knew something was wrong and this is his way of taking care of things."

Can I just say I hate it when people make comments like that? I know Dick was trying to comfort me, but it backfired.

"Then God should have known that I'd love the baby no matter what!"

"I had a feeling you'd say something like that," he half-chuckled through his own tears.

Dick called my parents and handed me the phone. My Dad answered, and I tried to explain what happened, but my speech was too garbled.

"What is it? Are you alright?" I could hear concern and strain in his voice.

"I lost the baby," I blurted.

"Are you okay?"

I didn't realize it before, but my mother was on the phone and piped in, "Oh honey . . ." I had heard that sigh before.

"Are you okay?" my Dad asked again, louder this time.

For weeks following the miscarriage, I was haunted by dreams of shrinking babies. I would be holding a baby only to look down and realize that it was a paper doll. The doll would shrink, and the closer I held it, the faster it would deteriorate. Eventually, the doll would become too small to see in the palm of my hand. It would dissolve completely, and my dream would end. I considered that this was God's way of telling me I was unfit for parenthood. Okay, I was completely messed-up.

In the outpatient wing of our local hospital, I was taken to a private recovery room where an anesthetist explained that I would rather undergo general as opposed to local anesthesia so that I wouldn't hear the sound of the vacuum. I agreed. Normally, I am terrified of any sort of anesthesia, but at that moment I welcomed the opportunity to remove myself from reality. I changed into the surgical gown, stuffed my unruly Mediterranean hair into the plastic cap, and reclined on the gurney. Dick gave me a kiss and said, "I'll be here waiting for you honey. I love you."

"I love you too."

Once in the cold, pale blue hallway of the surgery wing, I began to shiver. My hands were shaky and sweaty and my teeth began to chatter. Even though I was cold I could feel the dampness in my armpits soak through the thin material of the hospital gown. The gurney stopped, and a nurse approached me. "We're just going to give you a little something to calm you down," she said without looking at me. She handed me a small Dixie cup and a little white pill. I took it. In about ten minutes I felt sleepy. The nurse proceeded to take my arm and swab an area above my right wrist with a cotton ball. "You'll feel a little sting," she said.

About fifteen minutes later, she still couldn't find my vein. I wasn't sure how she could have so much trouble when I happened to be considered very vascular like my late Grandpa Ralph who was rumored to have veins the size of night crawlers in his hands and feet.

After switching to the correctly-sized needle as recommended by her supervisor, the nurse found my vein, and I was wheeled into surgery through two automatic doors. I noticed that most of the nurses in the bright blue room were male. One placed his hand on my arm and asked, "Was this your first?"

I awoke en route to my recovery room. I tried to lift my swirling head, but someone said, "Just keep your head down. You're all done." We turned a corner and were in the room. Dick's face appeared above mine, and he gave me a kiss on the forehead.

"All done honey," he said as he stepped to the side for the nurses to push the gurney beside the bed.

One, two, three, they lifted me onto the mattress. I noticed there was a thick paper-like pad beneath my bottom, and I was starting to shiver. One of the nurses covered me with a doubled up white cotton blanket that felt like it had been warmed in an oven. She tucked the edges underneath my legs and feet and gave my chin a pat with her hand. I could only keep my eyes open for a few seconds at a time, and then I just gave up and napped on and off.

Emerging from my haze momentarily, I noticed that our minister was at the foot of my bed. He said a prayer with Dick, patted my ankle, and I closed my eyes.

The bedside phone rang and Dick answered it; it was my parents. He covered the receiver with his hand and said, "Your parents are down in the lobby and want to know if they can come up."

I turned my head and looked at a spot of blood on the sheet. "No, I just can't have them here."

Dick uncovered the receiver and told my parents we'd see them at our house in an hour or two. How could I let them come up to this bloody room, this funeral parlor? What on earth would we talk about? I couldn't face them.

The nurse came in and gave the pad underneath me one more check and declared that I was fit to go home. She asked if I had a pad. I didn't. In my ignorance I had completely overlooked the fact that I may be bleeding. The nurse came back with gigantic hospital-grade diapers that are referred to as feminine napkins. They reminded me of the generic maxi pads that my mom used to buy before the self-adhesive ones were invented. I was sure these came in a box about the size of a hay bale that read Sanitary Napkins in large black letters.

"Is there anything else I can get you?" The nurse held the handles of the wheelchair as I lowered myself onto the swayed vinyl seat.

"Can you whip me up another baby?" I joked, but my voice cracked, and I grimaced to hold back tears. Dick gave my shoulder a squeeze and left the room in order to pull the truck around to the hospital entrance. The nurse leaned over and gave me a quick hug.

"I wish I could," she said before pushing me to the elevator and to the lobby. While waiting for Dick, a teacher I knew from the high school entered the sliding doors pushing a stroller. She saw me in the wheelchair with the nurse behind me.

"Ginger! What happened?" she asked in a high-pitched, singsong voice.

"I had a miscarriage and I . . ." I began, but her look said it all.

"Oh no. I'm so sorry." she cooed, leaning over me to give me a loose hug.

I wanted her and her precious, sleeping newborn to go away. Could anything worse have confronted me at that point?

Dick drove under the carport and I said, "Well, I gotta go." She just pulled away and gave me a grimace. "Hang in there," she offered with pity in her voice.

Riding home, I noticed how still everything seemed. It was unseasonably warm for May in Wisconsin, but it was overcast and the air was heavy and there was no wind. I could smell the dogwood and flowering crab apple blossoms. Everything appeared to move through a thick haze, and I felt heavy and empty at the same time.

There were my parents, positioned in lawn chairs in our driveway. I could see that my mom had placed bowls of nuts and snacks on a small table between the chairs.

My parents set down their gin and sours, walked over to my side of the truck, and waited for me to get out. I wasn't moving all that fast. I had started to feel cramping before I left the hospital, and now I was in serious need of Extra-Strength Tylenol. My parents hugged me but didn't say anything. My Dad set up two more lawn chairs, and Dick and I joined them around the snack table. No one mentioned anything about the hospital or the baby. My mother stood up and announced that she would set out dinner. An old neighbor had brought over casserole and friendship bread after she heard the news. She had called our house to invite me to a Tupperware party, and I had to tell her why I couldn't make it.

We sat down in the kitchen and ate the casserole. I took a piece of the sweet friendship bread and spread butter on it. It tasted wonderful. The inside was moist, and the sugary outside crunched slightly between my teeth. I finished the bread, got up from the table, and walked to our bedroom.

"She must be tired from the anesthesia," I heard my mom say from the kitchen before I dropped myself onto our bed.

My D&C was on a Thursday, and I didn't go to work on Friday. That day my mom made lunch and colored my hair. I had two more days to mentally prepare for school. My parents left for home, and I got back to my regular weekend routine of cleaning the house and catching up on chores. I was in the basement loading our khaki clothes into the washing machine when I had a horrible thought: *Was this it?* Was this all I had to look forward to from now on? Was I to fill my weekends with loads of laundry and housecleaning? I felt the prospect of parenthood drifting away from me. Was I to become comfortable with this routine? This wasn't what I wanted at all. I wanted small shoes by the door. I wanted finger paintings on the refrigerator, and I wanted bikes in the driveway.

Facing The Music

Three of my fifth grade orchestra students approached me that following Monday while other members of the class folded metal chairs and music stands.

"Mrs. Marten, our teacher told us your baby died. Is that true?"

"Yes," I confessed, exhaling.

"How come?" Their eyes were wide open, and their heads were tilted to the side waiting for me to answer.

"Sometimes it just happens."

"Is it still in your tummy?" Their eyes looked up, but their chins pointed at the floor.

"Not anymore."

"Oh. We're sorry." They stepped forward and hugged me around the waist. I touched the tops of their heads and looked up at the fluorescent lights, trying to blink away the tears spilling over my eyelids.

Their innocent question "How come?" echoed in my brain.

"You don't look pregnant," a librarian said to me later, meaning to pay a compliment.

"That's because I'm not," I said curtly. Now I was getting irritated by having to back track and do my own damage control. I was sick of the "everything happens for a reason" speeches and the sympathetic grimaces even from those who had experienced miscarriages themselves. I was sick of all of it.

In the Clear

The summer following the miscarriage, Dick's son (only four years my junior) and his daughter-in-law stopped by our house on their way home to Minnesota. At the end of our visit, they quietly informed us that they were expecting. I could tell that they were trying not to sound too excited for my benefit. They were already *twelve* weeks along! They didn't spread the news at six weeks like I did. They waited until they were in the clear. I felt my cheeks get hot and I began to blink rapidly, but there was no way I was going to get up and reach for a Kleenex. "I will not be pathetic!" I told myself as I sat on my hands. "I'm going to handle this like an adult."

We said goodbye, and they headed outside with Dick. I turned on my heel, went for the linen closet, and pulled out the vacuum even though I had vacuumed an hour before they arrived. I turned it on anyway and pushed it back and forth in front of the couch as if trying to erase their news.

I noticed that Dick had come inside and was standing behind me. *Just keep vacuuming, vacuum it all away.* Eventually I tapped the top of the vacuum cleaner with my toe to shut it off. Dick wrapped me in a tight hug from behind. I turned toward him slowly, and we stood there in our living room with me crying into his neck and shoulder.

It was time to move forward.

The Power of Suggestion

The Christmas prior to our third wedding anniversary, Dick, our yellow lab Lucy, and I traveled to the Upper Peninsula of Michigan to spend Christmas with my parents.

A few days after our Christmas dinner as we lay about the house groaning and chomping on Rolaids (really, my mom should just set them out in a candy dish), my mother suggested visiting their neighbors Ken and Christine, who had returned from Russia with their newly adopted daughters.

"Let's go see the little Russian girls!" my mother squeaked. Dick and I looked at each other. I looked at my mother and narrowed my eyes.

My mother turned and continued, "I have a little something for each of them. They have only been home for a couple of weeks, but they're probably settled in now. I called Christine and she said we could all come over after dinner."

I watched my mother from my spot on the couch as she scampered into our TV room and set about rummaging through her "blue light" closet containing her cache of sale items, some dating back to 1985. A few minutes later we were standing at Ken and Christine's front door with my mother clutching two pastel colored gift bags overflowing with pink tissue paper.

Ken answered the door. Christine was in the middle of unpacking groceries. Two little girls, one blonde, one brunette, both age two, ran in circles between the foyer and the kitchen. The Christmas tree stood in the center of the living room surrounded by the carnage of Santa's visit. Over the cream colored carpet lay toys, wrapping paper, and naked Barbie dolls. Ken and Christine introduced the little blonde as Alison and the taller brunette as Lily. Alison was shy, but Lily ran right up to me and wrapped her arms around my legs. Christine explained that the girls weren't cautious of strangers yet and that they were a little concerned. This was a concept that had never even occurred to me. I realized that these children were removed from the only home they had ever known and placed with Ken and Christine. Christine went on to explain that kids from orphanages may exhibit signs of reactive attachment disorder, a term that was unfamiliar to me. From what I understood, reactive attachment disorder occurs when young children aren't given the chance to form a bond with a caregiver. This isn't necessarily an orphanage issue; it can occur right here in the good old US of A if kids aren't cared for properly and provided with unconditional love. Basically, a child's brain has a certain window of time to learn affection. If a child doesn't experience or learn affection within the first few years of life and that window closes, the result is reactive attachment disorder.

"There are still presents under the tree for them to unwrap, but they don't even know they're theirs. They don't even know what presents are." Christine pointed to several colorful boxes under the tree.

Up until that point, adoption was only a distant thought, something my sixth grade cohorts and I aspired to while perched atop the monkey bars at recess. Being in Ken and Christine's house brought it to the forefront of my mind. Suddenly, I realized that perhaps my mother had engineered our meeting with Ken and Christine and their new family, the first intimation that my parents had suggested their desire to become grandparents. Unlike the parents of some of my friends, my mom and dad never pressured us into explaining why we didn't have kids right away and, when other people asked them the same question, my parents would just explain that it was none of their business and that we would have kids or not when the time was right. After our miscarriage my parents never again mentioned the idea of having grandchildren.

Jumping into the Pool

The following summer we were sitting in a nice restaurant on our third wedding anniversary with a white tablecloth stretched between us. I was working on my third glass of wine, had overshot the pleasantly flakey state, and was quickly entering the zone of pitiful and annoying.

"You know honey," I slurred while twirling the stem of my wine glass, "I just want to be a mom. I don't care how it happens, and I don't care about being pregnant. I don't want a pregnancy; I want a child. And I don't want another anniversary to go by without one."

Dick folded his hands on the table and made one of the most demonstrative gestures that a German-Norwegian male can make. He nodded.

"I want to stop trying to get pregnant," I swallowed. "Can we adopt from Russia? I need a plan. I can't keep going on like this." My face was now hot, and I was feeling more than a little bloated and uncomfortable in my little black dress, heeled sandals, and control-top briefs. My own outburst sobered me; I had been harboring this desire for months, and here I was blathering like an idiot in front of a waitress toting our dinner rolls.

"What agency did they use?" Dick looked up from his Greek shrimp.

"I'm not sure," I said, "but I'll get details."

*

During a visit to Escanaba following our anniversary, Christine and I sat together on her formerly white leather sofa while the girls played on the floor. She and Ken had applied through an agency in Michigan, and the process involved a three-week hotel stay in Russia with their girls. I listened to her tales of constant crying, brushing teeth with bottled water, eating pizza for days on end, and washing underwear in the sink. This didn't deter me in the least; I was ready.

As I walked across the field that separated my parent's house from theirs, I felt hopeful for the first time since our fertility treatments, and I couldn't keep from smiling. *We can do this,* I thought. *This is what we're supposed to do. Wait until I tell Dick.* Almost skipping, I decided to omit the part about washing underwear in the sink.

That night I shared all my new information with Dick and my parents. My parents sounded more than a bit excited, and Dick sounded optimistic. "We can take out a home equity loan," he said. "We can make it work."

Before leaving Escanaba, I drove to my grandmother's to say goodbye. I stood in her sunny kitchen with its old varnished cabinets, gave her a hug, and told her that Dick and I were ready to embark on an adventure. "Are you going to adopt a baby?" she asked in her quavering voice.

"How did you know?"

"I just had a feeling. I've been thinking about you a lot lately, and I just knew that you were going to share some good news with me."

CHAPTER 17

I made a phone call to the only adoption agency that I knew in our area, Lutheran Social Services (LSS). After calling during my lunch hour one afternoon, I was excited to discover that an informational meeting would be offered in two weeks. Fourteen days later, Dick and I headed to a city an hour north of our town to attend the meeting in the fellowship hall of a Lutheran church. People were positioned at clusters of tables in the large green-carpeted hall where prospective adoptive parents like us waited to hear first hand accounts from parents who had adopted. Dick and I circulated through the room and stopped to listen to these adoptive parents bare their souls. By the end of the meeting, we had decided to give domestic adoption a chance, even if we were a bit uncertain. We had just learned what open adoption really meant, and I could tell Dick was not exactly on board with that idea. However, two sets of adoptive parents told us that even though most adoptions now are open, the birth moms really only wanted contact with the baby during the first few months and after that contact tapered off a lot. The major plus was that the domestic adoption fees were half as much as those for international adoption. Dick's frugal, dark-Lutheran side prevailed and he suggested, "Let's at least give the domestic thing a shot."

The director of the LSS domestic adoption program told our group that LSS would only take on eleven prospective parents that year. To be considered for the domestic program, we would have to enter a lottery. This was news to us. If we were chosen from the lottery, we would need to create a portfolio of ourselves that would be placed in the LSS offices around Wisconsin. Birth moms would look at the portfolios and choose three sets of parents to interview. I must admit that I felt more than a little uncomfortable with the idea of trying to sell ourselves to a birth mother. Some of the domestic adoptive parents at the meeting told us that birth moms could be fickle. One adoptive mom told me they were chosen just because they owned a horse and the birth mom wanted her baby to grow up with horses. *We have a yellow lab—maybe that's a plus*, I reasoned. What if we weren't good-looking enough? I briefly considered getting a nose job to correct what I considered my biggest flaw, but what if that wasn't enough? Would I become addicted to plastic surgery after so many rejections and end up looking like the Cat Woman I saw on *The Learning Channel*? What if a birth mom didn't approve of the age difference between Dick and me? Despite my doubts, we signed ourselves up. We filled out the requisite forms and handed them to the director before leaving the church. In a week we would know if we were eligible to enter the domestic adoption pool.

After exactly one week, I called the LSS office during my lunch break. No, we had not been chosen from the domestic adoption lottery, yet we were relieved. I had been having dreams involving a sixteen-year-old tattooed-chain-smoking birth mother showing up on our doorstep in the middle of the night to tell us she wanted her baby back and asking us to co-sign a car loan. Now we could move forward with my plan, or rather, *our* plan. I went ahead and scheduled an after school appointment for December fifth to discuss international adoption with a Lutheran Social Services caseworker named Susan.

The LSS office was located in an old two-story house between a church and a parking lot. We parked in the street up against a steep snow bank and trudged through the slush to the front door. Once inside, we introduced ourselves to the receptionist and waited to be led up the creaky stairs to Susan's office. The second floor reminded me of an old high school friend's house with its dark, worn, varnished woodwork, small rooms and crooked floors. I could smell the aroma of coffee drifting into the hallway from a cozy break room. Susan, our caseworker, met us at the threshold to her office.

"You must be the Martens," she said cheerfully. She was on the short side with rosy cheeks and a slightly chubby build. She had bright blue eyes, and I liked her immediately. As she led us to her office, which consisted of a desk and three chairs, I hovered in front of the curled and faded photos of children tacked to a bulletin board. Susan noticed and mentioned that these were all children available for adoption. She pointed to one little girl, age 5 and said, "Oh, this one is really a sweetheart. It would be great to see her get a family. That's our motto here. We look for families for children, not children for families." I liked the sound of that.

We spent the next two hours answering questions concerning our motivation to adopt. She asked us specific questions about our failed attempts to become pregnant and how we tried to remedy the situation. She asked about Dick's previous marriage and why it ended in divorce. She also asked him about the relationship he had with his children now. Towards the end of our meeting, she asked us if we attended church and how we felt about religious education. After our little chat, she handed us a stack of paper work and explained that there would be a series of parent group meetings we would need to attend in order to apply officially to the Russian Adoption Program.

In the car on the way home, I perused our paperwork. Our first task was to answer a myriad of essay questions. As I looked them over, it occurred to me that any couple considering cross breeding should be required to answer these. One question posed what we thought of divorce and if we considered who would care for our child should we split up. There were questions about education, about day-care plans, about our childhoods, about our relationships with our parents and siblings, and about our medical histories. We each had to write a two-page autobiography. Two pages? I didn't feel there was enough "normal" information about my family to construct a paragraph. In the end, I fabricated a well-balanced, happy family, omitting all evidence of the abnormal like my brother's brief, but lucrative stint selling used porno magazines in the men's room at our church before confirmation class.

My parents were easy enough to describe. My mother was an artist and my father was a physical education teacher at the Escanaba Area Junior High for thirty-six years. He wore a polo shirt with a pocket and polyester pants Monday through Friday. Never jeans. My mother packed him a soggy bologna sandwich, a banana, and two cookies for lunch. And he ate it, everyday for thirty-six years.

When writing about Dick and me, I tried my hardest to make us seem like a healthy and happy All-American couple that ate organic, recycled, and attended church regularly. I even emphasized my Meals on Wheels volunteer work over the summer. There were things about myself that I didn't mention either, like the fact that I can barely balance a checkbook and that I'm still perplexed by standard units of measure in the kitchen. Just to be cruel, Dick will periodically quiz me with questions like, "Come on, how many quarts in a gallon?" Of course, Dick had nothing to hide, so his essay was a piece of cake (of the German-Norwegian variety, a bit dry, yet consistent).

Once we started attending our LSS parent meetings, we were overwhelmed by a slew of forms. While I don't mind filling out forms, these were the types of forms that required what I call digging, meaning Dick had to run downstairs to our basement office and dig through filing cabinets locating tax returns, bank statements, mortgage statements, and the like, dating back three years. In addition to the two identical dossiers (I believe *dossier* is French for "a packet of unnecessary red tape) that needed to be completed for the Russian government, we had to undergo rather extensive physicals that involved a 12-screen drug panel, including tests for AIDS, syphilis, and tuberculosis. I worried that our insurance company would take one look at the claim and drop us. On paper we looked like drug-dealing homeless prostitutes. Poor Dick had a very thorough doctor who checked every crack and crevice and even recommended a colonoscopy. And as if this weren't enough, we'd have to go through the entire physical and blood tests again no more than three months before we traveled.

Over time, much of the paperwork became a blur. Many nights after school, armed with paperclips and staplers, Dick and I would find ourselves at our kitchen table with forms and binders spread out on every surface. We had piles for copying, piles that needed to be notarized, and piles that needed to be certified, a process that involves sending a notarized document off to be notarized again by a state government official at ten dollars per document. We had lists of documents that needed to be authenticated, including our marriage license, birth certificates and Dick's divorce decree. A lot of it was truly tedious, not to mention expensive. Once we finished all the home study paperwork, the medical reports, the employment verification forms, and the two dossiers, we ended up spending over three hundred dollars on certifications alone.

Our next hurdle was the home visit. Would Susan look in our toilets? Would she notice the iron stain in the Smurf-blue bathtub? Prior to her arrival, we hid our liquor bottles, dusted the blades of the ceiling fans, and I wiped my long black hair out of the bathtub. While reorganizing our basement storage room, I came upon Fluffy, a taxidermy squirrel on a log that I had received at elementary school faculty Christmas party. Fluffy traveled from teacher to teacher every year and at every holiday his host would dress him appropriately. When I uncovered him, he was still clad in his Mardi Gras regalia. As fond as I was of this decrepit example of taxidermy-gone-wrong, he needed to be incognito for the time being. I stuffed him, along with his decaying tail and chewed-up paws into a Target bag and stashed him in a suitcase behind our furnace. Now we were ready.

Turning a Corner

After a brief tour of our house and some small talk about the neighborhood, Susan followed us to the kitchen and more questions arose. This was the single question I was anticipating; she asked if we would prefer a boy or a girl. I know an open-minded and grateful person would just say, "It doesn't matter," but I did have a preference. I really wanted a daughter. I also felt, unlike other members of our adoptive parent group, that we had the right to request a girl. Many parents at our parent meetings felt that requesting a specific gender was just not kosher and that we should all just be happy with whatever fate dished out. I agreed, to a point, but the truth was I felt we had spent so much money and jumped through so many hoops that the least the agency could do would be to grant us our request, and I wanted a daughter. Why? I always imagined having one. Even those paper dolls in my weird dreams happened to be female. Dick and I had discussed the gender issue at length, and he agreed. He reasoned that I would bond more easily with a daughter, a relationship that would become more important hinging on Dick's speculation that I could be widowed at a relatively early age. What a pleasant conversation that was.

Without hesitation, and in unison, we requested a girl. We also requested a child around fourteen months old figuring this would help make up for some lost time when considering Dick's age. Though I didn't tell Dick, deep down I wanted an infant. I ached for a child that was completely dependent on me. I longed to carry a baby in a sling, to feed it a bottle, and to rock it to sleep. More desperate than selfless, I agreed to go along with Dick's practical plan.

Hurry Up and Wait

In June that summer, we attended an LSS Adoption Festival with the hope of getting even more information on health concerns like vaccinations and attachment issues. We even arranged to rendezvous with friends we made at our adoptive parent meetings. Walking into the large conference center lobby, we saw Gil and Rory and Pat and Mary. They were in a sort of huddle, talking excitedly and giggling a lot. They all saw us approach and asked, "Are you coming with us? Did you get your referral? We're leaving for Russia on July fifteenth!" Dick and I were baffled.

"No, we didn't get anything yet! When did you find out?" I tried being happy for them, but I was just puzzled. We had worked so hard to get our paper work in, and I knew for a fact that we got ours in before many couples in our parent group.

"We got a call from Susan last night," Mary squealed.

We must have looked absolutely pitiful.

"Don't worry, you'll probably have a call on your answering machine when you get home," Rory interjected, attempting to reassure us.

"Hmmm," I murmured. "Well anyway, congratulations!"

Later that day, as we unwrapped our mashed submarine sandwiches from our pre-paid box lunches I admitted, "I can't believe it. How come they're going and we're not?"

"I don't know. Maybe we just didn't get it in fast enough," Dick offered through a mouth full of stale bread.

"I'm calling Susan when we get home."

"No you're not. Just wait. It'll be our turn next." Dick is always the voice of reason in our relationship and I knew I shouldn't get emotional over a mere technicality, but I felt like the last kid chosen for the kickball team. All that effort to be on time with forms; some forms that needed to be FedEx-ed, others that needed next day air and so on, for what? Ugh.

We returned home to find pictures of Rory and Gil's little girl Amanda in our e-mail box. She was cute, I had to admit, but I was too depressed to e-mail her back right away. No, that's actually not true. I was plain old jealous. How ugly is that?

So yes, our referral finally came three months later after Gil and Rory arrived home with Amanda. As it turns out, Rory actually knew about our child before we did.

Susan had called us on a Monday night to tell us that our referral was on the way and that she would call one of us tomorrow. "Whom should I call?" she asked. "Ginger," Dick said, immediately; he had picked up the downstairs phone when he saw the caller ID. Bless his heart, he really knew what this meant to me and he wanted to give me this moment.

"Call *me*," I said, sounding like a junior high school student.

"Okay, what time should I call?"

"I'll be in my office between eleven and twelve-thirty."

"Excellent, I'll talk to you tomorrow."

I gave her my office number, and we hung up.

Yeehaw! The wait was almost over. We hung up our respective phones and I jumped up and down with my hands clasped under my chin. Dick jogged up the stairs sporting a wide grin.

"Alright! Finally!" he yelled as we hugged each other.

The next day the phone rang in my office as I was giving one of my high school violinists, Karly, a lesson. I had prepped Karly; she knew what this call meant. When we heard the phone ring, she smiled and gave me a thumbs-up before slipping out the door. I looked at the phone and let it ring one more time before picking up the receiver. "Hello?"

"Hi, Ginger." It was Susan.

"Hi, Susan," I said in that expectantly corny tone people use all the time.

"I have your referral information. Are you ready?'

"You bet!" I sat down at my desk with a pen in hand as if I would need to write this down.

"What would you like to know first? The sex or the age?"

"Boy or girl?" I'm not sure if I even heard her.

"It's a girl."

"Yes!"

"Okay, now are you sitting down?" She sounded serious.

"Um . . . yes." *Oh my God, is this kid fifteen or something?*

"She's four months old today."

"Four months?"

"Is that okay?"

"Is that okay? Yes! It's perfect!" I was screaming. I could see Karly looking in through my office window from behind my lesson sign-up sheets. "Wow, a *baby*. We need a crib!"

"I'll be e-mailing her picture so if you want to get on your computer you'll see her in a few minutes."

"Great! When do we travel?"

"You will be flying to Russia on October twenty-first, so you have a few weeks to get your things together."

"Thanks so much Susan. This must be the best part of your job."

"Yes. It is."

I hung up and called Dick immediately. One of his eighth grade students answered. "Mr. Marten, please," the kid set the phone on Dick's desk, and I could hear the table saws in his technology room growling away.

"Mr. Marten," he said in his teacher voice.

"Hey honey, it's me."

"Hey, what do we got?"

"It's a girl!"

"Aw, that's great! Just what we wanted."

"And we need a crib!"

"Why do we need a crib?" Dick asked.

"Because she is four months old today!"

"Four months! Well, I think you got what you wanted."

"You knew I wanted a *baby* baby?"

"I had a feeling. Funny how things work, huh?"

During the summer Dick had fastidiously designed and constructed a beautiful bedroom set including a headboard, dresser with hutch, night table, and bookcase. While I painted the room three times over after a failed attempt at finding the perfect shade of periwinkle, Dick was actually being constructive. He made the new bedroom set of birch and designed it to replicate an expensive set that I had fallen in love with at an upscale children's furniture store. I knew that this set was quality in accordance with Dick's standards. The hutch for the top of the dresser had an adorable arch at the top of the frame, reminding me of the furniture from a marionette version of Hansel and Gretel I had seen when I was little. Dick had incorporated the arch into the headboard, the bookshelf, and the nightstand too. He had meticulously sealed it with three coats of glossy polyurethane. Now the bed would have to wait.

I told Dick that I was waiting for the picture to come through on my school e-mail, but it wasn't working. He told me to go home and try on our computer because our school server was most likely blocking the picture. I quickly hung up and waited for about ten more minutes. Since it was close to my lunch break, I threw on my denim jacket and ran to my car. On the way out of my office I saw Karly in the orchestra room. "Boy or girl?" she yelled from her violin locker as I sailed by the doors.

"Girl!" I shouted, running out of the music department. I broke out of the school, and into the bright noon sun beating on the blacktopped parking lot. I zipped home and barged into the house ignoring Lucy barking from her kennel in our backyard. While taking our steps downstairs to the office, I wondered what our daughter would look like. Would she be cute? Was that important to me?

I logged on and waited. I opened my e-mail and double-clicked on the letter from Susan, then the attachment. I waited for the photo to load. At first I saw black fuzz, then a high forehead, followed by a slightly furrowed brow, and then . . . beautiful, almond eyes that were almost black. I let out a sigh and stopped tapping my feet. I swear I had seen her face before. I quickly forwarded the picture to Dick and called his office.

Dick answered on the first ring.

"She's so cute! And I'm forwarding you the picture right now!"

"Okay, I'm logging on. What does she look like?"

I thought a moment and then I realized something very strange. "She kind of looks like me when I was a baby." *Now I really had lost my mind.*

"Let's see . . . here it comes," said Dick. "She *is* cute."

"She looks kind of serious, doesn't she? But I suppose I'd look serious too if I were in a Siberian orphanage."

"We'll fix that. We'll make her smile." I could hear the smile on Dick's face and I heard some unmistakable sniffles as well.

"I'm printing out her picture, and I'm bringing it back to school. I've gotta go. Love you."

"Bye honey, I love you too."

I grabbed my cell phone and placed the call I'd been waiting to make.

"Northwoods Manor," the receptionist answered. I asked to speak with my Grandma Dorothy who was recovering from a stroke.

"She's eating lunch right now."

"Well, this is really important. This is her granddaughter calling and I need to tell her that we just found out we're getting a girl!" I sounded a bit hysterical, I'm sure.

"Oh, well, of course, I'll bring the phone right to her," she said. I could hear cups clanging on saucers and forks tinging on plates as the phone traveling through the dining hall. "Dorothy, your granddaughter has some news for you," a distant voice said.

"Oh my," I heard my grandmother say in her quivery voice. I imagined her white, boney hand taking the receiver. "Yes? Ginger?"

"Hi Gram, I have some news! You better sew a pink quilt, it's a girl!"

"Oh, isn't that something? That's wonderful . . . ."

The phone was passed around and I could hear some commotion.

"You're grandmother is a bit overwhelmed," the nurse explained, "but don't worry, she's smiling!"

*

I kept Rachel's black and white photo folded in my back pants pocket for two weeks and accosted everyone I knew with it. I'd produce and unfold the creased picture with her thoughtful little face on it. I'd spent hours analyzing her face and comparing her features to pictures of children with alcohol fetal syndrome in the LSS parent packets. We made note of the perfect Cupid's bow on her top lip, and her well-balanced little ears.

When Dick and I returned home after school, we realized we needed to discuss her name. After much deliberation over what not to name her, we had narrowed it down to two choices. Finally, we decided that our quietist, nicest, and smartest former students were all named Rachel.

We took Susan's advice and called Dr. W., who specialized in international adoption medical issues. We e-mailed him our pictures of Rachel along with the official Russian medical report we received from Susan a day later. I must admit the medical report seemed downright scary. According to the Russian doctors, Rachel was afflicted with pyramidal insufficiency of the perinatal background, and we wanted to know just exactly what that was. Unfortunately, Dr. W. offered no explanation, nor did he do anything to put us at ease. His manner was almost terse, and I found myself feeling defensive. He informed us that he had adopted his son from Russia, and his tone seemed to imply that we weren't worthy of this venture. Suffice it to say, I just didn't like the guy or what he said.

"You really don't know. She could have cerebral palsy," he told us in his dry and dour New England accent.

We didn't know what to do. The only glimmer of hope Dr. W. gave us was this: he deduced that Rachel's parents were Muslim, having emigrated from Kazakhstan to Novosibirsk, Russia. I wasn't sure what he was implying, but then he spelled it out for us. Muslims don't drink or smoke. Chances were Rachel's birth mom had not abused alcohol or drugs during pregnancy or before. Whew, there was *something* positive to cling to.

We didn't sleep all night. What if our baby was sick? Could we provide the therapy she needed? Were we up to parenting a special needs child? We never considered rejecting her. It never even entered our minds.

The next morning we decided to get a second opinion. We made an appointment with a pediatrician in town who was recommended by an adoptive parent on my summer golf league.

About a week later, we were sitting in Dr. L.'s examining room with our pictures of Rachel and her medical report spread out in front of him. "Well, she sure is cute," he said looking through his bifocals. I liked him immediately. "I don't see any recognizable signs of alcohol fetal syndrome, and her head circumference looks normal." We were relieved to hear that a professional thought she looked healthy. As far as *pyramidal insufficiency* was concerned, he had no clue what it meant but explained that when a baby in Russia exhibits even the slightest delay developmentally, they are immediately labeled with an affliction. He figured this was the case with Rachel. From my own research, I had come across an explanation for some of these diagnoses by Russian doctors and realized that their approach to medicine is much different than ours. Basically, in Russia orphans are sick until proven healthy.

Dr. L. gave us several prescriptions for antibiotics. "Believe me," he said, clearing his throat, "you don't want to get sick when you're in Siberia." We believed him. Before leaving, he handed us tubes of cream for treating scabies and ringworm.

Deflation

The end of October was nearing, and we had purchased our airline tickets through the travel agency used by LSS. The ticket prices were insulting, but we gritted our teeth and slapped the balance on our credit card. We were scheduled to leave on October twenty-first.

As we were making packing lists that included Monistat 7, Pepto-Bismol, and travel toilet paper, the phone rang. It was Karen. She started by telling us she had bad news. Bad news? Of course, I thought the worst. Was something wrong with Rachel? Was the trip canceled? Was there a problem with our paper work? No, but our trip was postponed. Apparently, someone's math was way off because Rachel wouldn't be officially ready for adoption until after November first. I didn't know how we could wait until November when we were already jumping out of our skins. The next morning we called the travel agent first thing and transferred the tickets to November fifth. The transfer fee was two hundred dollars per ticket, but what was two hundred dollars here and there?

And of course, I had to backtrack and explain to my friends and anyone who would listen, that no, we would not be heading to Russia next week because there was a mess up, and yes, those international adoptions can be like that and we would be traveling in early November instead. People asked if this happened often and shared horror stories of friends and acquaintances waiting years to go overseas and adopt their children. "Thanks for sharing," I thought, "and go pee up a rope while you're at it."

In the meantime, we needed to get our Visas. The advantage of our travel delay was that our Visas would be several hundreds of dollars cheaper because we were farther from our travel date. I squawked out the LSS mantra, "Be flexible."

One night after supper, Dick made a call to the Russian embassy to order our travel Visas. I heard him say, "Hello, I . . ." and that was it. He paced around the living room with the phone to his ear. Every now and then Dick would say, "Excuse me. Sir, excuse me." This went on for about ten minutes.

"Are you talking to somebody? Is it a recording?" I was thoroughly confused. I could hear a voice coming from the receiver. "What's going on?"

Dick held the phone away from his ear. "I'm talking to Vasily. I mean *he's* talking. I'm not even sure what he's saying, his accent is so thick, and he's talking a mile a minute. I might hang up."

"You can't hang up!"

After about fifteen minutes, I heard Dick give Vasily our address and our credit card number. I heard the chirp of the cordless phone as he disconnected. He staggered into the kitchen, sat down, and blew out his cheeks in a long sigh. I wondered if our Visas would ever come.

As we were counting down to our travel date, we also scheduled new physicals, and I saw my doctor for an anti-anxiety prescription to get me through the flight. I have a slight problem with flying, mainly that the plane is going to fall out of the sky. This causes much anxiety, makes me sick, and drives Dick insane.

We prepared the house too. Dick bought a baby gate and built a custom extension for it so it would swing. I washed loads of pink laundry in Dreft and packed and unpacked my suitcase to see just how much it would hold. We decided to travel with our possessions in carry-on bags after learning of Gil and Rory's debacle with flight delays and lost luggage. There was no way I was going to risk having to wear our host family's sweat pants and underwear for six days. I finally decided to pack two pair of pants and five long sleeved T-shirts. I would wear a fleece cardigan if I got too cold. Like I said, everything had to fit in the carry-on; it wasn't worth the risk.

True to form, Dick handled the money for our trip. For the first trip, we were required to bring three thousand dollars in cash to pay our escorts, translator, and host family. The bills needed to be in pristine condition and in twenty-dollar increments. Dick called our credit union and ordered our money. The credit union president, who we know, jokingly asked if we were scoring some sort of drug deal. We told him of our travel plans, and he happily obliged by actually ordering the crisp new bills for us. Of course, Dick customized a cheaper and better money belt with a rigid plastic insert to keep the bills nice and crisp.

In addition to our clothing, Karen at LSS called and asked if we would bring some donated clothes to the orphanage. She stopped at our house a week later with several boxes and grocery bags of winter clothes. Dick and I stared at the pile of clothing in the middle of our living room floor and knew it had to be stowed under the plane. There was no way we could carry it on. We dragged out the most gargantuan suitcase we owned from downstairs and stuffed it with the little wool toggle coats, fleece hats, and mittens.

We were ready to go.

CHAPTER 18

Being Flexible

We sat across from each other at the table in the small airport coffee shop. I had just washed down my little blue pill with a five-dollar latte. Dick finished his dried out apricot Danish, and we dragged ourselves toward security.

The night before, we had driven two hours away and met my parents at an Applebee's. Over burgers and fries, my Dad wanted to know particulars like: when our flight departed, what time we'd land in Cincinnati, when we'd land in New York, when we'd land in Moscow, and when we would finally land in Novosibirsk. My dad is big on departure and arrival times. Perhaps wearing a stopwatch around one's neck for thirty-six years does this to a person.

The next morning we arose at five a.m. in our room at the Super 8. We boarded an eighteen-passenger plane for Cincinnati and had an uneventful flight due mostly to the Paxil I had swallowed at the airport. Once we landed in Cincinnati, we began our search for our travel partners Sherry and Shawn Olson. In an hour-long phone conversation the week prior, Sherry had describe herself and Shawn as "two very tall redheads. You can't miss us." And she was right. We spotted them immediately at the gate for JFK and hugged like old friends. We headed for a TGI Fridays, pulling our carryon bags along the dark blue industrial airport carpet.

Once at JFK, we met Kate and Al Kroger, both donning sweat suits and new sneakers. To pass the time, I read aloud from a new David Sedaris book I had purchased at the newsstand in Cincinnati and made a lame attempt at keeping a video journal. I don't think Kate appreciated the humor, but Sherry and I laughed until we drew attention to ourselves, and Dick told me to "tone it down."

The flight to Moscow was a ten and a half-hour experiment in sleep deprivation. I struggled to drift off, entangled in my blow up neck pillow and Dick's shoulder while staving off restless leg syndrome, but to no avail.

When we landed in Moscow, groggy and starving, Kate reminded us to look for our LSS assigned escort, Darya. In the crowd we caught sight of a piece of cardboard sporting the letters L-S-S. We pushed our way through the throngs of international travelers toward a petite brunette in a knee length white wool coat. We waved at her, and she smiled back while moving through the crowd.

Darya's English was pretty good, and she was extremely composed. She led us through the airport to baggage claim and finally to the exit. The air was damp and cold and the sky was deep gray. I was glad I had opted for my Columbia ski jacket instead of the more fashionable Russian looking jacket my friends had encouraged me to buy, but I was shivering just the same. We approached a van and Darya said, "He is taking nap," as she knocked loudly on the driver's door window. A shaggy looking guy in his mid-twenties unfolded himself from the driver's seat and limped toward the back doors of the vehicle. While he threw our luggage in the back, we threw ourselves into the seats and took in our surroundings. Orange shag carpeting climbed half way up the walls of the passenger van. Paisley curtains hung at the side windows and trim with little fuzzy balls draped from the ceiling. I closed my eyes.

Darya explained that we would need to stop and exchange our money before we did any sightseeing. *Sightseeing?* While we took turns nodding off, our driver navigated the potholes of the road into the city. At one point we stopped suddenly and the van stood still signaling that we had reached our destination. When I awoke, I thought I was still on the plane. My eyes burned, and my neck had an obnoxious kink. I'm sure Dick's back was hurting too. We blinked our eyes as we tried to figure out where we were. It seemed as if we were just parked in the middle of an intersection. Darya turned to the husbands and said, "Please give me your money, and I will go exchange for you."

I watched Dick lift up his shirt and pull at his money belt. Darya jumped out of the van, but the van stayed put. We watched as cars buzzed past us and honked horns as the van shook slightly from the wind sheer of the traffic. A woman in a small car behind us honked her horn and shook her fist in the air, but our driver just yawned and pulled his stocking cap over his eyes.

About a half hour later, Darya jumped into the front passenger seat, counted out the money, and handed it back to our husbands. "Now we go to Kremlin for sightseeing."

We bounced around the van for another hour or so before arriving at the Kremlin. I wish I could say I was awestruck by the beauty of all the cathedrals we saw, but truthfully, I was too delirious to enjoy any of it. At one point Dick grabbed me by the hood on my jacket to keep me from pitching head first through a glass case display of Faberge eggs.

After sightseeing, Darya took us to a popular Moscow restaurant specializing in Russian cuisine, and I swear to this day that I saw the Russian Olympic figure skater Maria Butyrskaya, but I kept drinking out of Dick's wine glass, so really who knows what I saw. We settled in around a long table in the center of the restaurant, and I could feel the tension in my shoulders from shivering all afternoon. The restaurant was warm, rustic, and dark, and it was all we could do to not push our place settings aside and drop our heads onto our folded arms for a nap.

After rounds of vodka and authentic goulash, we were happy to scamper back to our psychedelic van and head for the airport. At the stark, white, check-in counter, Darya wished us well, and we said our goodbyes. She told us she'd see us again in five days.

We slept about three-and-a-half minutes on the four-and-a-half hour flight east to Novosibirsk. As our plane made its final descent, I noticed passengers pulling large fur hats from carry on bags and men wrapping long wool scarves around their necks. I'm from the Upper Peninsula of Michigan, and I know cold, but watching these people prepare themselves for landing made me a bit nervous. I pulled my cute little felt beret from my pocket and pulled it over my head, but it couldn't compete with fox fur. If we thought it was cold in Moscow, then Novosibirsk was an absolute Arctic hell. It had to be about twenty below with a forty below wind chill at six o'clock in the morning. We had gone without a solid stretch of sleep for almost thirty-six hours.

The Novosibirsk airport was about as remote and primitive as they come. There was no accordion style ramp to connect to the plane and guide us into the gate. There wasn't even a gate. We simply walked stiff legged down the icy aluminum steps that shook with the Siberian wind. We all grabbed at the railing, and I could feel my thin gloves stick to it on the way down. I suddenly had a sadistic urge to put my tongue on it. Would they extend my Visa, I wondered? We stepped onto the tarmac and followed the crowd toward baggage claim.

Shawn reminded us all that we had to look for Sergei, our Novosibirsk escort. We had all seen pictures of Sergei at our parent meetings, so we at least had some idea who we were looking for. We approached a rusty chain link fence and saw hundreds of people pressed up against it in the early morning darkness shouting and waving at the other passengers. Then we spotted the familiar LSS sign and the short grey-haired man in a derby hat. We waved as if he couldn't figure out we were the Americans, and he yelled, "Hey guys!" We ambled over toward the fence, and he pointed at an opening. We pressed through the crowd, and he pushed through a clot of Russians to shake our hands. "We go in here," Sergei yelled, and he pushed us toward what looked like a dilapidated pole barn. I didn't have the strength to propel my way threw the throngs of people, so he grabbed the sleeve of my jacket and flung me through corrugated aluminum door. On the inside, the walls were framed with rusted metal, and it didn't look like there was a bathroom in sight though I was too tired to even know if I had to go to the bathroom. Sergei ushered us toward a fenced in area inside and pushed us into the corner. "Women, stay here together. Do not go anywhere." *Where on earth would we go?* "Guys, come here." He gestured for our husbands to follow him to the other end of the building.

The entire baggage claim area was about fifty by one hundred feet with a conveyor belt coming from the center of the wall opposite us. We watched Sergei talk to Dick, Shawn, and Al as the belt began to move. It took a long time for our baggage to appear on the belt, but Sergei wouldn't let the men walk over to us until all of them had their luggage.

We jumped into yet another van and drove about an hour into the city of Novosibirsk. We discovered later that Novosibirsk is about the size of Chicago, not as much fun but with the same number of potholes. After passing long stretches on a two-lane bumpy road with huge birch forests bordering grey fields, we finally began to see the lights of the city as our heads bobbed with sleep.

We were scheduled to stay with host families who would give us a room and cook us breakfast and dinner for seventy-five dollars a day. Sergei's first task was to get us to our hosts in one piece where we would have breakfast.

The van jolted us awake at our first stop for Al and Kate. Our van sat idling in front of a three-story rectangular apartment building that looked more like a bunker. The front of the building appeared to be concrete patched in spots with corrugated steel. I had learned that during the Stalin era, each Russian citizen was allocated only five hundred square feet of living space, heated with steam courtesy of the Russian government. The buildings reminded me of shoeboxes, and the wooded neighborhood with its winding, single-lane roads was reminiscent of a college campus.

After Sergei emptied the van of Al and Kate's suitcases, he said, "Krogers, I see you here at 9:05." We watched through the frosted windows of the van as Kate and Al gave their hosts hugs and picked up their baggage. We went through the same routine to drop off the Olsons, and then it was finally our turn to meet our hosts.

A stocky man was standing at the end of the short sidewalk in front of our building when Sergei pulled up. Dmitri, Nadia's husband, stood with his hands in his pockets, a large fur hat perched on his head. He waved at Sergei, and Sergei braked. As with our friends before us, Sergei got out and came around to open the sliding door of the van. He stood back to let Dick out and then gave me his hand to help me. Normally, I have a bit of an aversion to this type of chivalry, but I was so dead tired that I was grateful for it.

Dmitri said hello in a thick Russian accent and shook our hands. He took our large suitcase containing the donations for the orphanage in one hand and grabbed my carry on bag in the other. I figured there was an elevator in the building, so he wouldn't have to haul both suitcases up the stairs. I was wrong. After punching a code into a small box near the handle of the front door, Dmitri pulled open the rusty steel windowless door to the building. Once the door shut behind us, the hall was almost pitch black. Dmitri muttered something in Russian that probably meant "watch your step," and we followed him up three flights of stairs. Once we reached the highest landing, Dmitri pounded on a door, and it opened quickly. There was Nadia, just as I imagined her. She was on the shorter and on the curvy side with strawberry blond hair that was permed and teased. She held out her arms to us, and we stumbled into her embrace.

Thank goodness Nadia spoke English fluently. I was in no mood to mime and speak slowly for the rest of our stay. She knew exactly what we needed and directed us to the bedroom, which she and Dmitri usually occupied. She told us to shower, and after we would have breakfast. She also showed us a water cooler that was in their hallway explaining to us that the water had been boiled and that we could drink it and brush our teeth with it. "Sergei will be here for you at 9:15. You cannot be late for Sergei," she said with the wave of her index finger.

"What time is it now?" I asked.

"7:45," Nadia announced as she began to crack eggs in her tiny kitchen. We hadn't slept more than three hours in almost two days. We didn't dare lie down on the bed that looked so inviting for fear we would never wake up.

After our showers, Nadia served us eggs with sausage that resembled skinny hot dogs and toast with jelly. She sat with us as we ate and chatted about our flight and Rachel; she was surprised to learn how young she was.

Sergei was right on time, and Nadia kissed us on both cheeks before we trudged down the steps of the unlit hallway. We could hear three bolts lock behind her door. It was actually two doors. One was the kind of solid door that we have on many houses in the U.S.; the second outer door resembled that of a walk in freezer with the exception of three deadbolts.

Sergei jumped from the van, opened the door for us, and held my elbow as I stepped up and ducked my head before sitting down. We had been the last ones dropped off an hour and a half before, and now we were the first to get picked up. Our next stop was Svetlana's place where the Olsons were staying. Sherry and Shawn looked the way we felt, and I'm sure we looked just as raggedy. Sherry let herself fall onto the bench seat in the back of the van, and we all said our *good mornings* and *be flexibles* in the most syrupy sarcastic voices we could muster with forced smiles and cocked heads. Kate and Al were next to get on board. Al sat in the front seat beside Sergei and Kate squeezed in next me. I could tell immediately that Kate was one of those morning people even though this wasn't really morning for us. She was perky and bright-eyed and had restocked her purse and pockets with granola bars, fruit snacks, and candy.

Before we could do anything else, we needed to visit the Department of Education to formally accept the referrals for our children. We drove the van along a wide six-lane street in the center of the city. All the buildings were gray and no more than ten stories high. We parked the van and walked across the street to the Novosibirsk Department of Education.

Sergei explained that our interpreter Maria would be meeting us inside. Sergei's English wasn't fluent enough to navigate the jargon involved in the adoption process, and we were relieved that we would have another English speaker among us. The lobby of the building had a low ceiling and warped linoleum on the floors, the likes of which I hadn't seen since my parents remodeled an old rental house of theirs back in the late 1970's.

As we entered, Sergei pointed out Maria who was watching the door for us. He waved at her, and she walked forward in her long black coat and matching fur hat. I was surprised to discover she had Asian features, and I reasoned that she must also be Kazak like Rachel. She shook our hands, and we all said we were pleased and happy to meet her. After the formalities, she said, "Please come around me because I have something very important to tell you." We formed a huddle around her and bent our heads down so as not miss what she was saying in the crowded lobby.

"There eez problem. You are too earlee." We all lifted our chins and furrowed our brows.

"What do you mean?" asked Shawn, "We all had plane tickets and documentation."

"I know, but government officials do not expect you to accept your children until tomorrow."

"So do we wait until tomorrow?" Kate asserted with narrowed eyes.

"No, instead government assigned child for you. You go upstairs and sign papers to accept child. Then Sergei will take you away, and you will sign papers rejecting child immediately."

What?

This was insane. Did we all misunderstand her? After all, fatigue can cause hallucinations, and we hadn't slept since Monday and this was Wednesday, but really? Were we hearing her correctly? We were all asking questions at once, and Maria had to raise her hands to reign us in.

"The problem is with Olson baby and Marten baby."

My mouth hung open.

"Your children will not be ready to be officially accepted until tomorrow. Thees is why you need to accept different child today, then reject. Tomorrow we are here again, and you accept *your* child."

We bit our lower lips and shook our heads. What could we do? A woman we had just met was telling us to accept a different child then reject it. It was crazy, but we had no choice.

"Thees happen sometimes. It is only formality. Do not worry." She led us up three flights of stairs lined with floor to ceiling single-pane windows covered with frost. I tried to control a chill that overtook my body as I lifted each foot to the next step, but it was no use. By the time we reached the third floor, I was shaking and my teeth were chattering. Were we about to make the biggest mistake of our lives? Could we trust this person? Should we try to call Karen or Susan at LSS? How could we even get to a phone?

Maria went on to prep us, "Do not talk while we are in office. Do not say anything about thees not being your child. Do not ask questions unless she asks you something directly." We looked at her and nodded. "Remember, Sergei will take you to a place where you can sign paperwork rejecting thees child." *Oh brother, what have we done?*

We all congregated outside a nondescript office door and stood on the warped linoleum in a hallway lined with enormous ancient radiators. As we waited for the official in that office to open the door, we fidgeted to stay warm. Dick, Shawn, and Al shuffled from one foot to another with their hands stuffed into the pockets of their bulky winter jackets. Sherry, Kate, and I couldn't keep from whispering our concern over the situation.

"What's up with that?" Sherry hissed.

"I don't know. I don't get it. Do you think the folks at LSS know about this?" I wondered aloud.

"Why is Adam ready when your kids aren't?" Kate asked.

All we could do was scrunch up our shoulders in complete bewilderment.

"I'm pissed off," declared Sherry. So was I. And what was to become of the child we were about to reject? I tried to convince myself there would be a family for that child soon.

Kate and Al were called into the office first with only Maria to escort them. The rest of us stayed in the hall with Sergei. As he rubbed his forehead, I noticed that he had small tattoos on the tops of his three middle fingers just below his knuckles. Perhaps they were Cyrillic characters; whatever they were I wanted to know, but didn't want to ask.

Kate and Al emerged about ten minutes later. They said they just had to sign some papers, and Maria translated.

It was time for us to do the same. This time Maria had us go into the office with Sherry and Shawn. Inside there was a desk with a pretty but severe looking brunette sitting behind it. Behind her were bookshelves to the ceiling. In front of the desk were four chairs. Maria stood while the four of us tried to arrange ourselves into a sitting pattern in which our knees weren't touching.

Maria greeted the woman, and she introduced us. The woman didn't smile, and she didn't look at us. She pushed some papers to the edge of her desk. "Shawn and Sherry, this is the child that has been referred to you. You may sign this paper here at the bottom." Sherry leaned toward the desk and took a pen handed to her by the woman at the desk. I could see Sherry look intensely at the small picture in the upper left hand corner of the paper. She looked at Shawn then looked at me. I looked at her and widened my eyes but kept my mouth shut. She turned and signed the paper. Shawn took his turn, and then they both got up so that we could take the chairs that were closest to the desk.

Neither Dick nor I can recall the likeness of the child in the photo we saw. Now I can't even remember if it was a boy or a girl. But I do remember feeling awful about the rejection even if the circumstances were beyond our control. I repeated to myself, "There is a family for this child. There is a family for this child." I prayed it was true.

After the signing, Maria stood and ushered us into the hallway. Sergei was waiting with Kate and Al. "Guys, come with me," he said, looking over his shoulder. He took us to the stairwell, and there on the landing, we signed rejection papers using Sergei's back as a writing table.

We all needed a potty break after this adrenaline-inducing episode, and Maria pointed toward the public restrooms in the lobby of the Department of Education building. Sherry, Kate, and I pushed the swinging door open and walked into what looked like a normal public restroom. Then I pushed open a stall door. I backed out and said, "There's no seat on the toilet," and pushed open the next door. "Okay, there's no seat on this one either and there are some weird things next to the bowl." Sherry and Kate peeked in as I stepped aside.

"I guess you'll have to squat," said Sherry. "I don't know what those things are for, but they look like some sort of platform for your feet."

"I guess so, but I'm taking a picture first. I think I'll keep a public toilet photo journal. This could be interesting." Why would people stand and squat above the bowl instead of just sitting on a seat? We just couldn't figure it out.

We were starving, and Sergei told us he would take us to a place called New York Pizza for lunch. I was anxious to get another public restroom shot for my bathroom photo journal. When I did, I wasn't surprised to see a toilet sans seat, but I was astounded and comforted to find a paper towel dispenser, empty of course.

Following a slice of Hawaiian pizza, we all said silent prayers because it looked as if we were about to lose a game of chicken due to Sergei swerving wildly around the potholes in the road. My forehead rested against the frosted van window as row upon row of gray rectangular apartment buildings streamed past my gaze.

We Would Know Her Anywhere

Finally, the van bounced over a curb and into a small lot in front of a large white building. There was a single door for the entrance. We stepped out of the van, with Sergei's help of course, and congregated for a group photo taken by Maria before we stepped in to see our children.

As the door opened, I smelled something rather unsavory, a combination of sour milk, bleach, and dirty diapers. The entry was cold and the banister on the stairwell leading to the second floor had large chips of paint missing, exposing the dark iron underneath. We followed Sergei down the narrow hall to a lobby-like area with a small couch and a coffee table.

"Guys, stay here," Sergei instructed. "I find Dr. Eva."

Dr. Eva showed up and gave us all a quick nod. I already knew that she didn't speak English, but I knew somehow that even if she did, she wouldn't say much anyway. Al and Kate stepped into her office first. The door was slightly ajar leaving me a view of Al's face.

Sherry and I sat on the green couch with packing tape that sealed the ripped and discolored vinyl. The place had a closed-up smell and felt much like my parents' log cabin in the winter. I kept my jacket on and jotted some notes in my journal while Dick and Shawn paced. Several caregivers walked passed without giving us a second glance. Sherry got up and found the bathroom. She came back and told me it was a five out of ten. I decided to make a trip myself. Aside from the lack of toilet paper, paper toweling, and a toilet seat, the concrete floor was cracked and rough and looked as if it had had a run in with a jackhammer. A five was generous.

I walked back to Dick, Sherry, and Shawn and reclaimed my spot on the couch. I watched the caregivers walk briskly in and out of rooms and down the corridor, wearing white nurses' uniforms with black nylon stockings underneath. I noticed that they wore heeled, white, toeless sandals. Not a good look. I guess they didn't have *What Not to Wear* in Russia. From Dr. Eva's office, I heard Kate ask, "Do you have any history of his birth mother?" I heard Dr. Eva speak to Maria, then Maria translate to Kate and Al. "There is information on birth mother's height and weight. Records will come later."

We heard a baby's cry come from deep within the orphanage; it was very unsettling.

"Sounds like a newborn," Dick said, straightening up and rubbing the back of his neck. Kate and Al emerged from the office with Dr. Eva close behind. They looked worried.

"Adam has the chickenpox and he's in quarantine at the orphanage hospital," Kate blurted as Sergei whisked them away. "We're leaving now. See you later."

"Good luck." We all stared at them as they walked briskly down the narrow hallway toward the exit while throwing their scarves over their shoulders.

It was our turn next. We shuffled into Dr. Eva's office. I looked around and noticed the 70's style paneling and dented filing cabinets. Dick and I sat across from Dr. Eva's desk, and Maria sat behind us. She translated while Dr. Eva rifled through papers and talked with her head down. After a few moments, Dr. Eva looked up from her paperwork.

"She is very strong," Dr. Eva said through Maria. "She is also very healthy although she suffers from pyramidal insufficiency." *Whatever that means.* Dr. Eva continued, "This means she could not flatten her heal while standing." I looked at Dick with a cocked eyebrow, and Dick frowned at me as if to say, *Don't be a smartass and keep your mouth shut.* I clamped my mouth shut as Dr. Eva rattled on about Rachel having the chickenpox early but that she is now recovered. "Also, generally children born to Asian parents are intellectually strong." *Okay, okay, let's get on with it. We just want to see our baby!*

At last we were led upstairs to an area called the winter garden to wait for the babies. Sherry and Shawn were led into Dr. Eva's office. Like the rest of the orphanage, the floor was clad in warped linoleum, and it sloped down dramatically in the center of the room, as if the four walls were just plopped on top of the roof. There were blue fluorescent lights hanging on the walls, and I recalled my mother telling me about an article she read in the *National Geographic* explaining how Siberian children didn't get enough vitamin D due to lack of sunlight in the region. In contrast to the orphanage lobby, the winter garden must have been close to eighty degrees. I noticed the windows were fogged as Dick and I tugged on the necks of our turtlenecks and pushed up our sleeves. I shed my fleece and Dick unpacked the video camera. Sherry and Shawn came up about ten minutes later.

"Oh my gosh, I'm so excited I have to pee again!" Sherry squealed as she came into the room. She didn't try to make another trip to that bathroom, however.

"Ooh, it's kinda toasty in here, isn't it?" Shawn remarked, unzipping his ski jacket. Maria came in a few minutes later to tell us the caregivers were waking the babies up from their naps. She told us to give her the diapers we brought along so that the caregivers could put them on the babies. In Russia, babies are potty *conditioned* beginning at six weeks. The children aren't diapered. They are simply placed on a little pot a half hour after feedings. If the caregivers are lucky, the children will eliminate at that time. I was glad to learn that their little butts didn't have to sit on the cold porcelain of a seat-less toilet.

We handed Maria our Huggies size-one diapers and hoped they would fit. She left the winter garden, and we waited.

I filmed our little group as we sat on the sectional squirming on the edge of our seats. Dick, Sherry, and Shawn had their hands clasped in front of them. Dick's voice cracked as he said into the camera, "Rachel, we can't wait to see you. We love you already, Honey." As I stuffed the video camera in its padded case, we could hear footsteps coming from behind a door on the far end of the room. We stood up and watched as the doorknob turned, and the door creaked open. Two caregivers holding our babies stood behind Maria, who quickly stepped aside.

We would have recognized Rachel anywhere. The caregivers turned so we could see our children's faces, their round cheeks squeezed by the ties on the little bonnets they wore. She was the baby on the right, wearing the green terry cloth sleeper. She was the one with the huge, brown eyes wide open and staring. She was the one with the chubby cheeks. She was the one staring back at us. For a while I just stood there covering my mouth with both hands until Dick said, "You can hold her, Honey. She's our daughter!"

I reached out and placed my hands on her curved warm little back. The caregiver held her out to me, and I swiveled her around until she conformed to my shoulder. She settled right in, and I looked at Dick who was smiling but teary-eyed. All I could utter was "Oh, oh, oh." A huge wave swept over me. What was it? Was it responsibility? No, it was more powerful than that. It was motherhood. I knew I just couldn't let anything happen to the little person in the green terry sleeper on my shoulder. I'm sure I squeezed her too much because Dick told me, "It's okay, Honey. She's fine. You don't have to hold her so tight."

Eventually I handed her over to Dick. He held her up at arms length and gave her a little jiggle until a smile separated her chubby cheeks. Pulling her down to his chest, I watched her snuggle against him. I wrapped my arms around them both. So this is what almost a year of paper work was for.

Sherry and Shawn were already on the floor with Jacob, watching him teeter on his tummy and bat at his stuffed toys. Jacob was two months older than Rachel, very petite, but perfectly healthy and very responsive. Rachel, on the other hand, was not what we expected. This was not a typical orphanage baby that people had warned us about. She was a chunk with creases where her wrists and ankles should have been, and she was strong. I spread out the baby blanket we had stuffed in the diaper bag, and we pulled out the puffy plastic book and rattle toys placing them around her.

"Let's take off her bonnet," Dick said. "She's sweating!" I untied her bonnet and slid it off her head. Her brown fuzz was flat to her scalp, and she seemed relieved to lose the bonnet. We moved on to the rest of her outfit. We peeled off her sleeper only to discover another sleeper underneath, and under that we found a T-shirt. Wool socks covered the feet of the sleeper, so we pulled them off, rescuing her damp feet. Maria picked up our video camera and filmed us as we uncovered our child. I half expected a reprimand when she said from behind our video camera, "The Russian mothers believe that being very warm keep babies healthy."

We spent our time watching Rachel roll onto one side and coaching her to push herself all the way over onto her back. We remarked at how strong she kicked her little legs, and how she watched us so intently and seemed to take in her surroundings. I noticed a flat spot on the back of her head, but I was expecting this after going through the endless binders of prep material from LSS. Because Rachel probably shared a crib with three other infants, she commonly lay on one side, eventually flattening a spot on the back of her head. We checked her out all over, as Dr. L. suggested, even removing the diaper we brought. Rachel did appear to be perfectly healthy, but when I held her, I could hear a rattle in her chest. Every so often she would let out a gravelly cough, which alarmed me, being a childhood asthma sufferer. I mentioned it to Maria, and she assured me that she would ask Dr. Eva about it later.

After three hours, Maria announced that the caregivers would be coming back to take Rachel and Jacob away for their bedtime. I felt an ache in my chest. *Take them away? But we're their parents. Wow! I'm a parent!* We had to get them dressed quickly, much more difficult than I thought. Rachel began to fuss and cough, and she stiffened her chubby little legs when we tried to pull on her second sleeper. *I don't blame you,* I thought. *They have you wrapped up like stuffed cabbage. No wonder you were sweating.*

Reluctantly, we handed our children off to the caregivers. Maria told Sherry and me that we could follow them down to the children's "sleeping chamber" as she called it. We followed the two women through a room attached to the winter garden that was filled with mats and what looked like some sort of therapeutic apparatus. I noticed strange ropes and pulleys and hanging bars. It reminded me of the movie *One Flew Over the Cuckoo's Nest,* and I held in a shiver. We walked down the dark stairwell as Rachel and Jacob watched us from over the white-clad shoulders of the Russian women. We walked through another series of rooms and dark corridors, and after that the caregivers gave us a signal to kiss our babies and say goodbye for the day. I craned my neck around the doorway and looked into a large room holding about six cribs that looked more like play pens. They were square with white rails around each side. Each crib held four infants. I imagined Rachel rolling to her side and resting against the rails along with her crib mates.

"This place is huge," Sherry remarked as we tried to find our way back to the winter garden. I agreed. The place was like a maze with all its additions, narrow hallways, and dim lighting.

Sergei met us in the orphanage lobby with Kate and Al, who he had retrieved from the infirmary.

Kate greeted us with, "Hey guys!" in her usually chipper fashion that I had become familiar with in less than forty-eight hours. Kate and Al already had one child, a daughter named Alison, who had special needs. I could see right away that Kate was exactly the type of parent Alison needed. She was always prepared to whip out a handi-wipe or toss someone a pack of fruit snacks. I imagined her having those little secret pockets sewn into the lining of her jacket in which to stash her motherly cache of emergency items.

After offering everyone a snack in Sergei's van, Kate told us about the infirmary. "It was dark and had cinder block walls," she explained while opening Al's granola bar. "I think it may have been a prison before!" But she went on to tell us that her son looked to be in good shape except that he was covered in green spots. The green spots were actually a chicken pox salve that we would later see on Rachel in her passport photo.

All in all, we were happy with the way our kids looked, and despite my rather unflattering depiction of the orphanage, we knew that these caregivers truly cared about our children. Their schedules were rigid, and we knew that they were bottle fed by hand and rocked, not common in other orphanages. We also knew that even though there were a hundred children at this orphanage, there were two hundred caregivers to watch over them. Though it was run down by American standards, and the bathroom was really nasty, the rest of the place seemed clean and tidy.

We were dropped off at Nadia and Dmitri's last and told to meet Sergei at 9:35 the next morning. Dmitri met our van and led us upstairs. It was 6:00 or 6:30 p.m. when we reached the apartment, but it felt like 4:00 a.m. to us. The twelve-hour time difference had taken its toll; to say we were wiped out was an understatement. I felt like a dirty dishrag, and I'm sure Dick felt the same. Nadia had dinner ready and on the table for us; a goulash that tasted quite good and a coleslaw-type side dish. She sat with us as we ate and asked us about our day. It was hard not to like her. She shattered every stereotype of stern Russian women. She smiled and laughed while we talked, and I noticed she touched Dick's arm frequently. Don't get me wrong; I thought it was cute. Dick *is* handsome, and he has what one of my friends refers to as bedroom eyes. I could see Nadia's admiration.

After dinner we brushed our teeth with water from the water cooler and headed to bed. We were asleep before 7:30 p.m. When we awoke at 4:00 a.m., I remembered how long it took to get over jet lag. I figured we would be holding to this weird schedule for the rest of the trip. Dick was also awake, and slowly we began to move about. I went straight for the video camera. We lay on the bed, and Dick held the camera so we could watch all the footage from the day before.

Nadia had to work that day, but she had breakfast ready for us before she headed off to the university where she taught English to physics majors. We were staying in Akademgorodock, the Academic Village of Novosibirsk, which explained why the apartments were laid out like a college campus.

Sergei's van was ready to meet us at precisely 9:35. Our first stop was the Department of Education again, but this time we were going to officially accept *our* children. For the rest of the morning, Sergei planned on taking us to a "Toy Store" and then to New York Pizza for lunch.

We waited outside the same office door as the day before. For some reason, Kate and Al had no issues with Adam, so Sherry and Shawn and Dick and I were the only ones who had to go through this acceptance process again. Maria gave us the same instructions as before, "Do not talk. Only look at peec-ture of child and sign paper."

Once inside the office, the process was almost identical to the day before. The woman behind the desk slid a paper across with a photo of the child in the top center of the page. All we had to do was sign. Sherry and Shawn were first. I watched Sherry bend her head intently as she scribbled her signature. As she raised her head when she was finished, I noticed something rather odd. The pen she was using was topped with the head of a court jester, complete with jingle bells hanging off the ends of his pointed hat! *I'm going to sign my child's life away with this?* I thought. I looked at Sherry and her eyes went to the pen and back to me as Shawn was signing. She bit her lower lip and began to shake as her face turned red. *Do not laugh,* my eyes said to her as I opened my lids as far as possible while sucking in my lips. I had to control myself. Rachel's livelihood depended on it. *Okay, don't look at Sherry. Don't look at Sherry!*

It was our turn; when I looked at the paper, the humor melted away. I grabbed the crazy pen in my sweaty hand and signed. I handed it to Dick, and he did the same. He paused after just for a second and gave the pen a quick examination before handing it back to the lady behind the desk.

With that behind us, we headed to the toy store. It was like a small department store with diapers, toys, clothes, and accessories for children. Sherry, Kate, and I went right for a rack of clothes.

"Oh my. Look at this!" Kate said as she held up a tag from a jumper.

The tag was from Kohl's department store. "Are these . . . *stolen?*" She raised her eyebrows and began examining all the other outfits. They all had Kohl's price tags. What the heck? We decided to pass on buying these clothes and look at toys instead. I picked out something that looked like a large weeble but more like a mushroom. It wobbled back and forth but didn't fall over and made a subtle jingling noise. This one had a very friendly expression on its little yellow globe. I passed on some others that looked rather sinister. The store looked much like a scaled-down and less obnoxious Toys R Us, with the exception of little plastic toilet training pots. Unlike the American thrones with blinking lights and sound effects, these were basically Cool Whip containers.

The rest of the day played out much like the day before: lunch at New York Pizza, a visit to see Rachel at the orphanage, peeling layers of sweaty clothes off her, and entertaining ourselves by watching her drool on the bib we brought along.

It was the next day when everything went straight to hell.

CHAPTER 19

The van pulled off the two-lane road onto a gravel parking area strewn with litter. It was one of those painfully bright days, with the sun glaring off the snow and blinding us when we tried to look through the windshield. "Get out and we take peec-ture," Sergei instructed as we all looked around skeptically. "It takes only one mee-nut."

We got out of the van, leaving everything inside.

We were at a huge dam with what appeared to be a nuclear power plant across the river. After our photo, Sergei walked down an embankment for a few steps to show the guys his hot fishing spot. Naturally, the guys were intrigued and followed him. They walked ahead, and we all ended up arriving at the edge of the dam where about three fishermen stood with their elbows against the cement wall bracing long iron hooks that held long fishing poles. I looked over the edge and felt dizzy. It had to be at least a fifty-foot drop. (I consulted with Dick on this who has a knack for guessing measurements. Some people have perfect pitch; Dick has perfect calibration.)

Sherry sidled up next to me, "Interesting, huh? Doesn't this look like a great picnic spot?"

"Brrrr. I want to get back in the van. I'm freezing, and my eyes are watering from this insane wind."

"I hear ya," she said, squinting herself.

"And I feel naked without my purse," I added.

The guys and Sergei were heading back to the parking lot where a fish monger—yes an actual fishmonger—sold frozen fish hanging from a line across the street. I caught up to Dick, and he and Shawn and I went to take shelter from the wind on the side of the van while the others checked out the frozen fish.

Dick and I walked to the van hand in hand while Shawn lagged behind us with his video camera. We made it to the van and stood with our mittened hands shoved deep into our pockets doing the cold weather dance.

We turned toward the sliding door and noticed something. Actually, it didn't register at first. It seemed like I was looking into the van, but what's wrong with that, right? *Why isn't there a reflection? Oh my God, where's the glass? Oh my God.* "The window is broken!"

"Oh, shit!"

Shawn caught up to us by then. "Hey, what the h—"

"Sergei!" Dick screamed across the road as the others crowded around the frozen fish stand. "Get over here. Our van was robbed!"

I looked on our seats. They were empty. My backpack purse was gone. Dick's camera bag was gone. *Oh my God.*

Sergei ran over to us. His face was completely purple.

"What did they take?" He was yelling over the wind and squinting while he pulled his keys from his pocket. He unlocked the passenger door and reached around to unlatch the sliding door so as not to rip his jacket or scratch himself on the shards of glass.

After a quick scan of the van, it was clear that Dick and I were the only ones who had been robbed although it was evident that the crooks had tried to pry the handle of the passenger door first. All of our court documents sat in a briefcase on the seat. *What if they had gotten those?*

"Guys, what was in bags?" Sergei had his hands on my shoulders and was practically shaking me back and forth.

"Our passports, our plane tickets, our Visas!" I hollered at Sergei.

"I told you to always take with you!" Sergei hollered back, and then my sassy side made a guest appearance.

"But you left all our papers on the seat!" It gushed from my mouth followed by a gasp and tears. Dick stepped in front of Sergei, pulling me to him.

"Yes, you are right," Sergei conceded while rubbing his forehead.

"What about the police?" offered Al.

"Yes, I call police," Sergei nodded quickly while starring at the broken window and pulled his cell from his pants pocket.

As Sergei placed the call, we noticed a long rod like the one we saw the fishermen using lying on the gravel near the front of the van. We also noticed that the car we parked next to when we first pulled in was still there. I noticed Shawn's video camera sweeping over the car and focusing on the license plate for a while. He saw me watching him, and he pulled away from the camera quickly. "You never know," he shrugged.

Sergei spoke quickly and loudly into the phone. Every so often we caught the word *American* followed by what I imagined to be Russian expletives. He hung up and promised the police would be here soon but not to expect much.

"This happens sometimes," he said with his hands palms up in front of him. I thought again about the tattoos on his knuckles. "Sometimes things held for money, you know . . . ?" He made a circular motion with his hand compelling us to fill in the blank for him.

"Ah, you mean ransom. People kidnap stuff for ransom!" shouted Al like he was playing some warped version of charades.

"Yes!" Sergei pointed at him, like Al was on a game show.

As Sergei and Al held their dynamic exchange, two men approached the car next to us. They were rather non-descript; one was older than the other, but they appeared to be in their mid-twenties, and they both wore parkas but no large fur hats. They looked at us huddled around the broken window, then laughed across the roof of their car to each other as they slid into their vehicle.

While waiting for the police, we hobbled down the steep embankment toward the river. There were thick weeds and jagged rocks, but we held out hope that the culprits rifled through our stuff and then dumped it along the bank.

As we wobbled amongst the rocks, I wondered how on earth we would get home. Could we travel? Would we have to purchase new tickets? They had everything: our passports, our tickets, and worst of all to me, my journal. I felt violated, vulnerable. Were we going to be victims of international identity theft? I could see us now on *60 Minutes* being interviewed by Ed Bradley, Dick and me sitting side by side with our hands clasped in our laps, the center of an international incident. What a mess.

The police showed up in a white van. They appeared to be fifteen years old and have less facial hair than I, not exactly confidence inspiring.

Sergei spoke to the police, pointed at the fishmonger, and the cops walked across the windy road to question him.

*

Eventually we wound up at the Novosibirsk police department. Sergei ushered us in and told us to wait in the lobby while he went behind a counter to speak with someone who looked like a detective. The building was much like the Department of Education but with even less ambience, battleship gray with a hint of rusty steel thrown in as an accent. We stood around watching the sullen cops in their high lace-up boots walk briskly down the hall and through the doors to the inner office where Sergei was holding court. Every so often one of the detectives would look our way.

"Man, they look so serious!" said Sherry,

"Maybe it's because they're so ugly," offered Al.

We all began to snicker uncontrollably. Sergei glanced at us quickly over his shoulder then quickly swiveled on his foot and jogged toward us.

"Guys, come here and stand in hallway. No laugh here. No laugh in government buildings," he hissed at us then headed back toward the office.

Nadia showed up about an hour later with Sergei following close behind her as she clicked down the hall toward our bench in her high-heeled boots and fur coat. I stood up, and she enveloped me in a huge furry hug. After kissing Dick on both cheeks, she explained that Sergei had called her, and she was here to assist in translation for us.

A stern looking uniformed policeman came up behind our group. Sergei looked at Shawn. "Shawn, you must go," Sergei instructed. Then Nadia cut in.

"They need to ask you some questions. Bring your video camera."

We became even giddier after Shawn was taken away, and our topic of conversation digressed quickly from national security to circumcision. Sherry wondered if it was possible to perform a foreskin transplant if they had second thoughts when Jacob got older.

"I hope we can still see the babies today," I uttered despondently. That sobered us up for a while.

Thank God Nadia showed up. It turned out that Shawn's footage provided the police with information that was intriguing and incriminating. Shawn told us that the police in the conference room where he was taken became rather agitated and excited after seeing that he had shot film of the nuclear power plant across from the dam. Nadia did some fast talking and patiently explained that he was with us on an adoptive mission and was just being a dumb American tourist. No, Shawn was not a terrorist. Poor Shawn. But he did good work because the police were following up on the plate number.

Then came the bad news. There was really nothing else we could do. Nadia translated as Sergei explained how we could stay and file a police report, but we'd need to stay another five days. If we didn't want to go that route, we could take our chances on trying to fly to Moscow from Novosibirsk without passports or identification. This was a no-brainer. We couldn't stay another five days. I didn't have asthma medication to take me that far, and both of us had jobs waiting for us back home. We decided that we would try to sneak by security and make it to Moscow where we could get new passports at the American Embassy.

About four hours and one missed meal later, we headed out of the police station and into another van delivered by Sergei's son for another quick stop at New York Pizza for supper. He pulled the van into a slushy, angled parking spot in front of what was now becoming our regular hang out. Sergei and the guys got out of the van, but we decided to stay behind. "Guys, don't go anywhere," Sergei warned before he locked and slammed his door. *Oh, don't you worry.*

Sergei, bless his heart, made arrangements for us to go to the orphanage even though we missed our visiting hours. That evening at the orphanage we were allowed to feed the babies their bottles. The bottles were glass and had black rubber nipples about four inches long. Dick and Shawn speculated as to what sort of udder in nature it was trying to mimic. There were bits of bread floating in the milky liquid in the bottles, and both Rachel and Jacob sucked it down in less than two minutes. The babies fell asleep in our arms that night. Looking into Rachel's eyes that evening, I was so thankful that all of this mess didn't occur while she was with us and that she was safe.

Back at Nadia's, Dick spent two hours on the phone calling our credit union and canceling all of our credit cards. After he got off the phone, Izolda, the Russian liaison for LSS, called and spoke with Nadia. Nadia informed us that we would be leaving for Moscow in two days with our friends, but then we would be staying in Moscow to get our new passports at the American Embassy.

Sergei, Nadia, Izolda, and the LSS office in the U.S. arranged for us to fly with our friends to Moscow. They would fly to JFK, but we would have to stay over Sunday and most likely Monday night with a new host arranged by Darya, our driver in Moscow.

Our last day in Novosibirsk was spent traveling to the open market in the morning where Kate, Sherry, and I bought "fur" coats. When we asked Sergei what kind of fur it was he said, "forest creature," with a shrug and wave of his hand. That was good enough for me. I just wanted to ditch my Columbia ski jacket that seemed to make us a moving target. Sergei motioned for us all to make a huddle around Dick when it was time to pay for the coat. He told us not to pull out all of our money and to hand it to him quickly

With our new coats, we made one final trip to New York Pizza before our last visit to the orphanage.

People have asked us if it was hard to leave Rachel. At the risk of sounding insane, I'll be honest: my answer was "no." The truth was, we were hoping that we *could* leave, so that we could turn right around, come back, and bring her home. Sergei had told us that we would be coming back on December fifth, less than one month after we were to arrive in the U.S.; we just needed to get there first.

Our last visit to the orphanage was rather bleak. We had no diaper bag with diapers or toys. Sherry gave us an extra quilted blanket that she had brought along, and we spread it on the floor for Rachel. Kate and Al loaned us some toys from their supply and because Adam was now out of the infirmary, we were all able to play with our children together in the winter garden.

Saying Goodbye, For Now

At the Novosibirsk airport, Sergei spoke rapidly to the stewardess collecting boarding passes. Kate, Al, Sherry, and Shawn had already boarded the plane without incident. We, of course, were in the middle of negotiations with the Russian transportation board. After some deliberation and the handing over of our photocopied passports and Visas, Sergei motioned for us to get on the plane. We practically galloped onto the tarmac and up the steps to the small aircraft.

In Moscow, Darya met us again and took us by van to the other airport where our friends would board the flight to JFK in New York. They hugged us tightly and gave us all of their extra rubles. We said thank you with quavering voices, and they told us it was nothing and wished us good luck, their faces reflecting their doubt and concern. Then Kate handed me her last cereal bar.

Believe It—It Can Happen

Darya took us to our new host where we were to stay until we got new passports and Visas. Because it was a Sunday, she, of course thought we could go sightseeing after we got settled. Being the flexible types that we were, we agreed.

Olga, our hostess in Moscow, had a huge apartment by Russian standards. It was about twelve hundred square feet and had hardwood floors, something we had not seen since leaving the U.S. She met us at the door and quickly ushered us in. She was a large woman with even larger hair who talked incessantly while we ate our breakfast.

After touring a famous art museum where nothing was written in English, Darya dropped us off at Olga's and told us she'd see us the next morning for our trip to the American Embassy. I awoke around three a.m., not yet adjusted to the three hour time difference from Novosibirsk. I heard some strange noises and felt the bed shaking. It took me a while to remember where I was until objects in the room came into focus. I rolled over and saw Dick sitting on the edge of the bed. His head was in his hands and his elbows rested on his knees.

"Honey, what's wrong?" I crawled over to him and put my arm around his shoulders.

"I want us to go home, and I don't know how we're going to get there. I don't know what to do. I can't help us." He was crying. I hadn't seen him cry like this since the miscarriage. I realized how truly scared he was and somehow the direness of our situation finally struck me. This wasn't an inconvenience. This was serious stuff. How would we get out of Russia?

"We'll get our new passports and Visas tomorrow, and everything will be okay." What was I talking about? "We'll get home, honey. I know we will."

We lay awake until it was time to get up and shower. The shower was located in a separate tiled room next to the room housing the sink, toilet, and cat's litter box. Although this couple was rather affluent, the apartment was filthy. When getting undressed, I hung my dirty underpants on the towel bar for fear of them touching the floor. I let the water run good and hot in an attempt to sanitize the bottom of the tub before stepping in. Later, I discovered Dick did the same. We ate our typical breakfast but passed on the orange caviar Olga had set out for us. We waited for Darya.

The American Embassy opened at eight a.m. We were there early, waiting on the frigid sidewalk with Darya. She had picked us up and driven us in her vehicle, a small blue station wagon belonging to her and her fiancé. She explained that in Russia, people don't buy cars with loans like they do in the U.S., instead you "wait until you have money, then buy." What a concept! We sped to the center of Moscow. She explained that she would be waiting for us outside because only American citizens were allowed inside the embassy. We walked through the gate and up the steps by ourselves.

The inside of the embassy was bright and overly warm from the steam heat provided by the Russian government. We stood in front of a long white counter until a chubby, young woman wearing a baggy sweater and black rimmed glasses walked in and took a seat behind it. It was such a relief to see an American in clothes that looked comfortable.

"What can I do for you this morning?" she sat down in a swivel chair as she addressed us with a warm smile.

We explained our predicament. Then *she* explained our predicament.

"Getting new passports won't be a problem. They'll cost you about $180. Do you have that money?" We told her we had just enough.

"The problem will be getting your Russian Visas out of the country. The Russian officials will take their good ole sweet time because you're American, so you could be here up to three more weeks."

What? She mentioned this as if she were telling us to bring our own silverware to a potluck.

Oh my. I was going to run out of asthma medication. Where would we stay? What about school? What about Rachel? Would this affect the adoption?

She gave us forms to fill out declaring that our passports had been stolen, and we turned from the counter to find a spot at the long table in the lobby. As we turned, a man in a trench coat approached us.

"Hi there, my name is Tom. I overheard your story. I'm from Iowa. Where are you from?"

We told him.

"You know, I'm here on business, and I come here a lot. Somehow I feel it is my duty to help out fellow Americans, and I think you could use some help." He pulled back his coat and reached into his back pocket, pulling out his wallet. He opened it and handed Dick a one hundred dollar bill. "Look, you need this. Please take it."

Dick reached out his hand and took it. Tom and Dick shook hands. I croaked out a thank you as Dick clamped his lips together and bowed his head.

Darya was waiting for us where we left her. We walked to a small convenience store a few blocks away to have our new passport pictures taken. After waiting for the photos to develop, we walked back to the embassy and turned them over to the young woman behind the counter. "This kind of thing happens here," she told us apologetically. "I hope everything works out and you can get your Visas quickly." Her empathy was not a good omen. It would be about an hour until the passports were actually assembled, so we decided to go outside and wait with Darya, but not until I used a restroom. It was an absolute pleasure to let my butt touch the pristine white toilet seat!

We met up with Darya outside in the overcast late morning. We were discussing our timetable in regard to the situation and when and how we would state our case of desperation to the Russian officials in order to expedite issuance of new Visas. Darya said she would do the talking. We were fine with that and had become used to keeping our mouths shut. We were watching her intently and nodding dumbly when her cell phone rang. She reached in her pocket, opened it, and brought it to her ear in one swift motion.

She spoke in typical clipped Russian at first, and then her end of the conversation became quite animated. She looked back and forth at us and started to smile and nod. Her fist went into the air, and she became more animated than we had ever seen her. We realized that this news might actually have something to do with us. She pulled the phone away from her ear and snapped it shut. "Guys," she grabbed our shoulders, "eet is Izolda on phone. She talk to Sergei. He find passports and Visas!"

For the second time in five months we cried for joy. We all embraced and jumped up and down on the sidewalk. I felt my muscles relax as Dick pulled me off the ground. It was nothing short of a miracle. We were going home!

Of course, the fact that our belongings were recovered made things a bit more interesting. We had to go back into the embassy and explain this to our compatriot behind the desk. Her response took us by surprise. "Hey, this is Russia. I've seen stranger things happen. No problem. This is what we need to do." I liked the way she said "we." She leaned forward onto her elbows and explained in detail what to do to get back into the U.S. now that our old passports were reported stolen and an alert for them was on the U.S. databases at every major U.S. airport.

We would use our old passports and Visas to leave Russia from the Moscow airport, but once we landed at JFK, we needed to hide those and use our new emergency passports so that we wouldn't get detained (fancy embassy lingo for arrested) at the airport. At this point we would have hidden our old passports in a body cavity we were so happy.

Sergei would be putting our documents on the late afternoon flight in Novosibirsk and they would arrive in Moscow that evening. Darya would pick them up and bring them to us in the morning before taking us to the airport.

To celebrate, Darya said she would take us out to lunch. I hate to say it, but we opted for McDonald's. And I'm not too proud to say it tasted great. We chatted about our jobs and life in the U.S. with Darya as I happily chomped on my ice cubes sweetened with Coke-a-Cola.

When we reached Olga's apartment we began packing immediately, and though I considered sleeping in my clothes to expedite our departure in the morning, Dick convinced me that I was, in fact, being dramatic.

The next morning Darya rang the doorbell, and she had our documents as promised. She told us that Sergei had the rest of our belongings, and he would have those for us on our return visit in December. No problem, we thought as we rifled through the large envelope she handed us. There were our passports, Visas, driver's licenses, and plane tickets. My journal wasn't among these items, but I hoped Sergei would have it for me on our second trip. Dick stuffed everything into the large pocket lining of his jacket, we thanked Olga's husband for the breakfast he prepared, grabbed our luggage, and never looked back.

The Moscow airport was relatively empty when we arrived with Darya. We handed her our documentation under the fluorescent lighting while we stood in front of the check-in counter. We listened as she explained our situation, the ticket exchange, the fee waiver for the transfer, and something about a letter from a senator. *Letter from a senator?* Our ears perked up. Darya passed a faxed document to the un-smiling woman behind the chin-high counter. The woman took her time looking it over, handed it back to Darya, and then dismissed us with a wave of her hand.

After turning to head for the gate, Dick asked Darya about the letter. "Oh yes, there eez letter here from senator." She pulled it from her messenger bag and handed it to Dick. We stopped, and Dick read aloud, "To Whom it May Concern: It is my understanding that two of our citizens have been detained in your country as victims of a crime. It is my hope that you will do everything in your power to expedite their safe return to the United States of America." Dick looked up at me and continued, "Signed: Senator Russ Feingold."

My jaw dropped. "Holy shit!" The expletive rang out in unison.

"Thees very important matter," Darya nodded in explanation.

We said our farewells to Darya, she wished us luck, and we passed through security into the concourse. The final test was presenting our boarding passes with our old passports. I watched Dick's hand shake as he handed his passport and boarding pass to the stewardess. My palms were sweating, and I could feel my cheeks flush. The stewardess looked over his papers and handed them back with a smile. She did the same for me, except for the smile, and I followed Dick along the downhill ramp toward the plane, practically skipping.

We walked sideways down the aisle of the plane with our gear hanging from us. Dick found our seats and I scrambled in first, close to the window after stuffing our things into the overhead compartments. As soon as my rear hit the seat, I grabbed for the seatbelt. Dick watched in amusement as I connected the metal ends with a satisfying click and pulled the strap tight. I leaned my head against the seat and looked at Dick. "I'm not getting off this plane."

He grabbed my hand and squeezed. "I'm not either."

CHAPTER 20

One More Time

From the time we arrived home until it was time to leave for Russia again, we kept busy with four baby showers thrown at three of my elementary schools and the junior high where Dick taught. We regaled our friends with the tale of our harrowing first journey to Russia and set the record straight on what actually happened. No, we were not robbed at gunpoint and kidnapped; no, the bandits didn't get $10,000; no, we didn't think the Russian mafia was involved (although, we couldn't really be sure); and NO, SERGEI WAS NOT INVOLVED! It bothered me that our friends immediately assumed Sergei had something to do with the theft, and we found ourselves defending his reputation. They didn't know how honored he was to work for the Americans and how he made more in one day from LSS than most Russians made in a week. They didn't see the tattoos on his knuckles from his former career with the KGB. Dick and I both knew in our guts that he would never do anything to jeopardize his position with LSS.

The three week waiting period was a blur of stuffing our truck with pink gift bags and doing loads of pink laundry. Soon after we emptied our suitcases, we kept them open in Rachel's room in her crib, and we started packing all over again. We started replenishing the essentials first, toilet paper, travel size baby wipes, and diapers. Rachel's suitcase was by far the largest. This was it, we realized. This time we'd be bringing Rachel home. Panic set in. I found myself singing under my breath *"Hold on . . . I'm comin' . . . hold on . . ."*

One night, Dick ripped open the cardboard packaging around the Baby Bjorn we acquired from a recent shower. He told me to put on my new Russian coat from the open market. I knew Dick was on some sort of rampage, so I just went along. He strapped the baby Bjorn to my chest over my big coat and then ran to the kitchen. I could hear him rummaging through the crisper drawer of our refrigerator.

"Where are you going, and what are you getting?" I asked in a slightly hysterical tone. He came back into Rachel's bedroom with a ten-pound bag of baking potatoes.

"Here we go. This is what you need." He grunted while stuffing the plastic sack filled with potatoes into the Baby Bjorn. "You should walk around like this for a while. Sure, the weight is off by a few pounds, but it's pretty close." Dick adjusted the straps as I stood with my arms out, sweating up a storm in the twenty-pound coat. Our yellow lab Lucy sat in front of me and cocked her head as if to say, "What on earth is wrong with you people?"

After amusing ourselves with potatoes, we got back to making preparations. We needed a lot more money this time. Once again, Dick made the trip to our credit union and returned home with $8,000 in clean new bills and feeling like Tony Soprano. We also needed to bring gifts for Nadia and her family. The people at LSS told us we should ask them if there was anything they needed. That was fine, but I was expecting something like a new set of dishtowels or a coffee pot. Instead, we found ourselves forking over hundreds of dollars on Clinique Happy perfume for Nadia, and Clinique Happy cologne and after-shave for her son and husband which made Dick anything but "happy" after entering the credit card receipts in the check book. Since we were on a spending frenzy, we picked out some nice perfume and a small stuffed animal for Darya. We'd still be looking for the American Embassy if she hadn't been with us.

Quicker than I could imagine, the time came for us to make arrangements with our respective schools for maternity and paternity leave again, and I called my mom and dad for our Lucy exchange.

Flying to Cincinnati was a piece of cake. We met up with Sherry, Shawn, Kate, and Al. As we sat in a pub for a quick drink before getting on the plane, we all speculated as to how Sergei managed to recover our belongings from the first trip. Shawn and Al came up with scenarios that involved Sergei doing some bone crunching. And although we laughed about it, perhaps it wasn't far from the truth. During our first trip, Olga had confided in us that Sergei used his influence with the KGB to "get things for people." Eek.

I couldn't imagine traveling with anyone else. There is a certain kinship formed by adoptive families, and Dick and I could tell we would all be friends for a long time. Once we landed at JFK, we would be meeting another couple, Phil and Cindy.

The guys watched the weather channel as the girls discussed the decorations for our babies' rooms. On the way to the gate Shawn mentioned that flights were backed up at JFK. We all bristled at this news. We were due for our official parental court hearing in Novosibirsk the day after our scheduled arrival. There wasn't much room for a delay. With crossed fingers, we waited for the plane to take off.

JFK was in the middle of a total white out when we landed two-hours late. The arrival and departure screens listed one cancellation after another. I started to sweat. Our flight was way overdue and Cindy and Phil were nowhere to be seen. We figured they were on the plane that we saw leaving as ours pulled up to the gate. If this flight out of JFK was cancelled, there was no way we were going to arrive for court in Novosibirsk on time. If we missed this hearing, we knew that the Russian judges would not be sympathetic. Oh brother, just when we thought we'd been through the worst. We looked at the screen and watched the green lettering flicker and change from DELAYED to CANCELLED. Ugh!

"Al, go do something." Kate pushed him in the direction of the ticket counter. We saw Al move faster than ever toward an Air France gate, his jacket flapping around him. We were close behind him tugging our carry-ons and lugging our heavy coats. As we approached the counter, we caught the beginning of his conversation with the perfectly coiffed ticket agent clad in a navy polyester uniform.

"We are an adoption group. It is absolutely crucial that we get on a flight out of here." Beads of sweat were running down the sides of Al's face from under his salt and pepper side burns. The woman behind the ticket counter nodded her head and called for another flight attendant. She turned to her computer, and we could hear the furious click of keys. "We need to get to Novosibirsk for our court hearing and we cannot be late!"

We stood back for a while and listened to Al's heavy breathing. The clicking of keys came to a halt, and the agent said, "We have a flight boarding now for Paris where you can connect and fly on to Moscow. I am transferring your luggage. Please produce your driver's licenses and passports. I need your credit cards, also." Dick and I tugged at the cords around our necks that were connected to our very nerdy, yet necessary identification holders. We took care of the ID first, slipping it safely inside the clear plastic pockets, then we added our credit card. We needed to pay extra, but what was a couple thousand dollars anyway? It was worth it. We had gotten on the last flight out of JFK before it shut down for two days.

I awoke with one leg on Dick's lap and the other underneath the seat in front of us. We sat in the three middle seats of the plane even though the one next to me was empty. Dick's head was tilted back on the headrest, and I could hear a soft snore coming from his throat. I untangled myself and stood to regain the circulation in my lower half. What a crazy way to become parents I thought. I squinted at the face of my watch. We would be landing in Moscow in about four hours where Darya would pick us up and take us to a hotel. The next morning we would take a flight to Novosibirsk on the Russian airline Aeroflot.

Darya was at the Moscow airport to pick us up, but this time, she hugged us immediately and said, "Guys! You are here!"

"Yeah, the Martens are bad luck, but we managed," Sherry winked.

We checked in to the hotel around midnight Moscow time and quickly ordered room service. This was a luxury I never would have considered in the U.S., but the rules didn't apply when we were in Russia.

The next morning we caught a flight from the airport that serviced Siberia. Instead of Siberian Air that we used on the first trip, we needed to take an Aeroflot flight. While squished against the window beside Dick, I kept repeating to myself, *Hold on . . . I'm comin', Hold on . . . I'm comin'.*

In three and a half hours, we landed in Novosibirsk and were reunited with Sergei, who held a box of our recovered items. Rifling through the box, we discovered our disposable camera that once contained our first pictures of Rachel, ripped to pieces, the film gone. Most importantly, there was my journal, among our packets of travel toilet paper and my redeemable Subway card. I grabbed it with both hands and kissed the cover without shame.

"Sergei, how did you find our stuff?" I looked up from the box while Dick kept digging.

"Ah . . . it is, how you say . . . interesting."

Keep a Straight Face

While Sergei drove us to our hosts' apartments, we discussed our schedule. We would go to court after breakfast and celebrate at a nice restaurant afterwards. The next day we would get the children's birth certificates then head to the orphanage to get our children in the afternoon. On the way to the courthouse that morning, Sergei stopped the van at an intersection, and Maria jumped in. She always seemed to appear from nowhere; we speculated that she jumped out of a manhole. What's really odd is that we never picked her up in the same place, and we never had to wait for her.

We couldn't laugh in the Novosibirsk courthouse either. We rose stiffly and clutched the instant coffee, the recommended gift for the judge, and allowed Maria to escort us into the courtroom. I would have thought the judge would want some good coffee, like Starbucks or Gloria Jeans, but no, she wanted instant. How bizarre that we were trading instant coffee for our daughter. As I stood to recite my name and date of birth to the judge, I stammered and my knees shook. She didn't smile, and she didn't look up. She just looked over her bifocals at the papers in front of her. Dick went through the same routine, stammering while he stated his place of birth and country of origin. After we emerged from the courtroom into the waiting area, our friends and Sergei patted us on our backs and wished us congratulations. *Where was our daughter? Why wasn't she here to celebrate with us?* I felt uneasy, as if this whole arrangement could fall apart at any moment. I didn't want to celebrate. I wanted to go get Rachel.

We all raised our glasses and shouted "to parenthood" at the restaurant following the hearings, but I just wasn't in the mood. I noticed I didn't feel all that great and was experiencing some stomach cramps, but I shrugged it off and downed my champagne. After my eighth trip to the toilet at three o'clock in the morning, Nadia met me in the hallway and offered me some medicine she said was stronger than Pepto-Bismol. Going against my better judgment to ingest something I couldn't even read, I swallowed it with bottled water. I had to get over this or there was no way I could make it to the orphanage to get Rachel.

In the morning, Nadia had hot porridge ready for Dick, and dry toast for me. "Today, you bring your daughter home," she said, holding me by the shoulders at arms length. It made me feel more like a child than a parent. She gave Dick a kiss on each cheek and sent us on our way.

We spent the morning back in Sergei's van traveling to each quadrant of the city to get birth records for our children. All but two of our kids were born in different quadrants of Novosibirsk. Dick and I sat in the back seat, letting ourselves get jostled around while I kept my arms crossed over my stomach. At each stop, we waited for about thirty minutes, until it was Phil and Cindy's turn. They came out of the office with Sergei in about *ten* minutes.

"How do you rate?" Sherry asked as they climbed into their seats.

"Sergei told us we go to the head of the line because he bought the doors for this building!" Phil grinned and winked.

Of course, we were last. The inside of the office was rather dumpy, go figure. Warped paneling covered the walls and cement covered the floor. Sergei handled everything, and told Dick that only the father's signature was required for the release of the birth records. My mouth hung open in indignation. When Sergei noticed, he gave me a mock punch on the shoulder. "Sorry, Mama," he whispered.

We took a seat at a table in the lobby as a woman turned to go into the records room for us. Here was our chance. Dick leaned forward on his elbows, "So Sergei, how did you get our passports back?"

Sergei squirmed a little and looked over each shoulder. "It is funny. I get phone call. It is young girl I think." I noticed him looking down at the tattoos on his knuckles. "So, I call police. I go to house and . . ."

At that moment the woman came out of the back room with Rachel's birth record. Ugh! We'd never really find out what happened, but maybe it was better that way. Maybe my conscience couldn't handle the truth.

At New York Pizza, I nibbled on a cold slice of buttered toast that Nadia packed for me while Dick dutifully munched on his slice of Hawaiian delight. My stomach was still feeling rather jittery, and there was no way I could force down a slice of pizza. As the others finished, Sergei and his assistant Ivan approached Dick.

"You ready to go to orphanage?" Sergei asked.

"Yes! We're ready!" I replied as I pushed Dick out of the booth.

"You go with Ivan. I take others," Sergei said, loosening his scarf.

We followed Ivan outside to the curb where his small station wagon was parked. On the drive to the orphanage, I filmed non-stop with our video camera as Ivan dodged the potholes. Russian pop music was playing on the radio, but I blocked it out; all that ran though my head was *Hold on . . . I'm comin' . . . Hold on . . . I'm comin.'* We passed the vacant apartment building on the hill that I came to recognize as the halfway point between New York Pizza and the orphanage. After ten minutes, the pinkish stucco house with the curved window shutters and wrought iron fence came into view. It was next to the orphanage. We were there. I turned off the camera and stowed it in the bag before jumping out with Dick.

The smell of the orphanage was exactly as I remembered, the combination of disinfectant, dirty diapers, and something else, was it formula? I was still trying to figure that out while we all stood together in the lobby waiting for our tour of the orphanage to start. Yes. A tour. What was it with Russians and sightseeing? I just wanted to get my kid and get out of there.

We were led from one room to another along the crooked and winding corridors of the orphanage. Each room housed some sort of therapy equipment and was eerily tidy. There was a room for water therapy, one for physical therapy, one for tactile therapy, and even a Montessori room. Kate remarked that her daughter, who had been born prematurely, had been in many rooms much like these. Also encouraging was their music room that contained a piano and small drums.

When we toured the infant area, we saw first-hand how early children are potty trained or *conditioned.* A tiny boy not more than ten months old and dressed only in an undershirt sat slumped on a small pot near an open bathroom door. He gave us a forlorn look as we walked past.

After the tour, we headed back to the winter garden where Dr. Eva was to prep us on our children. We sat on the battered sectional sofa, and she gave us the schedules for each child as we took copious notes. I was astounded by how involved this was. Rachel woke at 6:00 a.m., had a feeding at 7:00 a.m., and had a nap at 10:00 a.m., followed by a feeding of porridge. And on and on until 10:00 p.m. when the babies were awakened and given Kefir to help their digestion.

"Before you see children, you have opportunity to see special needs room," Maria told us. "It is not obligatory, only voluntary."

I looked at Dick and cocked my eyebrows. He scrunched his chin in thought and offered an "okay, let's go" shrug.

Only Kate, Al, Dick, and I went into the room. Immediately, I noticed the crying that ensued as we walked through the doorway. There were about four caregivers in the room and maybe eight children ranging from nine months to four years. Some wore braces on their legs, and some were engaged in physical therapy with a caregiver. I noticed a boy, a toddler, in a wheelchair.

Looking down at his feet, I noticed they were twisted backwards. I blinked, thinking that I wasn't seeing correctly. Maria kept talking, but I didn't hear her. This little boy had clubfeet I realized, although I had only read about this affliction. It was probably a relatively inexpensive surgery in the United States. He looked toward me while he screamed. The sight of the tall Americans in thick sweaters must have terrified him. *There is a family for him somewhere*, I chanted to myself.

We emerged from the room quietly and shuffled into the winter garden where Sherry, Shawn, Kate and Phil were waiting for us.

"Pretty tough?" I heard Phil ask Dick who was ahead of me.

I heard Dick say, "Yeah," and saw his elbow rise as he wiped away a tear.

Maria instructed all the mothers to follow her downstairs to fetch our children. The fathers were to stay in the winter garden and wait for us. We walked down the dark stairwell to the first floor where we could hear the clank of bottles. Maria and Dr. Eva stopped just outside Dr. Eva's office in front of a group of brightly colored boxes. Maria explained that the boxes contained cakes for us to bring to the caregivers of our children. My box was emerald green with colored ribbons swirling around it. I didn't want to open the box, but it turned out that I didn't have to. We then followed Dr. Eva into the other wing of the orphanage where our children were waiting for us. Sherry and Kate found their boys and ran to the cribs that resembled low wooden playpens. I looked around for Rachel, but this must have been the wrong room. Maria noticed I was looking a bit confused, and she told me that Rachel was in the next room. I looked across the hall and took off toward the doorway. From the doorway, I saw a dozen playpens. Where would I start? I looked in the first crib; all four babies in it were blond. From the corner of my eye, I noticed some movement. I straightened up and headed toward a crib with a chubby leg clad in a green sleeper sticking out from between the vertical slats. The leg wiggled up and down. My pace quickened, and I reached the playpen in about three steps. There, waiting for me, was our daughter.

"Hi, Rachel honey!" I said as a reached into the crib and put my hands around her middle, preparing to lift her.

"No, no, no!" I turned to see a caregiver coming at me quickly with her arms open. She bent over the rail and scooped Rachel up and into her arms. She held a blanket out to me with one hand and motioned for me to put it over Rachel's head. I set the cake box on a rocking chair and arranged the blanket carefully over Rachel's head so she could still peek out the back, and then I followed the caregiver up the steps to the winter garden. Rachel didn't take her eyes off of me as we climbed the steps and didn't make any noise. I kept smiling and talking to her, half expecting her to say, "Yeah, I remember you. You're the one with the diapers. What took you so long?"

Hi, Bye

The winter garden was in a state of chaos. Jacob was there with Sherry and Shawn; Kate and Al had Adam, and Phil and Cindy had Brian and Natalie who were both crying and hanging onto Phil's legs. Maria came in and announced, "You must take children's clothes off, then dress them in new clothes you bring. You have ten minutes."

Without thinking, we moved into parent mode. Rachel wasn't wearing her diaper yet, so we needed to act fast. Dick unzipped the new diaper bag and pulled out the burgundy velvet dress my friend Kirsten had made. I stood clutching Rachel to my chest and tears spilled out. Kate saw me from across the room and shouted, "Congratulations first-time mommy," as she stuffed Adam's legs into a new snowsuit.

Dick pulled me back to reality with "Hurry up and get her undressed!"

We pulled off her three layers of clothing, slapped on her diaper, and pulled the new velvet dress over her head. I turned her over in my arms and tried to button it up the back, but could not. The fourteen-pound baby we had seen a little over three weeks ago had packed on some weight. We left the back of the dress open and pulled on her tights. I could see that Phil and Cindy had put snowsuits on Brian and Natalie, so we got the snow gear out too. We carefully stuffed her chubby little legs into the pink fleece bunting but decided to stuff her into the pink downy snowsuit once we got downstairs.

Outside Dr. Eva's office, we were greeted by the caregivers who had watched our children so vigilantly. Six or seven women in white uniforms reached for our babies to give hugs and secure hats. Rachel's caregiver held her as we threw on our own coats, and then helped us get Rachel into her snowsuit. We gestured thank you to her in Russian and said farewell to the caregivers, Dr. Eva, Maria, and the entire orphanage by waving Rachel's down-covered hand.

It wasn't until we stepped into the van that I realized there were no car seats in Russia. In fact, I didn't recall seeing seatbelts either. On several occasions, I had noticed children in the backs of cars jumping on the seats at stoplights, but it didn't register until now. We would be bringing our child into a death trap. I held Rachel tight to me as she swiveled her head to take in all of us stuffed like sardines into the van.

During our first evening as a family, Rachel let out a wail that lasted for three hours. We tried everything to comfort her, but Dmitri seemed to be the only one with the magic touch. He soothed her by walking her up and down the short hallway in their apartment until she fell asleep. We heard him go into our bedroom to place her in the small grey crib that had been occupied by Nadia and Dmitri's children years ago. We heard the squeak of the mattress and a "shhh" from Dmitri. Silence. Then a wail from Rachel. Several hours later, Dick, Rachel, and I all passed out on the bed. I knew that other parents warned about the hazards of letting your children sleep with you, but I reasoned that those parents probably hadn't flown halfway around the world to get their children, and they could stick their advice where the sun never shone as far as I was concerned.

We settled into a comfortable routine during our four day stay. Nadia and Dmitrii went off to work while we lounged about in our pajamas and played with Rachel. Olga showed us her collection of American videos, and we watched *Conan the Barbarian* and *The Breakfast Club* twice. Before leaving to teach her morning classes, Nadia prepared a pot of porridge and left it on the stove for us to feed Rachel when she awoke. Nadia helped us so much that I was considering buying her a one way ticket to the U.S. and offering her free lodging with us for a year.

Cabin fever set in and one day we called our friends and arranged a rendezvous at the nearby New York Pizza, about a one-mile walk from the apartment. We tried to squeeze Rachel into the Baby Bjorn, but she was too big with her down snowsuit on, so Dick decided he would carry her. When we got to New York Pizza, sweat had seeped through Dick's sweater and soaked his jacket.

On the final day at Nadia's, we all made a trip to Izolda's apartment to finish the immigration and Visa paperwork that we had started in the States. We came back to bowls of warm borscht and pear tarts at Nadia's. After lunch, we began packing that afternoon for our flight to Moscow where we would get physicals for the kids and secure their passports and Visas. Always thinking ahead, Dick slipped outside to fill a plastic bottle with snow for Rachel's baptism two months later.

The next morning, Sergei was outside the apartment to pick us up for the last time. Nadia and Dmitri gave us hugs and kisses and wished us luck with parenthood. We traveled to the Novosibirsk Airport through the dark on potholed roads and past ominous birch forests as our children dozed in our arms. Every now and then Rachel would have a short crying jag. I hoped it wasn't a sign of more to come.

Be Flexible

The snow drifted down as the plane's wings were sprayed with antifreeze. Poor Dick didn't know what weather lay ahead, and I'm sure that was killing him. After the plane reached altitude, we took turns holding Rachel and keeping her entertained. She seemed like such an easy baby until the crying started again. We jiggled her and bounced her on our knees as we watched the little screen toward the front of the cabin that displayed the planes air route.

"Hmm, that's funny," Dick stretched his neck as he gazed at the in-flight monitor. We had been in the air for about two hours of the four-hour flight. "It looks like the plane is turning around."

I looked at the screen, and indeed the little plane was turning around on the screen. We looked at the other passengers. No one else seemed to notice or care, except for Shawn whose red-haired head poked up and turned to make eye contact with Dick. He mouthed, "What's up?" and pointed toward the screen.

Oh man, we're probably being hi-jacked. I thought things couldn't get much worse than having our passports stolen, but I guess a hi-jacking trumped theft of personal property.

As the plane tilted, the captain's voice came on over the intercom. We couldn't understand a word because he spoke Russian, but I noticed that the rest of the passengers appeared agitated. We sat still and waited for an explanation.

Svetlana, Shawn and Sherry's host, came up the aisle from the back of the plane. She was heading to Moscow with us where she'd catch a connecting flight to Saint Petersburg to visit her sister. "The plane is going back," she explained as she clutched the headrest of the seat in front of Dick. "There is much fog in Moscow. We wait at airport in Nizhiny Novgorod."

You've got to be kidding!

*

After seven hours, running out of formula, singing happy birthday to Dick, and subsisting on Ding Dongs and Pringles from the kiosk, our flight was called. Because Rachel's snowsuit was stowed in our luggage, under the plane, she wore only her fleece bunting. I strapped on the Baby Bjorn, Dick squeezed her into it and buttoned my furry Russian coat around her.

We were waiting near the exit gates of the terminal when Rachel began to scream. I tried to divert her attention by bouncing her, while Dick fished for our boarding passes in his coat. Not being an experienced parent, my goal was for her to stop crying so that everyone would stop staring at us. After about fifteen minutes I looked down at her fuzzy head and said, "I'm sorry Baby Rae, I don't know what to do." She looked up at me from the sling on my chest, her face red, and her fists clenched. Kate recommended giving her some gas drops, guessing that she had gas pains. Dick rummaged through the diaper bag and found the drops. He squeezed the dropper over her gaping mouth, and she gulped the medication down between sobs. It didn't seem to help.

Instead of walking to the plane, we were herded onto a tram. Dick and I were the last ones in. I was sure everybody else wanted to get away from us. The tram glided over the snow-packed tarmac and stopped near the plane, but the doors didn't open. People craned their necks to see out the fogged up windows and watch as two airport personnel tried unsuccessfully to align the aluminum stairs with the exit door. This lasted about twenty minutes, and Rachel wailed non-stop. Finally, the stairs were in place and the doors of the tram opened. Everyone got up and headed out into the cold dark night. Dick and I sat back and let everyone else get off the tram without us, figuring this was the least we could do. I was bouncing Rachel again when I heard, "Go mama, go!" I looked out the door and saw Shawn waving for us to come out. Dick stood immediately and grabbed our stuff. I stood with Rachel and stepped onto the snow. I couldn't believe what I saw. All of those people who had gotten off the tram first were standing at the bottom of the stairs in two groups forming a chute for us to walk through. They patted us on our backs as we passed them to get to the steps chanting, "Go, go, go!" They could have chosen to be in the warm cabin of the plane, but instead they put us first.

Rachel continued her screaming when we got on the plane, but we found our seats quickly and many passengers offered advice. One young woman, who looked far from matronly in her tight jeans, tight sweater, and high-heeled pointy toe boots asked, "Is she Russian baby? Russian babies like this." She cradled her arms and gently swung them back and forth. I tried it, and Rachel's screaming seemed to drop one or two decibels. A man seated behind us offered to trade places with us because he had two empty seats on either side of him. We thanked him profusely. He said, "My son used to cry like that. All I could do was walk with him." I picked Rachel up and walked her up and down the aisle before the plane took off. I was reaching the breaking point. What did people with no coping skills do in situations like this? I was beyond frustrated. I could feel my cheeks getting hot and my eyes begin to sting.

"Hang in there, Mom, you're doing fine," I heard Kate holler over the din of the engines. I looked at her and bit my lip as she gave me a sympathetic grimace.

It was time to sit down and buckle up. I handed Rachel over to Dick and by the time my seat belt was buckled, she was curled up asleep against him. I collapsed against his arm and sobbed as the engines roared and the force held us against the backs of the seats during our ascent. With his free hand, Dick reached under my chin and pulled my head close. It felt great to leave that place behind us.

Good to Go

The next two days were crammed with visits to the Russian Embassy and the American Embassy. Our kids needed physicals before they could get their passports and Visas. We followed a doctor into a white room with a gurney. He instructed us to set her down and undress her. He cooed and handled her gently while he listened to her heart and lungs and checked the movement of her joints. We dressed her and he pronounced, "Very big and strong for orphanage baby."

After three days of appointments, we were ready to go home. While waiting in the vast lobby for Darya, we made small talk with a myriad of other adoptive couples. Some had been staying at the hotel for weeks waiting for the paperwork on their children to be completed. When we mentioned that we went to the Russian and American Embassies the day before, one set of parents asked, "How did you get there?"

"Our escort picked us up," we replied as if it were obvious.

"You have an escort? What agency are you with?" It was evident from seeing those parents, that not all agencies were as thorough as ours. I felt so lucky and so grateful that we had chosen LSS.

When Darya met us in the Marriot lobby, she looked at Rachel in her denim bib overalls and exclaimed, "She looks like American girl!" She would truly be American once we landed in New York.

Boarding the plane to JFK, Kate ambled back and forth in front of me holding her son in front of her. An old woman reached out from her aisle seat and lightly tugged at Adam's stockinged toe. "Oh little boy," she said, "You're so lucky. You don't know how lucky you are to go to America!" There were about forty adoptive couples with babies on the plane, and I was glad to hear other children crying.

When we landed at JFK we touched Rachel's feet to the floor of the ramp after stepping out of the plane. "You're now an American citizen," we cooed. We picked her up quickly and caught up with the rest of our group as they stood in line at customs.

The plane began its final descent into our small, local airport. Dick reached across the narrow aisle and grabbed my hand as the plane bounced down on the runway.

A few minutes later we landed and the stewardess wished us luck with parenthood. We gathered the diaper backpack, folding stroller, and carry-on bags and clambered off the tiny plane. The entire terminal was quiet and dark. All eleven passengers on the plane had cleared out and were on their way home by the time we emerged from the bathroom where we had stopped to change Rachel's diaper before her debut as grandchild number one. As we walked toward the dim baggage claim area, I wondered where my parents were and started to panic. As if reading my mind, Dick said, "There they are, see the balloons?"

Sure enough, my parents stood alone in the barren baggage claim area with balloons and a sign in my Dad's handwriting that read, "Welcome Home Rachel." Their faces brightened, and they waved the sign when they saw us. When we finally approached them, we all embraced each other at once in a huddle with all our bags hanging from our bodies. Oohs and ahhs broke the silence as Rachel was passed to my mom and then my dad. I looked at Dick, and tears ran down my cheeks. "We're home, Honey!"

The stewardess from our flight took a picture of our new family. Months later, when we looked at this photo I realized how awful we looked. Dick looked like he had slept in his clothes for two weeks, and I looked like I had given birth to a whale. Our faces were flushed, our eyes were bloodshot, and my hair was completely out of control. Finally, we all separated, wiped our eyes, and retrieved our luggage from the carousel. Dick and my Dad threw our suitcases into my parent's van, and I walked around to the open sliding door to give our dog Lucy a kiss and a scratch behind the ears while my mom held Rachel.

Pulling into our neighborhood, I felt like we had been gone for years. Dick slowed the truck and, in a familiar gesture, hit the garage door opener on the sun visor. I relished the echo of the engine as we pulled into the garage; the garbage cans illuminated by the trucks headlights. Dick turned off the truck and pulled the keys from the ignition. We let out loud sighs as we opened our car doors and slid off our seats. I shut my door without making any noise and moved to the back passenger door to get Rachel. Slowly, I unstrapped the five-point harness of her car seat and pulled her to my chest. She felt warm through the snowsuit, but I quickly covered her fuzzy head with her hood and shuffled carefully toward the door to our house. As we stepped through the threshold into the kitchen, I was greeted by the familiar smell of our furnace and the hum of our refrigerator. I turned the light on over the sink and basked in the florescent glow while I adjusted her in my arms. I carried her into the dark living room and lay her on our leather sofa where the light from the kitchen cast a soft glow onto the carpeting. Her arms were still sticking straight out in her pink quilted snowsuit, and she resembled one of those little snow baby figurines my aunt collects. Her large brown eyes circled the room, taking everything in. She looked up at me. I looked back at her and whispered, "We're home."

*

Bikes in the Driveway

Four and a half years later, I stand at the kitchen sink, stirring the second pitcher of Kool-Aid in two hours. I turn off the kitchen faucet, wipe off the outside of the pitcher with a checked kitchen towel and grab a clean stack of plastic cups. I step out the door with the pitcher in hand and cups under my arm and walk through our garage. I hear Dick on the lawn mower in the front yard and smell the fresh cut grass. On the way to our inflatable pool containing Rachel and four neighbor girls all between the ages of four and seven, I step quickly across the hot asphalt decorated in pastel sidewalk chalk. I smile as I weave my way around the pink and purple bikes in our driveway.

PART V

Grace

"Hope is the thing with feathers—
That perches in the soul—
And sings the tune without words—
And never stops—
at all—."

~Emily Dickinson

I was that friend, the one whose story was different from all the others.

When my book club read the best-seller Marley and Me, Grace invited us to join with her book club who had read the same novel and planned to meet at a local coffee shop. I had known Grace both professionally and socially, and whether she led a training on health management or met for our monthly card club, she usually showed up late, armed with bags of candy or plates of homemade cookies. Grace's refreshing optimism, however, always excused her habitual tardiness. This, and the fact that the only reason she was late was because she possessed that people-pleasing gene that continuously put her in two places at once.

For her planned book talk, Grace encouraged all of us to bring photos of our own pets, but I had no photos to share. As Grace and my friends affectionately described the shenanigans of their beloved canine family members, I laughingly recounted tales of an exuberant toddler's first bike ride and a messy baby's encounter with a frozen banana. Because I spent my nights reading bedtime stories rather curling up with an intriguing Jodi Picoult paperback, I would have been more comfortable discussing Clifford the Big Red Dog. Unlike me, my closest friends' lives centered around pets, not children. I hadn't realized it at the time, but many of them, including Grace, had desperately wanted to conceive; it just wasn't happening. I now understand that while my life resembled a cheerfully simple children's storybook, their sagas, especially Grace's, had the elements of a complex Brothers Grimm fairy tale.

~Jenny Kalmon

CHAPTER 21

Three Too Many

Marty's Liquor. The neon liquor store sign blinked pink and green down on my windshield as I stared at the six pack of beer sitting on the passenger's seat beside me. It was 6:00 p.m., too early to call a friend to go out to a bar and too late to call it Happy Hour. I picked up my cell phone.

"You'll never guess where I am," I challenged my friend on the other line. It was the third baby shower that did me in. I had happily (okay, maybe happily is too strong a word, but I still believed that I had camouflaged it well) planned two other baby showers for my close pregnant friends, and this was the third one in three months. We're talking about a lot of pink and blue streamers, a lot of tasting of jarred baby food to guess the flavor, a lot of ooh-ing and ahh-ing over little bunny outfits with matching bibs, and a lot of cake. A *lot* of cake.

Keeping a positive attitude is usually not that difficult for me, but by Baby Extravaganza #3, I had pretty much had it. The veneer of my rubber-stamped smile and forced cheerfulness was beginning to crack. Worse, I was becoming less and less patient with the "We'll be planning your party next!" predictions from well-meaning friends who didn't know my situation—and sometimes from those who did.

As my exhaustion was manifesting itself into snide comments and greedy looks at all of those baby gifts, I planned my escape. I was finished cleaning up, nearly out of there, when I saw them all talking together. All three of them. The three mommas-to-be who had no idea how fortunate they were to be in their situation. The three lucky sorority sisters who had pledged a club that I was not allowed to join. There they were, chatting about their due dates, their inability to sleep at night, and their baby room decor. There they were, not thanking me for their parties, for wringing out the last ounce of genuine happiness and generosity I had left. There they were, and there I wasn't. And that was it.

Let me clarify that the liquor store is not my usual first stop on the way to coping with my problems. I am an occupational therapist by trade, and am well aware of the risks involved with relying on alcohol to solve life's problems (why use alcohol anyway, when using food to drown sorrows is so much more socially acceptable?). On this particular night, however, I knew that my Pity Party needed some refreshments, and I was not going there empty-handed. It was just a six pack of beer, after all, and didn't I deserve it? I had survived three baby showers, and I deserved a night of self-indulgence. I deserved to treat myself. Never mind that drinking that six pack wouldn't make me any more pregnant than I was before—unless I had accidentally picked up a pack of Fertility-Friendly Pale Ale that some forward-thinking micro-brewery had created. At least I could indulge as I pleased. I summoned the battle cry that my husband and I had employed so many times in the past months: "Since we're not pregnant, we might as well drink/shop/go on vacation/spend/indulge as much as we want!"

I drank three beers and cried myself to sleep.

*

This thing called infertility, it's not for wimps. My husband and I never thought we'd be in this situation. A friend who had experienced infertility once told us, "This won't happen to you; you'll be pregnant within the first three months of trying." And secretly, I agreed with her. At the time, though, a small part of me got nervous. Was I ready to give up the freedom of being on my own? Was I ready to face the responsibility of raising a child? Did I even think I'd be a good mother? Little did I know that these doubts, which are probably common for many women thinking about starting a family, would be the least of my worries over the next months and years. As our childless time dragged on and on, I began to feel nostalgic for the days when my only worry was if I would know how to handle a baby. Even worse, I began to wonder if my initial fears had somehow jinxed us. Was fate implying that I wasn't cut out to be a mother?

Oh, the questions, some of which were answered by time, love, experience, and soul-searching; some of which have never been answered to this day. I am okay with that. I am here to tell my story so that other women don't have to feel alone. I am ready to reveal our path through the forest of infertility, and the signs that helped us navigate our way. To be clear, this is *my* story, not my husband's, who saw this experience through his male-colored glasses and, despite his best intentions and his testosterone-driven proclivity for fixing things, couldn't fix this. Nor is it my daughter's story, who burst into our world like a fire-cracker three years ago, leaving everything in her wake sparkling with glitter. This story is simply, and not so simply, mine to share.

Once Upon a Time

And so we begin, in a small, one-bedroom, starter apartment that my new adult self had rented upon first arriving in a city far from the civilized world. The paper mill smell in my new town was so foul on the day I moved in that I thought that the landlord had helped himself to the bathroom prior to my arrival. Perhaps the small size of the town only amplified the foul smell. My new hometown was so small that anywhere you go, you're literally ten minutes away from anywhere else you'd ever want to be. My friends, living in more metropolitan areas, laughed out loud when I told them that the parking meters here took pennies, and that was before they were removed altogether!

Small-town living was meant to be a pit-stop for me; I took my first job offer out of graduate school in order to gain some experience, build my resume, use it as a stepping stone to the job and life I *really* wanted, which was anywhere but here. Somewhere with coffee shops, book stores, museums, activity—and most importantly, cute single men. This was not the place where I was to meet my soul mate and fall in love. Surely, my soul mate wouldn't have found himself in this uncultured little town either. So, I had nothing to worry about. I'd get some experience, get a better job, and get on with my life.

Until, much to my surprise, this little town started growing on me. I watched kids riding their bikes to the library, families lined up at the local Dairy Queen walk-up window getting ice cream on a hot day, and teenagers throwing Frisbees around and flirting with each other at a small, local lake. What a great place to raise a family, I thought to myself. That's when I noticed it—the alarm on my biological clock was blaring, and I couldn't hit the snooze button.

I remember sitting in that little apartment, looking at the cracks in the plaster walls, and realizing that I knew two truths about myself: I really wished my newly adopted town didn't smell so bad, and I really wanted to be a mother. The rest was going to have to figure itself out as I went along. After taking a long hard look at my life, I began to focus on starting a family. Not in a run-down-to-the-sperm-bank type of way (although if I'd wanted to, there was one just ten minutes away), but in a break-up-with-my-current-boyfriend-who-doesn't-want-to-get-married-or-have-kids-and-start-fresh kind of way. That kind of way is never easy to do, but it was where I had to start. I knew my future husband was out there somewhere, maybe even in my foul-smelling town, and somewhere deep within me, I knew my baby was out there too.

Much to my surprise, my soul mate did live in my new little hometown. Our love story was five years in the making. We met, became friends, and one New Year's Eve, realized that we belonged together. Three weeks later, he came over to my apartment with bagels and coffee and never left. Like so many great love stories, ours felt like a fairy tale: a whirlwind engagement, a gorgeous wedding, a charming honeymoon complete with carriage rides and candlelight dinners. Life was smelling better and better by the minute.

*

Fast forward six months. We are sitting at dinner, another candlelit restaurant, holding hands across the table like two annoying lovebirds. Yes, we were *that* couple, the type of couple who we'd long to throw dinner rolls at years later as our infertility problems began to seep into our marriage. The type of couple that would make us whisper, "Suckers!" to each other as they strolled by hand-in-hand. Multiply this activity by ten and add some choice swear words if they had their children with them, and that was us.

So, there we were, sitting at dinner, planning our future together. And we began to do the math. The equation went something like this:

> *(my age) + (the number of years we want to spend alone before having children) ÷ (the number of years I took the pill)—(how long people said it would take until the pill was "out of my system") x (the time of year we'd want to deliver a baby to have the maximum time off) = (We'd better get going right away!)*

Strangely, this freaked me out.

"Holy cow," I uttered, slowly withdrawing my hand from his to wipe the sweat forming on my upper lip. "Is that really accurate? Did we forget to carry a number or solve for the lowest common denominator or something? Wow, start right away, huh?"

"Yep," he replied, with a new gleam in his eye. "Let's get to it."

What did he know that I didn't?

Well, turns out that trying to have a baby involves sex. A lot of sex. A lot of sex in really strange places and at strange times. In the ferns out back behind our house in the middle of the afternoon. On the basement rug as we unpacked our new house. In my car. In his car. In any car (okay, that isn't really true, but it might have been, given the opportunity). In the morning as I watched the clock, so that I wouldn't be late for work. At night, when he'd hug me goodnight and we'd (sometimes) turn off *Sex and the City* to have sex in our own city.

And after each time, we'd wonder aloud, "Wow, we may have just made a baby."

With romance in our eyes as we uttered these magic words, we savored the moment—so mysterious, so mystical, so right. So Hallmark card perfect. What a fitting end to our fairy tale, to have the perfect wedding, the perfect honeymoon, and to have all that perfectly good sex lead to a baby. What other possible ending could there be?

Missed Conceptions

The sign on the marquee of the Holiday Inn beamed proudly, "Congratulations, Ben and Allison!" The words literally glowed with joy, while inside, I felt just the opposite. There I was again, fake-fake-faking it through another glorious gathering. Only this time, there was a timeline attached. This was scheduled fakeness.

I first realized that something wasn't right that fall when I began making plans to attend Ben and Allison's wedding. We had it marked on our calendar for months in advance (since my husband was going to be a groomsman), and in my vision for this wedding, I pictured myself demurely drinking ice water and Sprite. According to my fertility math (again with the math), and accounting for several months of trying and letting the pill get out of my system, I would be about four months pregnant by then. Hmmm . . . something wasn't right. And it's not because of what the calendar said or what I heard from my friends about how quickly they had become pregnant. It was because I could feel that it wasn't right. Women know their bodies; they just do. I never realized it more so than going through our fertility dance—women just have a sixth sense of when something is off-kilter. And I just knew.

This was the first time that I felt that icky sad-in-my-gut feeling that I would experience so many times over the next several years. It's a cross between panic, fear, envy, and worry, throw some stress-eating on top of that, and you're in for a stomach full of fun, believe me. This feeling would reappear at baby showers, at holiday gatherings, at friends' houses when I saw baby toys strewn about, on my job when I worked with pregnant women (some still in their teens) who were depressed about adding another child to their already over-burdened lives. Oh, that feeling became very familiar—a character who invited himself over to my house, plopped down on my couch, and wouldn't leave despite every hint that I dropped. An unwanted presence waiting to snatch away my very happiness. Old Rumpelstiltskin.

We made it through Ben and Allison's wedding despite my depression and over-the-top drinking (I might as well as I certainly wasn't drinking for two). Fall turned into Thanksgiving and then Christmas, and still, nothing. Now we knew something wasn't right. It was time for medical intervention, but neither of us wanted to make the call. That would make everything suddenly real and scary. But, we told ourselves, it could be something so simple and small, and we'd get our adjustment and be on our way. We'd just have to do it, face it head on.

Soon, every form of medical professional entered into our lives.

Our first stop was to see my kind and sweet OB-GYN, which I am convinced stands for Oh By Golly You're Not (pregnant, that is) at our local clinic. My kind, sweet and accommodating (at this point, anyway) husband, came with me to the initial appointment. My doctor asked the usual questions: when was my last Pap smear, how regular were my periods, blah, blah, blah. Then came another question.

"How old are you?" he inquired.

"I'm 34 years old," I replied sheepishly.

"You know," he said in his cool, doctorly way, "if you plan to get pregnant and give birth to a healthy child, you need to get going. Every year that you wait to get pregnant, you increase your chance of having a child with a genetic abnormality such as Downs Syndrome exponentially."

He handed me a photocopied sheet of paper from a text book, smudged along the edges, that laid out with precision how screwed we were. Not only was I having trouble getting pregnant in the first place, but I was seemingly being punished for it by having an increased chance of giving birth to a baby with a serious health condition. Panic rose up into my throat, and the room seemed to close in around me.

"Do you think that this is even a safe thing to do?" I asked, my voice an octave higher than usual.

"I think we'd better get started," he stated crisply, and that was the end of that discussion.

Filled with a strange brew of panic and hopefulness churning in my stomach, we left the doctor's office armed with the tools we needed to start our War on Infertility. Our doctor had given us the following (in addition to heartburn):

1. *chart paper*
2. *a recommendation to purchase a Basal Body Temperature Thermometer*
3. *a prescription for pre-natal vitamins (here's hoping!)*
4. *the dreaded graph of how I was too old to be doing this in the first place and getting older by the minute*
5. *a business card from the clinic with a follow-up appointment scheduled in three months*

Not wanting to lose another second of precious, non-genetic-deforming time, we got started right away. The chart paper, we found out, was to graph my temperature at the same time every morning, to see when during my monthly cycle I would have the highest temperature, i.e., be the most fertile. This was when my husband and I were supposed to have sex for optimum egg/sperm partying in my ancient uterus. Every morning (did I mention that it was every single morning), my husband awoke to the sound of *beepbeepbeep* as my thermometer hit the right temperature, and I studiously marked it down on the graph paper, hoping that the very act of my punctuality and adherence to the task would be rewarded by pregnancy. Isn't that how it works—the best student gets the best grade? And I'd always been a good student, top of the class. I was NOT going to slack at this.

After months of *beepbeepbeep*, my thermometer grew sticky as my morning breath caked on it every day. I reached for it instinctively in my sleep, and knocked everything off my nightstand. I would forget to bring the damn thing when I went out of town, and have to borrow thermometers from my friends and family, most of whom we hadn't told we were doing any of this, because of course we would be pregnant soon and still get to have that magical moment where we tell everyone with a cute little grandma book or bib wrapped in a box. Yeah, lots of people thought I was sick a lot during those months, borrowing all of those thermometers. How many times can you fake having the flu? I was on my way to becoming an actress quicker than a mother.

Meanwhile, to rule out the possibility that it was my husband's duct work that wasn't performing up to capacity, he had to get tested as well. Yes, the dreaded Cup O' Sperm had to be collected, then quickly presented to the lab at the hospital at just the right temperature as to ensure maximum accuracy for the required tests. Leave it to the men to think up a test that is not only fun for them but can also be performed at home and will involve driving to the hospital at a break-neck speed, Jeff Gordon-style. Except in this case, my husband (who, in his defense and attesting to his extreme social nature, was afraid that he would run into someone that he knew) needed me to fast-track his boys to the lab. Off I went, with my special to-go cup tucked neatly under my warm arm until I could present it grandly to the lab technician. And of course, everything turned out fine. Mission accomplished.

I would come to envy my husband over the next months, not because of the quick and painless procedure that he had to "endure," but because procedures were so cut and dry when it came to him; either his body was working or it wasn't. Just like men, very black and white. Maybe they need it to be that way. Maybe women just handle the gray areas better.

Regardless, there seemed to be no answers to my questions, only more questions leading to more tests, more drugs, and more questions yet again. I went through the months on Clomid to see if that would improve my egg production, and nothing changed. More medications were added, to kill bacteria, to improve my uterine lining, to help ease the side effects of my other medications. Still nothing. Months passed with no change. I forgot to fill my prescription before we went camping one week in the summer, and I was relieved. I would have to skip a month, and I needed it. I had become Grumpy, Snappy, Weepy, and Dopey—the mutant dwarfs that nobody talked about, all rolled into one. Living with me was like encountering the Evil Step-Sister every day—the shoe was fitting someone else, and I was bitter. I needed answers, or at least a new direction.

Finally, that fall, I had my first laparoscopy, a simple out-patient procedure to see if I had blockage in my uterus that was causing my eggs to not fertilize. I had an ominous feeling that cloudy, cold day. Even though we'd finally be getting some answers, I sensed that the news would not be good.

I was groggy but strangely alert as the doctor came into my recovery room after surgery. Despite the cloud of anesthesia still hovering over my eyes and dulling my senses, I felt very aware that this was an important moment. Excited and anxious, I would finally learn something about my body, my underachieving, remedial body that was not performing up to its potential and worst of all, not correcting its work. I sat up in anticipation of my doctor's diagnosis.

"Grace, the surgery went well. We did find some major blockage right away typically caused by endometriosis. I think it's time we talk about getting you to a specialist who can perform the surgery to remove it."

There was Rumpelstiltskin again, perched in the corner of my dark hospital room.

My Knight in Shining Scrubs

Six weeks later, we entered the fertility clinic for our one o'clock appointment. The sign in the hospital's lobby that gave directions to the various clinics in the facility looked like a page out of my parents' World Book Encyclopedia, the one with the picture of the human anatomy, with all the skin taken off—arteries and veins crisscrossing every which way, creating a mixed-up maze of undecipherable colored lines. Only we needed to decipher the lines we were looking at: the blue line led to the Women's Endocrinology Clinic, to our appointment with our new fertility specialist. Where was the World Book Encyclopedia for Reproductive Losers when we needed one?

How did we even get here? Hadn't we just been frolicking like two reckless teenagers, creating our love child and hoping not to get caught? When did our love story stop starring ourselves and start starring doctors, nurses, lab technicians, well-meaning relatives, pharmacists, and store clerks who seemed to give me snide looks or, even worse, looks of pity whenever I purchased fertility indicators, pregnancy tests, and maxi-pads all at the same time? When did our privacy become anything but private?

Our new specialist was completely different from our kind yet firm and borderline disapproving doctor. He was young, friendly, and had even adopted two children, which we thought was an unusual choice for a fertility doctor. That had to be a good sign, right? We sure were looking for one.

The first words he spoke to me after reviewing my charts and taking an oral history were, "Well, let's get to work and get you pregnant."

The word jolted me out of my fog, which had seemingly begun rolling in right around the time of our friends' wedding and had been billowing around us ever since. "Pregnant?" Did he actually say the word, the forbidden word that was no longer uttered in our house or in my mind? Apparently, somewhere along the way, I had stopped believing that I was actually capable of becoming pregnant, that I didn't deserve it, wasn't trying hard enough, wasn't worthy of being a mother because my body and mind and heart were failing. Was this actually a possibility for me? A spark crackled in my heart. It was faint, but it was there.

I had to address the other concern that had been worrying me. "What about my age? Is this even a responsible thing to do?" I asked.

He looked at my chart again. "Oh, you're on the young side of the patients that I see," he replied, almost jovially. "Many women have healthy babies well into their 40's. I see no reason that you shouldn't move ahead with us in this clinic."

I could feel actual heat coming off my body as the spark grew into a nice, healthy fire inside of me. This was the first time in months that I really felt like this could happen for us. Here was my Knight in Shining Armor who could get us knocked up; I just knew it. At that point, as he scheduled procedures, I almost suggested he take out some extra unwanted organs and maybe a kidney for good measure. Strap me to a gurney, cut me up, take out whatever you want—just be sure to leave behind a baby, or at least a nice home for one. I was hopeful putty in his hands.

When we finally arrived at the date of my surgery to remove the endometriosis, which had been my reason for not getting pregnant, I was ready. I felt like a warrior going into battle. I had everything arranged at work in order to be gone for a few days. I had prepared meals in advance. My thoughtful husband had even gone out and gotten me a recovery bag filled with my favorite treats, magazines, etc. This was the time, this was the place, this was the moment. Something big was going to happen. I knew it like I knew my own body, my own heart. This was it.

The surgery, which was supposed to be short and comprehensive, ended up lasting four hours, such was the extent of the damage that endometriosis had done to my uterus. Huge brown cysts called chocolate cysts were removed one after the other. One of my fallopian tubes had been completely blocked by cysts, making it entirely useless. Only surgery could reconstruct that tube. But finally, the villains were gone. In my center was a uterus lightened of its load of angry cysts, ready to perform the task that it was created to do. But the battle had been fierce. I was sicker than I had ever been before. Puking and crying, I was released from the hospital—after all, this was still outpatient surgery. I don't remember a single detail of the two-hour ride back to my hometown, except that I could smell it as we drove into town, and never had a smell disagreed with me more. This surgery had knocked me out.

I lay down on our living room couch, which my husband prepared with sheets and blankets, and didn't move from that spot for a week. I could barely eat; the snacks in the recovery bag sat untouched. I used an umbrella handle to get myself on and off the couch to go to the bathroom and only with my husband's help and in the direst of needs. My poor husband didn't know what to do with me; snacks and hanging out on the couch could usually cure any ill for me in the past, but this was different. He brought me a stack of twelve movies from the video store, hoping they would keep me entertained. I sat there, lonely and helpless. As I watched him go off and continue with plans we had made before the surgery, when the recovery time wasn't a significant concern, I stared at him incredulously, mouth gaping, as he offered me the use of his hunting rifle if an intruder broke in, since being alone in the house made me feel very vulnerable and exposed. He spent the next day fetching me maxi-pads to catch the post-surgical blue dye that was leaking out of my body. Oh, I was a warrior all right—beat-up, bruised, and apparently blue on the inside.

Several days after the surgery, I spiked a fever. As I have learned through this whole experience, post-surgical fevers are not good. Nobody really told me why (I was probably wearing my Girl Scout Hypochondriac Badge that day), but it's definitely not safe to have a fever after your body has just been cut open. Following my knight's orders, we reported directly to the emergency room.

Our ER doctor was greeted with quite a sight: husband panicking and swearing, woman zoning out and shivering with unwashed hair and blue-stained panties. Oh, we were a sight to see that night. "We should never have done this!" was my husband's battle cry, angry that I had to go through this and helpless to do anything about it. Tears sprung to my eyes when the doctor told me he was going to give me another pelvic exam. I realized as I sat with legs spread open yet again that practically anyone with any kind of medical training had seen this particular view. I was devoid of shame, numbed to the indecency of it all. My crotch was everyone's business. Come one, come all, I thought to myself. Take a good look; here it is, in all its useless glory. After the doctor pushed on my recently sutured stomach and laser-beamed a spotlight on my private parts, he prescribed a medication and sent me home. It was at that moment that I realized there was nothing I wouldn't do to have a child.

Battered, bruised, yet strong and determined, I sat on that couch, watching my eleventh movie, making plans. This was it—this was going to be our time. Something was happening, something big. This was the start of a new era for us. We had made it through our toughest challenges and had become closer because of it. We had persevered and found the source of our infertility and had corrected it, and we had the knowledge and experience to move forward. We were ready for good times ahead. We were ready to embrace our future family. We were ready to make a baby!

Then we found our golden egg.

CHAPTER 22

Golden Eggs and Poisoned Apples

Seventh Street, Tenth Street, Water Street, Elm Street, Pine Street . . . Where was Madison Street? While we had been living here for almost ten years now, we hadn't spent much time in this neighborhood, and the green, shiny street signs reflecting the bright sunlight were unfamiliar to us. But we were headed somewhere, that much at least we knew. Taking time to get there was turning out to be a hidden blessing, helping to calm our nerves. Silently we drove up and down streets, looking for the one sign we hoped to find.

There it was, Madison Street. We turned left toward the adoption agency.

Two days ago, I had been lying on the couch, still aching from surgery. As I tried to distract myself with yet another video, my husband entered from the dining room, turned off the TV, and sat on the couch, facing me. The deliberate act of ensuring that he had my full attention came from a man who had always assured me that he was listening when I talked about my day while he read the paper and kept one eye on *SportsCenter*, so I knew that whatever he needed to talk about was big. Nerves scratched at the palms of my hands as I sat up, tense and quiet.

"What about adoption?" he asked.

My mind swirled with this new information. The possibility of adoption was one that we had discussed with our infertility specialist, mostly within the context of how we would spend the limited amount of money we had to add children to our family. We'd never really had the adoption conversation with each other; however, without asking, we both just knew we would be completely open to it. Both of us had even, at various points in our single lives, investigated adopting children on our own. Maybe it was because we both had a love of people, or maybe it was because we were rescuers by nature (dogs, bunnies, people, whoever needed a hand), or maybe we were just lucky enough to be that in sync with each other. We both knew we could love any child, adopted or not. So we opened the phone book to the yellow pages, found the ad for the adoption agency with the friendliest-looking people, and started planning for this entirely alternative route to parenthood.

*

Even though we were still pouring our hearts and souls into becoming pregnant, adoption had always been an option for us. We first thought seriously about it when our specialist sat down with us, pen and paper in hand, and showed us in dollars and cents what our options were. What we had done so far, my surgery, all the appointments, all the tests, had been mostly covered by insurance. The next step down the ladder of medical intervention would be a less expensive, elective procedure called artificial insemination. The infertility problems that this procedure was meant to correct were never the problems we had, so this step wasn't an option for us. Our doctor explained our last two options. We could spend upwards of $15,000 on in vitro fertilization, or we could put that same amount of money towards adoption. Yes, our infertility doctor, to whom we are still grateful for laying it all out on the table, actually talked with us about the adoption option. It was one of those rare moments in our journey through the forest of infertility that we actually saw a clear path ahead of us.

The longer we thought about adoption, the longer the list grew of couples we knew who had difficulty conceiving, a surprising number, really. We began to catalogue the choices they made. We knew some friends who had adopted from foster care and who could become true mentors for us. Some couples adopted through traditional means, while others have found themselves pregnant after years of trying. Still others put their hearts on the line and went the route of IVF, with both wonderful and devastating results. In any case, without exception, people formed deeply strong opinions about what was best. I had friends who had adopted by choice, who believed that there were so many unwanted children already in the world that they felt a moral obligation to raise one of them. Other friends had a deep desire to be pregnant, to feel that life growing in their bodies, to be able to say that their child was a tiny reflection of the two of them and their unique traits. We even know others who chose to remain childless rather than raise "someone else's child." They, or in some cases, their partners, could not imagine loving a child that they did not conceive.

But for us, as we studiously pondered the chart that our specialist had laid out, one path seemed obvious. We would try the realistic medical options that had a good chance of working, but we would not invest in IVF. I was not one of those women who always dreamed of being pregnant, of wearing the maternity clothes and sending my husband out for pickles and ice cream in the middle of the night; I simply wanted to be a mother. That I knew in my bones. Pregnancy was one means of getting there; adoption was another. We knew that when the time came to make the choice, when our reasonable and realistic medical options had run out, that we would choose the route that would bring us to parenthood most quickly and successfully. We also knew that putting all of our eggs in the precarious basket of IVF and then experiencing a miscarriage would break us, specifically me. Depression was already a real possibility for me, and even more so if I were to miscarry our baby. I feared sinking into a hole so deep I wouldn't be able to claw my way out of it, so in spoken and unspoken ways, adoption had always been in our plans. We just didn't know that our alternative route to parenthood would be quite so alternative.

*

The day of our initial meeting with our adoption social worker finally arrived. Unfortunately, we nearly walked away from the whole thing following that first appointment. Immediately after meeting her we knew it wasn't a match. Young and inexperienced, she greeted us with, "Oh, how lucky you are to have off of work today," not realizing that we were both using personal days that we would have to pay for, and would rather be pretty much anywhere else than in a social worker's office discussing how and why we couldn't get pregnant. She took down the facts of our battle with infertility with the bored expression of a student waiting to get done with class so she can go check her email. For the majority of our session, she told us how expensive adoption is but that couples don't have to "pay it all right away," that people love to adopt from certain countries because the kids "look like you," but that other ones are bad because the birth parents "drink too much," so we'd want to steer clear of those places. So insensitive was she to the delicate emotional balance that we were trying to maintain that she told us stories of these horribly abused, unwanted children in the inner city, where she'd been a social worker, and how deft she had been at getting the parents to do whatever she wanted them to do. We sat there together on the musty, plaid couch in her office, knees touching, knowing without talking about it that we would never want to deal with this woman again.

"Means to an end. Means to an end," I repeated to myself all the way home, fighting back tears.

Despite our reluctance, we did send in our application material and were added to the extensive waiting list. We knew that if we waited, the right child would come to us, that it would all be okay, that this would be our golden egg.

We had no idea how right and how wrong we were.

*

The next several months were spent filling out one piece of paperwork after another. On the suggestion of a friend who had adopted through foster care, we thought we'd become licensed foster parents, too. That way, we could be open to any options. After several hectic months, everything seemed in place. The long, arduous process of being licensed for foster care was done (including physicals, home studies, social worker contacts, even a veterinary check for our cocker spaniel Charlie) and all the paperwork had been filed. Our castle was ready.

Then it got quiet.

Our adoption social worker stopped calling. Our house seemed brutally quiet. We came home every day to an answering machine full of messages except the ones we wanted to hear. The lack of phone calls was the hallmark of that fall—where was everyone? We were ready to go. We knew this would take time, but the waiting was so difficult. Where was our child?

Finally, reality set in. This just wasn't going to happen for us, I thought to myself. We couldn't get pregnant, and we were getting nowhere with our attempt to adopt. This reality crushed me. Once I came to accept it, I lay on our couch and cried for hours, my dog panting beside me, sympathetic. I felt sick, worried, broken. We were good people with loads of love to share, not to mention the child-proofed castle. Where was our little prince or princess?

This was when I really started hating my body. I hated it for letting me down, for not being capable of creating life inside itself, for not even being able to do anything to speed up the adoption process. I saw teen parents everywhere, every day—how could these young, foolish teens be able to create life, while I could not? I hated my worthless, cut-up, scraped-out, under-achieving uterus. Food became my epidural for the pain. I fed and fed myself, not caring about the consequences to my body, just wanting not to feel sad, even for just that moment. But as I learned (and I really knew, deep down), food didn't fill my emptiness or repair my broken heart. Nothing could, until I got what I needed.

In the meantime, Rumpelstiltskin had moved back into our house, and seemed to have taken up permanent residence. Old Rumpelstiltskin, that uninvited presence who failed to leave and sought to annoy, had moved in, unpacked his bags and settled in for the long haul. And he was a terrible roommate; he eavesdropped on our conversations, stayed up too late and kept us awake, instigated fights between the Wicked Witch and the Big Bad Wolf at all hours, and worst of all, he never left us alone. He never had the common courtesy or social graces to stay in his room when we had friends or family over, he came with us on vacation, and he never had holiday plans other than hanging around us. Nothing could get rid of this roommate.

"Don't you have somewhere else to go?" we'd ask. "Our house is small. We don't have much in common with you. We think it'd be better if you moved on." The answer was always, with a shrug, "No."

We found out that Rumpelstiltskin, with his greedy nature and conniving antics, was also a magnet for perpetual bad luck. When a child finally became available through our agency several months later, and we prepared for her to come, the placement fell through. When my husband's father became very sick and needed surgery, we took care of him. When hoodlums needed a backyard tool shed to break into, they chose ours. And finally, after we'd pulled ourselves together through these events and done our best to muddle through, Rumpelstiltskin laughed in our faces while telling us that our beloved dog had cancer and would die within the month.

There were poison apples everywhere.

It had been six months since we had made that first call to the adoption agency. Six months of trying to hang on and stay positive, trying to smell the roses through the stench of reality. This felt like a slap in the face. Could there be anything more to handle? Yes, I realized that people had much worse tragedies happen in their lives, and they survived them every day—as an occupational therapist, I saw that constantly—yet it felt very different to be on the receiving end. Surely there was a purpose to all of this. What more could happen?

At the end of March, we buried our dog—the one who welcomed my husband into my life when I was ready for marriage and a family, the one who comforted me after surgery, the one who sat with me on the couch when I cried over adoption delays—under a garden stone in our backyard. To memorialize him we stood together and read a book called *Dog Heaven*. The book described a place where dogs go when they die, where they can run and play and chase geese whenever they want. If hope really is "the thing with feathers," as Emily Dickinson once wrote, then this was the time we needed it the most. Just as the part was read about the geese, a large flock of them flew over our heads, calling to each other and, we felt, to us. It seemed to be a sign that, despite recent evidence to the contrary, God knew where we lived and understood what we'd been through lately. He knew our hopes, desires, and deepest wishes. He knew that we needed comfort, and a change in direction, just as the geese seemed to know that in the spring it's safe to head home. It was time for Hope to fly home to us. And we were ready for her.

CHAPTER 23

A Pouch of Magic Beans

The sign loomed over our heads. With hands gripping the hard metal shopping cart handle, we took deep breaths and surveyed the lay of the land, eyes wide with fear and heads filled with questions. Yes, my husband and I were entering that department where we'd never before dared to tread. The land of all things pink, blue, and mysterious. The land where the word "pooh" held multiple meanings. We were about to enter . . . The Baby Department.

Never in our adult lives have we felt so much like fish out of water. A mere six months ago this was a place to be avoided like the plague, filled with emotional land-mines, screaming children, and know-it-all mothers with an air of efficiency about them. A place where hopes and dreams came to die. A place where, before you were allowed to enter, you were issued a button that read: "I'm a REAL parent" or "I'm just a childless loser shopping for a friend, and I will never know the joy and fulfillment of parenthood." A place where expectant mothers-to-be were issued Mary Poppins as their personal shopper, complete with bluebirds to dance above their heads. An enchanted forest for the fertile. Most definitely not for us.

So what were *we* doing here? We were asking ourselves the same thing. We stood frozen on the edge of the diaper aisle, peeking around the corner at the rows and rows of delectable, soft, sweet-smelling items that lay before us, luring us in. We were Hansel and Gretel, tempted fiercely by this sugar-coated land, but fearful that our hope would eat us alive.

Hope won. Shopping began. Life changed.

Everything started happening that cool, drizzly spring. Our hearts were still healing from our recent experiences of losing the monthly battle to conceive, losing our dog, even losing our faith in the adoption process. To keep our foster care license current, we were working with a social worker from the local social services agency, a friend and someone we trusted, who would call us occasionally about children in need of foster homes. So far, though, there hadn't been the right child for us. It was spring, the time of year of rebirth, yet we still felt heavy and dull.

Easter came, and with it the visits to our families. We stayed overnight at my mother-in-law's house and went shopping the next day. I was at my favorite place to lose myself, Barnes and Noble, flipping bargain books through my hands and drinking my freshly brewed Starbucks coffee. Suddenly, my cell phone broke the silence of the afternoon. My husband had gotten a call from our social worker.

"What did he say?" I asked warily.

"He said there is a baby being born soon, and he asked if we were interested in taking her in foster care."

My heart stopped a little when I heard those words. We'd been licensed foster parents for several months by this point, and while we'd received these calls more than once, I never got over the feeling of nervous anticipation that came over me when we got them.

We had heard about this baby before, my husband reminded me. Our social worker had contacted us a few months ago, letting us know that there was a baby due soon who would need a foster home. We listened at the time and absorbed that information, but we'd also learned not to trust it; we had learned not to count our chickens before they hatched. Eggs weren't always reliable.

To find out that this may actually happen and that we were still being considered as this child's foster parents was quite unexpected. And to our great surprise, this birth was going to happen in about a week.

"What do you think?" I asked my husband.

"I don't know . . . he said we should call him when we get home, and he'll set up a meeting with us to tell us more," he answered.

A million thoughts swirled through my head, but I tried to suppress them all. Could this really be it? I didn't know. I had been disappointed before, but something in that moment, smelling my coffee, hearing my husband's anxious voice on the phone, looking out the store window and seeing the springtime sun peak through the clouds, allowed a kind of hope to bubble up inside of me.

*

The next step was to meet with the social worker at my office. He confirmed everything that had been stated over the phone. Yes, the baby was coming soon; yes, they were going to place the baby in custody right at birth; yes, they knew the sex of the child—it was a girl. He said he needed an answer from us within a day or so because, otherwise, he'd have to find other foster parents to take this child immediately.

We weighed this information in our heads, and then with each other.

"What do you think?" I'd asked my husband privately.

"I don't know; what do you think?" he'd asked me back.

We went back and forth like this for hours, not knowing what to do. This was different than being pregnant; this was a choice. There were so many unknowns to consider. We felt as though we were being offered a pouch of magic beans. These beans could grow into a healthy vine that winds its way up to the clouds or into a vine which would grow beyond our control, choking back the family life we'd always dreamed of. It was our moment to choose.

In the end, the answer came simply. After struggling to see into the future and weigh the invisible options, we decided to meet with our pastor for advice. Our pastor was the man who had married us and who met with us when we needed support. As we sat on his couch, knees touching, holding hands, our decision to take her into our home suddenly seemed clear. My husband would later describe it as a feeling of peace that just came over him, covering him like a warm blanket. This was our family. This was what we needed to do. We were chosen for this girl. And we were all going to be okay.

Immediately, I sprang into action. I ordered my father-in-law to paint the old dresser from the spare bedroom and my husband to call my brother-in-law to see when we can pick up the crib.

"I'll start making a list of baby items we're going to need, and see what we can borrow and what we'll have to buy. Let's get going!"

We had only a little time to prepare for the arrival of our future daughter, the infant who would change our lives forever.

A flurry of activity began at our house that lasted into the wee hours of the morning. My husband and I didn't realize that we should have been getting extra sleep rather than squandering it. It was a double-whammy for us not really knowing exactly what we needed to care for a baby and not having enough time to figure it out. For me, a perfectionist with a propensity for wavering on every decision, this was probably the best way to welcome a baby into our house—we would have to wing it, rather than worrying over every excruciating detail. This was guerilla preparation, with all hands on deck and no time to lose. This was why we plunged ahead into the baby department that day, with neither a button to wear nor a wand to wave; we were in our own new kingdom, an undefined, unfamiliar land far, far away that we were going to have to figure out on our own.

As we prepared for parenthood, we puzzled over so many questions: What exactly did we need Vaseline for, since everyone insisted we it have on our changing table? Why do we need a bassinet *and* a crib? Were we the first people in history to actually read the directions on a can of formula, so that we wouldn't make her bottles wrong? While looking through a box of sleepers that someone gave us, we came across this weird, hourglass-shaped rag with duckies on it—what the hell was this thing? Was it a burp cloth, a cloth diaper, a baby mini-skirt? Panic set in as we realized that we didn't know what it was for. What if the baby desperately needed the hourglass-shaped ducky rag at some crucial moment, and we didn't know how to use it? Worse yet, what if our social worker knew just what it was for, and we had it pinned on the baby like a toga when he came for a visit? Would we lose our foster care license on the spot? Our answer was to hide that ugly rag under a pile of receiving blankets (at least we knew what those were for) and pretend we never saw it.

We quickly put together a room for her, again putting aside our dreams of wallpaper borders and baby decor. We simply needed a place for our girl to sleep, some diapers to keep her from leaking, and a Diaper Genie to keep them from stinking up the house. We needed bottles and formula. We needed sleepers to dress her in, and a car seat to bring her home in. Beyond that, we would just have to fill in the blanks.

The week before she was born was the slowest and fastest week of my life. I couldn't stand the wait anymore. Now that I knew that this was *really* happening, I wanted it to happen immediately, although I still wouldn't feel completely confident until that little girl was in my arms. We just wanted her to be born so that we had some answers to our many questions. Oh, how much control we always want, and how little we actually have. Isn't that true for all parents, whether they give birth to the child or not?

*

The day of her birth finally arrived. "What am I supposed to do today?" I asked myself. Technically, I had no reason not to go to work since I couldn't be at the hospital, so off I went, distracted thoughts and worry clouding my mind all day. More waiting. Still nothing, nothing, nothing. No word from our social worker or anyone. We knew we had no rights yet as foster parents, but it was so difficult to wait and worry and have nothing to do.

Finally, when we came home from work, there was a message on our answering machine from our social worker: "Hi, a baby girl was born at 12:10 p.m. today. She weighs 7 lbs., 15 oz., and is 19 1/2 inches long. Her Apgar scores are good so far. I will call you later so we can make more arrangements. Talk to you soon. Bye."

Relief flooded over me like a wave of warm water. She was here, and she was okay! A prayer flew out of my lips, "Thank you, God!" And I sunk onto the couch. Wow, she was actually here. I was aching to meet her.

So again, what do we do now? We couldn't go to the hospital—it would seem like we were panthers sneaking up on our prey. After all, the birth mother was still at the hospital, recovering from the birth and spending time with the baby. It would be inappropriate to go and press our noses up against the nursery window with potential grandparents in tow. We couldn't help but think of the birth mother, and what she might be feeling. Back to the question: What do we do now?

Enter . . . our spy.

She was one of my best friends and greatest supporters in every way, she had been with us for each step of this journey so far, and her involvement wasn't going to stop now. Fortunately for all of us, she had a friend who had had a baby the day before who was still at the hospital. After listening to me lament about how anxious I was to see the baby and how frustrated I felt that I couldn't, she came up with a plan to go and visit her friend's baby, and at the same time sneak a peek at our foster baby. This sounded fine to me, although I was a little jealous that someone else was going to see my baby before I was. Still, I was trying hard not to think of the child that way, since we were technically only her foster parents. I gave my blessing to the plan, and off my spy went to the hospital.

"Grace, I saw her," she said breathlessly when she called me an hour later from her cell phone.

"Well, tell me," I begged, nervous knots in my stomach.

"Okay, picture three babies in the nursery. One was my friend's, so I knew that wasn't her. The second baby was really small and sick and was having a hard time breathing. That baby was hooked up to all of these machines, and I just felt so bad because obviously something was really wrong."

I could feel my heart start to pound in my throat. My stomach flipped and flopped like a fish out of water. *Was that our foster child? Oh my God, what was wrong with her?*

"But then, while I was there, that baby was taken out of the nursery and airlifted to another hospital. That's when I saw the name on the third bassinet in the nursery, and it was your foster baby. She is perfect and gorgeous and beautiful. She looks like a little angel."

I burst into tears right then and there. The relief, oh, the relief. It never even occurred to me to be worried for that other little baby, so sick and frail, which prior to this moment would've been second nature for me. That baby was not my child. I only thought of my foster baby—a child whom I'd never seen, yet to whom I felt an instant connection. Through my tears of joy, I was now beginning to realize what we had signed on for: foster parenting, not parenting. Could we really handle this roller coaster? We had every reason to believe that this baby could someday become our forever child, but what if it didn't turn out that way? Could we handle having no rights, no control? Were we selfless enough to care for this child, to give her the early intervention that she needed, even if we couldn't keep her forever? We'll give her a good start in life, no matter what—that was what my husband and I had been telling ourselves and other people in order to justify this decision that could turn out to be completely wonderful or hugely devastating; did we really mean it? Our hearts were already tethered to this girl; would we really be able to ever let go? A huge problem floated to the surface of my mind, making every other thought irrational: I already loved this child. I loved a child that I had no right to love in that way, and I knew I couldn't stop myself. I only prayed that I had the strength to hold on and see this process through to the end of the ride.

Two days, two excruciatingly long days later, we found ourselves sitting in the hospital lounge, waiting to take her home. We were impostors again, but this time with no shopping cart to hide behind. There we sat, our emotions naked and exposed, waiting to meet this precious baby and also her birth mother. Electricity filled the space between my husband and me, sitting on the orange vinyl couch; sparks crackled as we hissed words at each other under our breath. We felt like two naughty kids at the library, like anytime now someone was going to catch us trying to get away with our delinquent act. We were there to take someone else's baby home; what gave us the right to do that?

A more terrifying thought hit me just then—did we even know what we were doing? We sat and watched *Taking Care of Your Baby*, the training video that a nurse had set up for us, but my God, I didn't know how to do any of this stuff. This video was created to show even the most inexperienced mother the absolute basics of baby care, yet it all seemed like brand-new information to me. It was like getting one lesson on quadratic equations and then being given a 24-hour-a-day exam on it. I kept wanting to rewind the video and cram so I had something to cling to in my panic.

After our social worker arrived, the panic lessened; finally, someone was there who knew what to do! He told us it was time to meet the birth mother. My husband and I got up and followed him down the hall of the maternity ward, rooms filled with balloons and people and laughter. We walked past all of these rooms to a quiet, dark room at the end of the hall, no balloons in this room, just the quiet feeling of sad sleep. We walked in to find the birth mother lying on her side in bed, and when she rolled over to shake our hands, we found ourselves looking into the face of an exhausted, disheveled, beautiful young woman who was clearly trying to sleep through the whole experience of turning her newborn over to strangers. I ached for her.

"It is nice to meet you," I said, feeling ridiculous. This wasn't a job interview after all, or was it? "We are going to take wonderful care of her. We really will."

She turned back on her side and wordlessly closed her eyes.

We all walked out of the room. I felt strange and somewhat relieved. Now that that part was over, it was time to meet our foster baby.

We walked past the nursery where all the newborns were sleeping in their little bassinets, and I dared to take a glance inside. There she was, swaddled close, a little white caterpillar snuggled into her cocoon. She was so tiny. I could see the little features of her face, her little wisp of hair on her head. I ached again, this time from wanting to hold her.

Several minutes and a lifetime later, I was able to do just that. The nurse wheeled her into our room, and after a few awkward moments of hesitating, I gently picked her up. She felt so little and fragile in my arms. I was never going to be able to do the duties that the video showed me to do—she would break. She just seemed like a little china doll, a little borrowed china doll.

As we stared at her in awe, the nurse asked if we knew how to give her a bath. The dazed look on our faces must have been her answer because she immediately sprang into action. With practiced efficiency, the nurse scooped the baby up, unwrapped the swaddling clothes, and washed her with the expertise that only experienced hands could know. She tipped her head back and washed her hair with shampoo that smelled like sweetness and love. She offered us some of the bath supplies, and I snatched up that bottle of shampoo—I wanted my baby to have that same smell, so that even as my inexperienced hands were messing up the whole bath time encounter, she'd know that I loved her by making her smell so sweet.

Finally, and too soon, it was time to take her home. We carried her out to the car, locked the car seat into the base in the backseat, and drove off. I never felt so odd in my life; it was like we had landed in a foreign country. Nothing looked the same out the car window on this short and previously familiar drive home. The whole world had flipped upside down during those couple of hours that we were in the hospital.

The next days were a blur of bottles, diapers, cuddles, crying, and learning what our house looked like in the middle of the night. The sound of late-night infomercials played in the background of my deep knee-bend lunges as I tried to get her back to sleep, or I heard those same muffled sounds as I lay guiltily in bed while my husband took his turn with her. I wondered if the few people driving by our bay window at that time of night wondered why every light was on.

Many of our friends and family came to meet our new little girl as if they knew that she was an important person in our lives already and wanted to treat her as such. "Foster" didn't hold a lot of meaning in any of our lives; she was a baby in need of love and attention from those around her, and that was easier than anything in the world to provide. Friends brought over gifts for her and meals for us. I will never forget the sight of my friend walking up the driveway with a pan of lasagna, the apparent dish of choice for families in need. After seeing that freshly prepared food accompanied by a homemade apple pie, gratefulness washed over me. Our eyes were opened at the level of love and acceptance of our foster daughter by our family and friends from the very first moment she crossed the threshold into our house. This child belonged with us, for however long we were blessed to have her.

CHAPTER 24

Mama Bear, Papa Bear, and Baby Bear

PUBLIC HEALTH DEPARTMENT, the sign screamed in black shiny lettering. As if we weren't intimidated enough already. At least we had found the place, a building constructed no later than the early 1970's; it's possible that Mike Brady himself designed the architectural structure. Yes, we'd found the place alright. And we were right on time to meet her.

Two weeks after becoming a full-time foster mother, I found myself in a large, brightly painted, toy filled room that was trying desperately not to seem institutional. At my side, a car seat that held a little sleeping baby, who had freshly clipped fingernails and wore a brand new sleeper. Across the conference table (disguised as a kitchen table) sat two people; one a frazzled yet competent person who had the aura of someone overworked and underappreciated, and the other a beautiful, young woman with dyed hair pulled back in a pony-tail, whose dark-circled eyes glanced suspiciously around the room at everything and everyone but me.

It was our foster daughter's first supervised visit with her birth mother.

I had dreaded this day since we learned that the birth mother wanted visits. I knew I would be scrutinized as her caretaker, for that was all I was at those visits; someone else was the mother. I also knew that I would be handing my foster child over to someone I barely knew and who I knew I didn't trust and then walking away for two hours. Worst of all, I didn't know what would happen in those two hours. Would the smell of the baby's skin and the feel of her soft breath on her face make this birth mother all the more motivated to get her act together and try to gain custody of this child? Or would she get frustrated at the constant, colicky cries and do something impulsive, irrational, hurtful? I didn't know how to frame this up in my mind.

Before I left, I watched the birth mother pick up the baby out of her car seat and hold her against her chest. Immediately, the little body curled up into her birth mom as if she recognized her and found comfort in the familiarity. Her little legs folded up into a fetal position, her head tilted gently, and she rested in her birth mother's arms. And my heart broke. Not for myself, although that would happen regularly over the next months as foster care, custody, visits, and the court system worked itself out at an excruciatingly slow pace. Not for the birth mother, even though I could certainly understand the difficult life she'd led and the domino effect of bad decisions and victimization that had surely led her here to this room and this place. No, my heart broke for my foster daughter. Despite all the love in my heart for her, and despite every ounce of my being that ached to care for her and nurture her for the rest of her life, I could not give her that familiar comfort of being with the person inside of whom she'd grown for nine months and whose heart had beat above hers for all of that time. I could not give her what her birth mother could in that moment, and I didn't know if or when her birth mother would be capable of giving it to her again. My heart broke out of grief for this foster child's loss, and I wondered if all along her colic had really been her own grief for her birth mother.

I guess that's what being a parent is—wanting your child to have everything they want or need, even at your expense.

There were good outcomes from that first visit, too; the birth mother expressed appreciation at having a foster parent for her daughter who was caring and conscientious (she would later tell me that she knew I'd be a good mother when she saw how I put all the items in the baby's diaper bag in little Ziploc baggies), and when I came to pick the baby up after those two hours, she was safe and her birth mother was ready to put her back in her car seat and have me take her home. But most of all, I made a decision that day to become my foster baby's memory, to write down and try to recall as many details about her birth parents as I could—what clothes they wore, what they talked about, words they spoke to her. Mostly, it gave me something purposeful to do besides just panicked waiting.

Even though it was very hard to put the fate of our family in the hands of another, fortunately, we were working with a social worker whom we trusted very much. We believed that he knew the real safety elements involved and would do everything in his power to protect the baby's best interests. My husband and I were willing to accept that too even if that meant that she wouldn't be with us forever. We trusted our social worker, because really, when it came right down to it, we had no choice. We'd gotten used to his visits, frantically cleaning up the dirty bottles and the spit-up stains on the furniture before he'd arrive, making sure that the Diaper Genie had been recently cleaned out and that chunks of strained carrots were carefully combed out of the child's hair. We'd asked guardedly optimistic questions about the status of the case: was the birth mother fulfilling the expectations of her court order, was she still around, did she want to have more visits? After several months, we were finally figuring out how to navigate this delicate foster care maze when we got a message that the birth father wanted visits.

The birth father? Who was this guy, and where did he come from? My husband and I closed our eyes, gripped each other's hands, and jumped Thelma and Louise-style into the birth father's world.

*

We agreed to meet him at a park in a nearby town, and before we even had the stroller unfolded, we knew who he was. A slim, tentative-looking man with a scruffy goatee waited in the park, looking as uncomfortable as a priest at a bachelor party. He stood amongst the joggers, the picnicking families, and the children feeding the ducks, looking as if he'd have given anything to be smoking a cigarette. He wore a watch on one wrist and a baseball cap on his head, and stared at us as we walked toward him.

"Is this her?" he asked.

When we confirmed that, yes, this was his birth daughter, he reached into the stroller, undid the straps with the ease of someone who'd done it a million times, and cradled her in his arms.

"Hi, beautiful," he sang, gazing at her and gently rocking back and forth.

Thus began visits with the birth dad. We would meet at the park, spread out a blanket, and listen to him talk and coo to her as if he'd been a parent his whole life. Of course, our enjoyment of these visits was made entirely possible by the understanding that this man had no intention of trying to get custody of our foster child; he merely wanted to see her and spend time with her. He made it very clear from the beginning that he understood that we wanted to adopt her when we could, and he was very glad that we would be the ones to do it. He seemed especially glad after talking to my husband and realizing that they had the same taste in rock bands. Did my husband really like those bands? At this point, I really didn't care if he had gotten tattoos on his body to match the birth father's; I was just glad that this was going so well. The birth father, a really interesting, likable character, truly adored his birth daughter just as we did—that we most definitely had in common.

"Want to go see the ducks?" he'd ask her, and he'd carry her off to a group of ducks feasting on picnic lefovers. She would reach down to try and touch the soft, white feathers, and their faces shone as they as they watched together, almost touching them.

At least we knew that our foster daughter would have at least one connection to her birth father—a shared love of animals. My furiously scribbled notes in my visitation journal would hold stories and details like this, so that one day she would be able to learn interesting facts, quirks, or funny anecdotes about the people to whom she is genetically connected besides what she will have to learn from official paperwork.

*

While traveling this road towards adoption, our lives intersected with so many people that we never expected to meet – doctors, lawyers, social workers, well-meaning strangers and curious friends. The birth parents were by far the most intriguing, mysterious, and significant people that we had met, or would ever meet, along this road. They came into our lives from very different roads that diverged into ours, roads surely littered by rocks, potholes, tangles, maybe even a wolf or two who were perpetually huffing and puffing and blowing their houses down. Surely there were no heroes in their stories, galloping up on their valiant steeds to rescue them.

We will never completely know the path these two people took to get to the place where we all intersected, and they will never completely know ours. It would be condescending to try to speculate on why they made the decisions they did—after all, they were parents, too. They had every right to make decisions for their lives and this child's life and not be judged, just as we deserved not to be judged either. While it seemed hard for others to understand, it was not difficult for us to at least respect them for who they were and love them for their love of their birth daughter, for they both absolutely did, in their own ways. That fact did not have to be written in any journal; that fact we knew to the core, as our foster daughter would someday know as well.

Deep in the Haunted Forest

Visits continued, colic dissipated, and months passed. By now I absolutely knew my girl; I knew her different cries, her moods, her favorite toys, and her favorite position when I rocked her, with one arm tucked behind my back, head resting on my chest, looking up at me with her beautiful blue eyes. Life just completely revolved around her now, and it was glorious, tentatively glorious. We still didn't know what the long-term plan would be for her, which was difficult. My husband and I didn't know what to think; every time the phone rang, our ears twitched and our skin prickled nervously. Yes, it was a glorious time in our household, but nervousness and doubt were always at the back of our minds. Rumpelstiltskin had taken to sitting on the bench outside our house, leering in through the bay window the moment we'd start to relax. We were getting really tired of him showing up.

This was a time when I needed something to cling to, to feel confident in, to *know*. As much as I loved so many aspects of having this child in our lives, I didn't know who I was to her. Was I just a caretaker? It didn't feel like that. She was already living in my heart, and I felt as protective of her as a mama bear. Was I her mother then? I certainly craved to be with every ounce of myself, but I didn't have the right, the legal right, to call myself that. And if I did think of myself as her mother, how shattered would I be if it turned out I couldn't raise her after all? I was not sure I'd ever be able to recover from that.

One deep, dark night, I crept into her room as usual to check on her before I went to bed. As I adjusted the covers, the smell of her powdery diaper, of her milky breath, of *her*, wafted up at me. In that instant, I recklessly let it seep into the room of my heart already filled with her, and the flood of emotion released sent me reeling. A tidal wave of love overcame me, and my hand gripped the rail of her crib for support. If that's the intensity of love that I felt when I even allowed myself to feel it, *really* feel it even for a moment, oh, how that love would break me if the source of it was gone. I hoped and prayed that she could feel that love from me even as I carefully repackaged it for my own self-preservation. She certainly heard the words from us enough, and felt our many hugs and kisses all day long, so I knew that wasn't lacking. It was just scary to acknowledge how full that mother chamber of my heart was for her.

The Light at the End of the Tunnel

On a particularly bleak day in early fall, we went to church. I went through the motions of singing the songs, sitting primly in the pew, yet inside I felt rotten and dried up. I had used every ounce of faith to get me to this point, and that was it—the well had run dry. For the first time ever, I began to question if God really knew what was going on for us. Didn't He see how much we loved her and how good we were for her? We're good people—didn't He see that? Why us? Why do we have to be the ones to wait and hope and worry, when there were people out there, young, foolish, drunk, stupid, ungrateful people who seemed to get pregnant simply by sharing the same can of Miller Lite at a house party? I had done everything right: I had waited for the right guy to start a family, I had gotten my career off the ground and had found myself as a person, I had even taken prenatal vitamins from the moment we had even started trying to conceive, for Pete's sake! What in God's name was going on?

I got my answer.

"Sometimes in life, our prayers often contain requests for what we want," our pastor stated thoughtfully in his sermon, interrupting my thoughts. "We think we know what we want and what we should have, and we want it right now. But God really knows us, knows what our life will be. He may not always provide what we want at the time we want it, but He will always provide what we need."

"And you," he said, seemingly speaking directly to me, "have everything you need."

It was one of those moments in life when you know deep in your heart that you are not alone. A spring tickled in my stomach, and my well started filling up again. My eyes pricked with tears as I snuggled my foster child against my chest and leaned into my husband, who felt suddenly warm and solid. Okay, maybe this wasn't the fairy tale I had pictured, but it was *my* story, her story, our story, and I was going to hold on and see it through.

That afternoon, the phone rang. It was the birth mother, crying.

She told me that she loved her birth daughter very much, but she knew that we would give her the life that she deserved, and that she wanted us to adopt her. Through my own tears, I told her how much we respected her decision, and that her birth daughter would know many wonderful things about her. On went the fairy tale phone call until I was emotionally drained. Then the tears started again as I told my husband, who stood listening in disbelief. We couldn't fathom it. This seemed too good to be true.

The plan was for the birth mom to call our social worker and tell him of her decision, and then we would schedule a court hearing so that both birth parents could legally and voluntarily terminate their parental rights, called a TPR. After that, we would be free to adopt her. This was the moment of our lives that we'd been waiting for, that would remove all the worry and stress and heartbreak. Finally, we were going to be parents.

The day of the TPR, after dropping the baby off at a friend's house, my husband and I drove silently to the courthouse. We were two bundles of frayed nerves riding up that ancient elevator to the courtroom. The air sparked with electricity as we entered the waiting area, checking and double-checking the list of court appearances for that day, making sure that our case was in fact on the agenda. The smell of musty paperwork permeated the air. High-heeled shoes clicked business-like up and down the hall. Men in suits hurried by distractedly, briefcases in hand.

We dropped our held hands as we saw the birth father sitting on a bench, slumped over, head hanging, baseball cap in his hands. He had not wanted any of this, to be a father, to fall in love with his child, to watch people he barely knew become her parents for life, to say good-bye to her. His voice shook as he spoke with us, and even as we reassured him that we would stay in contact, he nodded and stared at the paint chipping on the wall as if eye contact would have been painful. He was there to do his duty and nothing else.

And we waited.

Finally, the birth mother arrived. She shuffled nervously into the courtroom, never looking at us, keeping her eyes focused straight ahead. We all sat in our appointed seats, and the judged walked in and sat down.

I felt a tightness throughout my whole body, as if I was being squeezed from all sides. With crossed fingers, I listened as the judge read the opening statement in a monotone voice. I looked down at myself, realizing that I had crossed my whole body—my arms, my legs, my feet, all wound around each other, desperate to have some kind of cosmic control over the whole situation. I listened as the judge called the first witness to the stand, our social worker, who recounted the details of the case thus far.

Then the judge called the birth mother.

*

In stunned silence, we left the courtroom later that morning. The birth mother had changed her mind; she did not want to go through with the TPR. She had every legal right to do this. This was what we had signed on for. This was foster care. We asked our social worker a few tense questions, gathered our belongings, and walked back out to our car, willing our tears to wait until we got there. Rumpekstiltskin waited for us in the backseat, just smiling and nodding—what else had we expected, he seemed to say.

And once again, we were broken.

CHAPTER 25

Her Happy Ending

The sign, lettered in pink, read "Welcome, baby!" Pictures of a happy family, a curly-haired girl with her mom, dad, social worker, and friends, were displayed proudly. Tables sagged under the weight of food, drinks, and gifts wrapped in pink paper. A guitar player offered music to brighten up the occasion. And from everywhere came the sound of laughing children as they raced around the party, their faces shining with the pure joy of running, just running. Our friends had adopted a little girl.

From the matching hair color to the curve of her cheekbones, this child resembled our friends in countless ways. Watching them beam at their daughter as well-wishers pressed in closer to congratulate them, it was clear to us that this child was exactly where she belonged. Celebrating their adoption of her felt like coming full-circle, knowing that their childless, painful past had turned into a present that was exactly right all along.

What about our foster daughter's circle? What was going to be exactly right for her?

After the first TPR hearing, life took on a strange, hazy quality at our house. The atmosphere got quiet, just really quiet besides the noise and clatter of daily life with a growing baby, just shy of her first birthday. Without much warning, my husband and I got quiet with each other; we retreated into ourselves to deal with our recent set-back. Independently, we tried to figure out how to handle the disappointment of that TPR hearing, as well as the looming, unspoken disappointment that hung over our heads on a daily basis. The household literally jumped every time the telephone rang. We braced ourselves for the loss that we felt could be just around the corner.

Mirror, mirror on the wall, what would happen after all?

It was not long after our court hearing that our foster child got a terrible case of stomach flu—even more proof that we lived in a Murphy's Law household.

Even though the poor girl had had colic and many ear infections, she'd never had this before. The first time it came shooting out of her like a possessed Chuckie Doll, it seemed to surprise her as much as it did us. "Burp," she would say in a dreary voice, and we could do nothing but just hold and console her. We were back to the colic days of sleeping with her in the Lazy-Boy chair at night, afraid to let her sleep in her crib.

Late one night, after another "burp," I snuggled her up and held her to my chest, settling into the recliner for a long night. I suddenly realized she was snuggled into me, legs curled up, head resting contentedly on my chest, as she had at that first visit with her birth mother, shortly after her birth. A miracle had happened; I had become her comfort, her resting place, her home. As her warm body rested against mine and she slept, I soaked in the realization that the transformation had happened, and that I could give her what she needed, a mother. I knew absolutely that I would do anything to protect her and keep her in our lives.

Shortly after the flu went away, we were back in the daily routine of life, still with no solid ground to stand on, and more at stake than ever before. There was no answer to the question that people most frequently had: "Is this your daughter?" I felt like she was, but saying I was her mom was not right, and it was also not *my* right to say.

I ended up answering as generally as I could the long list of questions that followed: how old was she, was she walking yet, how many teeth did she have, where did she get that wavy hair? I went through my days feeling so fake, desperate to claim her as my own but feeling I had no right to. The word "mother" became sacred to me. Saying it out loud felt somewhat dishonest, yet to go into an explanation of our situation with every person who asked, would have been exhausting, not to mention a breach of my foster daughter's privacy. I let people believe what they would, and we would go on our way. But I felt false, like an impostor. I was fake fur and costume jewelry.

But this girl, what a bright light! She was every bit the party girl as the holidays approached. She loved her two-toothed match-'em-up pumpkin that we carved for her on Halloween. She spit up carrots and squash for her first Thanksgiving and turned up her nose, as we all did, at the baby food jarred turkey that smelled like dog food, with the consistency of something worse. And she made a brief, photo-op appearance at the choosing of our first family Christmas tree, swaddled in blankets due to the sub-zero weather and another raging ear infection. It's true, Christmas is for children, and with joy in our hearts we made plans for the upcoming holiday. All we wanted for Christmas was to spend it with her and her two new front teeth.

It was the last day of work before Christmas, and my husband and I came home exhausted with our foster daughter raring to go as usual. It was one of my favorite days of the year, with holiday lunches and shared homemade treats.

The sugar crash was hitting us full-force as we waited for our scheduled visit with our social worker, who we saw every couple of weeks.

"Come on in," we said to him as we greeted him at the door.

Once he made it through the door, he picked up the baby in his arms. "Hope your family is ready for a Christmas present."

We held our breath, "What do you mean?" I asked hesitantly.

"The birth mother called me this morning. She is ready to do the TPR, and this time she really means it. The birth father is ready, too, but you know that. He's always been ready. The court hearing is already scheduled," he said, a smile spreading across her face.

"No way," we said, shocked. We couldn't believe it. Could this be it, for real this time?

"Yes, it's true. The birth mother said she really loves her daughter, but she knows she can't provide the kind of life that she needs, and she's ready for you guys to adopt her."

Joy to the world! Our arms opened wide to hug her and our social worker at the same time. He truly had been our daughter's guardian angel, we said, and we meant it from our hearts. Trying to remember that our gain was someone else's loss, we tried to remain composed during the remainder of his short visit then lost ourselves in joy after he left. Our baby girl looked at us, confused, as we jumped and hugged and jabbered loud and fast to one another about what this meant and what would come next—after all, it was she who was used to making all the noise in the house lately. What were these happy sounds coming out of my mom and dad, she wondered to herself. They are smiling and dancing—hey, that looks fun! And I believe it was from that moment that our dancing daughter was born.

*

Another court date, another TPR, only different. This time, snow, slow and calm, drifted past the windows as we took our familiar seats on the bench. This time, there were no last-minute objections. And so unlike before, this time, within five minutes, my labor was over. Nine months of labor, really, three years and nine months of labor if you count all the time since we first tried to get pregnant, and it was all over. Parental rights had been terminated; she was free to be adopted by us, and nothing was stopping us now.

My Royal Family

Fast forward six months to another court date, another set of people, another gorgeous day. Who knew that our version of happily ever after would include the stink of the paper mill wafting through the open courtroom window?

The same judge sat on the bench that day, looking bored as ever, but with a certain twinkle in his eye that showed us that this was a part of the job that he enjoyed. Another five minutes and our foster daughter was officially ours, finally bringing to congruence how she had been ours in our hearts since the day we knew of her. Family and close friends came to witness the grand event. My close friend, the trusty spy, and her family became our daughter's newly appointed adoption sponsors, a concept we developed, similar to godparents, so that our child would have someone to talk to someday other than her parents about her adoption story. Together, we smiled for photos with the judge. This small yet joyous group celebrated by lunching at an Italian restaurant—after all, our daughter had to learn to live up to her adopted heritage, just like I did when I married her daddy. We received flowers from my sister-in-law and my sister, both beloved family members who later became our daughter's godparents, just like they might have sent to the hospital room on the day of her birth. And my husband, my true Prince Charming, had the best surprise of all.

"This is for you," he said, handing me a small, black box.

I opened the lid. Inside lay a pair of diamond earrings, gleaming and delicate, with stones to match my wedding ring.

"I always knew that when we had our first child, I would give you this gift," he said proudly, "and today is the day."

Never had I felt more grateful to have chosen a man to spend my life with who understood the legitimacy and importance of what we had just done; we had our daughter, and while the means by which she came to us were unconventional, she was our daughter, our *real* daughter, and I was her mommy. I knew that I loved him not only because he was my soul mate, but because he was also now the king of my daughter's world.

And as for our little princess, well, how do I describe joy like that? How many times in life does a person really get to watch her dream coming true? God knew. He just knew this child was meant to be our girl. Not only does she have so many of my husband's qualities (she's social, outgoing, stubborn, forgiving, loving, funny, competitive, creative), but she actually looks like me, and not in that spouses-looking-like-each-other-after-50-years-of-marriage or people-looking-like-their-pets kind of way. We have the same coloring, the same expressions, the same features. With a trip to the salon every couple of months to get rid of the gray, I can even pass as having hair color in a similar palette as hers. God obviously chose her for us, of that we have no doubt.

I used to hate myself and my body for not being able to produce a family. Now I thank God for the body I have, and I realize that it DID give me the family I wanted and needed. My inability to conceive was what brought our daughter home to us. I no longer think of myself as broken, but perfect; even though my womb was empty, my heart wasn't, and that is where I grew my family.

Being with her had always been a humbling, overwhelming, emotional experience, and now that she was officially ours, it was absolutely and purely joyful as well. I was her mother, and I knew her. I knew that she preferred to wear just one sock instead of two. I knew the pattern of the little hairs that grew down her back. I knew how her face changed shape when she laughed, and I knew the feel of her hard, smooth cheek under my lips when she cried. I knew that when I said, "I love you," she would reply, "You're welcome," as she learned the right phrases for different expressions. This was our girl, my girl, and nothing would ever change that.

We celebrated her adoption by inviting family and friends to a party, strangely similar (even down to the guitar player) to the other adoption party we attended. It was a gorgeous summer day, and as we shared our joy with so many people that we loved and who loved us, it became clear how lucky we were in so many ways. Never for a moment would we take any of them, or anything in our lives, for granted again. Rumpelstiltskin was not invited. He had been banished for good.

And They Lived Happily Ever After

Several months later as I put my daughter to bed, paperwork for the next adoption rests on our dining room table, waiting to be filled out after she goes to sleep. Are we ready to go through this again? Only time will tell. Many years ago, I asked my own mother if giving birth was painful, and she said that she couldn't remember, that mothers forget the pain of childbirth afterwards. I think it's the same with adoption; love overrides fear, and you forget the pain while you bask in the joy of raising your child.

We'll work with a private agency this time, opening our home and hearts once again for the right child to find his or her way to us, with the help of a little divine intervention. Our daughter is ready for it, at least we think she is. When we go shopping lately, she wants to buy clothes and toys for the "new baby" even though we've rarely talked with her about this concept. Is it possible that, despite the fact that she ignores most of our directions all day long, as most good toddlers do, she can hear what we're not saying? Does she have a way to see into our hearts? Perhaps she has seen into mine and knows that she has taken up permanent residence there. Perhaps she can see that my mother chamber overflows with love for her every minute of the day, and there is plenty to spare for the new baby.

I tuck the covers around her and rub her back. "I love you," I say, closing my eyes and saying a silent prayer of thanks to God for the amazing blessing of my daughter.

A small, clear voice rises up into the dark night, "You're welcome."

CONCLUSION

by Jenny Kalmon

I was *that* friend, the one who watched helplessly as my friends struggled to create their families, the one who stood silently beside them through their trials, and finally the one who rejoiced with them when their dreams of having children became a reality. I am now *that* friend who joins in and organizes play dates throughout the year.

Once my friends and I completed the book in the spring of 2009, we vowed to continue meeting on a regular basis, but we decided to include our children in the gatherings. Throughout that following summer, we met on Wednesday mornings, and I soon became *that* friend, the one with the minivan who could car pool other families to our destinations.

On one August Wednesday morning, Ginger and I pulled up in my Ford Windstar, every back seat filled with children or gear, into a parking space near the playground's entrance. I reached for the bottle of sunscreen as Kyra shouted, "There's Wyatt!" and took off running. Ben climbed out of the van and ran toward the playground as soon as I released him from his car seat. Braeden and Rachel, now kindergarten classmates and good friends, rushed off to join the fun and to help entertain the little ones.

"Hey, I'll be right there," called Ginger, poking her head out the passenger side window. "I'm just confirming dinner plans with Dick," she explained with a hand pointing to her cell phone.

Trying to catch up to my family, I gave an enthusiastic wave as I walked toward the group of friends sitting under the only shaded picnic table in the park. Kayden sat on Jen's lap with Colton to her left, racing a Matchbox car over his brother's leg. Riley, sporting a fishing hat and first haircut, kept all eyes on Amy, who pointed in the direction of the huge sandbox. I spotted Grace in the middle of the playground trailing her daughter as she eagerly explored.

"Come on, Wyatt!" Ben called, and the two of them chased each other in the sunshine. After watching the boys race over a bridge, through a tunnel, and down a slide, I found my place among the group of smiling moms.

"Riley is getting so big," I told Amy.

"He's already outgrown his nine month outfits," she explained, a habit of proud moms, always revealing the size of clothes.

"Speaking of clothes," I announced, smiling at Laura, "I have a box of maternity clothes in my van. You won't need them for a few months yet, but I wanted to get them out of *my* basement!"

I sat down on the edge of Riley's blanket as I scanned the group of giggling toddlers and children to make sure my own were within eyesight. I spotted Ben with six-year-old Rachel, so I felt immediate relief. Braeden and Kyra held hands with Colton and Kayden, helping them navigate the curvy red slide. Thank goodness for our big helpers, I thought to myself. Parenting required so much energy, but I knew I wasn't going to hear any complaints from this group. They all fought long and hard to reach motherhood.

Once Ginger joined the table, I looked around and couldn't help but feel a sense of wonder for the paths we all took to get here: Laura, who became a parent overnight to her precious Wyatt; Amy, who lost Atticus but gained Riley; Jen, who found Colton right in her own classroom; Ginger, who traveled halfway around the world—twice—for Rachel; Grace, who finally found her fairy tale ending—complete with a true princess; and me, who was lucky enough to be blessed with three healthy pregnancies, but who also knows that families are born of love, not genetics.

I'll be the first to confess that parenting is full of many challenging moments, of tantrums to calm and fevers to break. But because my friends and I wanted these experiences so much, because we supported one another through the creation of our families, and because we have each other to count on, we will likely always parent with a bit more compassion, a little more gratitude, and a lot more hope.

LaVergne, TN USA
16 June 2010
186351LV00004B/77/P